The USCTA Book of Eventing

The USCTA Book of Eventing

*The Official Handbook
of the United States
Combined Training Association, Inc.*

Edited by Sally O'Connor

Photographs by Sue Maynard

Addison-Wesley Publishing Company, Inc.

Reading, Massachusetts • Menlo Park, California • London • Amsterdam • Don Mills, Ontario • Sydney

Design and Art Direction: Dianne Schaefer/
Designworks, Cambridge, MA

Typesetting: ITC Garamond, by County Photo
Compositing Corporation, Jefferson, MA

Paper: 70 lb. Glatfelter Offset, supplied by Pratt
Paper Co.

Printer: Halliday Lithograph Corp. West Hanover,
MA

Portions of the text originally appeared in the *USCTA
News*

"The Unsung Hero of Eventing" by Edward E.
Emerson originally appeared in *The Chronicle of
the Horse*

Information about the USCTA can be obtained by
writing:

The United States Combined Training
Association, Inc.
292 Bridge Street
South Hamilton, MA 01982

(617) 468-7133

ISBN 0-201-05447-7
ABCDEFGHIJ-HA-898765432

Acknowledgments

This book has many parents, all of whom deserve a heartfelt thank-you from those of us who put the book together.

Addison-Wesley editor Anne Eldridge originated the whole idea, and Eileen Thomas, the USCTA's Executive Director, shepherded us through the innumerable stages of accumulating text. Joan Fulton, my agent at Harold Matson Company, struggled through days of negotiation to draw up a contract agreeable to all concerned and deserves a special vote of thanks. Neil R. Ayer and Paul Weaver also provided invaluable help in getting this project underway, and *USCTA News* editor Fifi Coles commissioned much of the original text for the *News*.

The riders and experts whose words make up the text gave freely of their time and knowledge to help all eventers understand the intricacies of the sport. A special thanks to the course builders; without them the sport would not exist. My thanks, too, to those organizers who cheerfully provided information for the course sections: Dr. and Mrs. Lang, Kate Lindsay, Gary Goodwin, Sallie Robertson, and Edith Harrison-Conyers.

Former event rider Brian O'Connor undertook the task of typing a tidy version of the manuscript and enjoyed reading the rough draft. Copy-editor Barbara Stratton pruned and polished the final manuscript, and Dianne Schaefer of Designworks expertly transformed the mass of text and photographs into a beautifully designed book.

Special thanks to Sue Maynard, who gave countless hours to this project; her photographs capture the essence of the sport. Thanks also to Jack Burton for the loan of some early photographs, and to photographers Mike Noble, Ed Lawrence, Susan Sexton, Irene Cromer, E. C. Rainey II, Judith J. McClung, and Warren Patriquin who contributed photographs to the book.

My thanks to USCTA President Denny Emerson for his support and encouragement, and to USCTA Education Vice-President Roger Haller, who, along with Denny, approved the final version.

Finally, a thank-you to Pat Marshall and Linnea Wachtler who rendered lovely drawings for the course section upon barely a moment's notice.

Sally O'Connor
Gaithersburg, MD
July 1982

To the "unsung hero" of eventing—the volunteer

Contents

The Unsung Hero in Eventing

Edward E. Emerson, Jr.

President, United States Combined Training Association

Edward E.—Denny—Emerson

The unsung hero of American eventing, the one who makes the sport possible, is the volunteer worker. The whole sport runs on the backs of thousands of largely unthanked and unrecognized support personnel, virtually none of whom receive a penny for their services.

What sport requires more man hours of labor for each minute of actual competition than eventing? What sport makes its organizers less rich and famous than eventing? And what sport would fold up and disappear more quickly without its labor force? Think of the logistics. To run even a Pre-Training horse trials requires acres of land. Trails must be made, trees cut, grass or brush mowed, a cross-country course planned and laid out. Then the course has to be built. Logs are cut and dragged into place, post holes are hacked through rocky soil, the simplest fence can take a couple of hours of labor, and even Pre-Training requires fifteen of them. The dressage rings must be constructed and painted, the area measured and laid out, the judge's equipment assembled. The stadium fences have to be purchased, built or borrowed, lugged into place and assembled. But even well before this, others have spent hours in an office and on the phone dealing with entries, arranging stabling, ordering ribbons, hiring officials. The list is endless. And all of this precedes the actual competition, when we get the really major manpower requirements, with the jump judges, the couriers, the timers, scorers, starters, medical personnel, and veterinarians.

I was at a little event in Vermont one time when Paul Popiel jumped a water jump too boldly and disappeared. Obviously, from a purely technical viewpoint, the water was too deep to be legal for the level of competition. I blithely said to him later, "Why don't you complain?" I've never forgotten his answer. "Denny, I've run an event, I'll never complain again." I only wish every competitor in America could sometime be on the other side of the fence. Neil Ayer told me that some motor racing or motorcycle group has worked out a system where in order to enter a competition a competitor must include with his entry a form signed by a rally organizer stating that the competitor has put in a certain number of hours as a helper. This may be tough to administer, but I certainly see merit in the spirit of the concept.

Yet, tempting as it might be to coerce people into helping run the sport from which they derive pleasure and benefit, the world "volunteer" is derived from the Latin "voluntas," meaning free will. And this willing commitment to eventing, multiplied by its thousands of proponents, is eventing's greatest strength. People get involved because they like the sport, they believe in its merit, and they freely and cheerfully give themselves to it. Here we see graphically demonstrated the power of the single individual to bring positive good to hundreds of others through his personal efforts.

I think of men like Ray Holland in Michigan or Glenn Fischer in Colorado who have spearheaded local combined training associations. I think of organizers like Sis and Albert Gould, who have run good events for years, or superworkers like Vermont's Betty Booth, who does everything for everybody! This is just a tiny segment of my list; each person has his own list.

So, from all of us who ride, thanks are in order to you thousands of workers throughout America who make eventing possible. And finally, I would like to give recognition to that individual (a different one each year) who has always symbolized for me the ultimate example of the selfless volunteer. There is an area of the Doornhof Farm cross-country course near the water jump where even the bravest course walkers never linger for fence analysis. No horse would be stupid enough to refuse there. I speak of mosquitoes as big as hummingbirds. And yet, I am told, someone sits all day as the jump judge at that fence. To you and all those volunteers who share your dedication to the sport, I dedicate this book.

Introduction

Neil Ayer

USCTA President, 1971–1981

Neil R. Ayer

Fifteen years ago, this book couldn't have been written—at least not by Americans. In the 1960s, in spite of the perseverance of a handful of dedicated and undaunted pioneers, there simply was neither the interest nor the expertise in eventing that now exists in this country.

Many of those who have contributed to this volume were, a decade and a half ago, just beginning their careers. Even Alex Mackay-Smith, Jack Le Goff, Mike Plumb, and Jimmy Wofford—the most knowledgeable and experienced people at that time—were yet to see the sport grow in popularity to the extent to which it has.

What is it about the sport that holds such an attraction? The clear-cut challenges at all levels have great appeal, as do the goals which are as attainable for the weekend rider as they are for the serious three-day eventer. Youngsters and adults alike can compete in divisions and at levels geared both to their skills and their experience. Whole families can and do become involved, and the ladies ride under the same rules and conditions as do the men. The judging is very straightforward: You either pass between the flags or you don't. You either perform a given dressage movement or you don't—and how well you perform it is scored from 1–10 against an objective standard of excellence. How fast you ride the course is accurately recorded by the clock, and in stadium jumping, style matters not—so long as neither disobediences nor knockdowns occur. In fact, there are few other sports where so little is left to "politics" or to the subjective interpretation of the judge.

Combined training does much to develop the participant's character, patience, courage, and sense of responsibility. It stimulates the best in sound and humane training methods and develops among all of us a profound respect for the horse. It is unique as a sport in that a competitor can measure his success not just by where he finishes in the ribbons, but, more importantly, by how well he has performed in terms of what he rightfully expected to be able to do. Many a rider has headed homeward at the end of the day well down in the standings but triumphant all the same, because his dressage ride showed greater accuracy, or because he finally jumped his horse through water, or because, after weeks of gymnastics, he completed his stadium round without a rail down.

Eventing not only offers these challenges, but also holds for all the elements of danger and uncertainty. The apprehensions that accompany the cross-country rider, in particular, bring both excitement while they are being endured and a sense of achievement when they have been overcome.

Cross-country is what the sport is all about. It's what sets both the event horse and the event rider apart—perhaps even beyond—most others. It's the phase a competitor remembers best about a horse trial. It's what gains a reputation for an event. It's what the rider most wants to know about as he trains and schools his horse. And it is for these reasons that this book gives such extensive coverage to preparing both horse and rider for the challenge of the speed and endurance test. So little has been compiled about this phase; so many books are already on the shelves that deal with dressage and show jumping.

Why do so many of us become involved? The competitor we've already talked about, but there are thousands of others who devote hours and days in the wind and the heat and the cold and the rain, judging fences and keeping score, setting up dressage rings, punching stopwatches from dawn 'til dusk, manning radios on distant hilltops. Basically, I think we become involved because we all enjoy being associated with and working for an activity that has structure and purpose and dignity; for something that makes it possible to participate with others in a project that fosters camaraderie and good sportsmanship; that places a positive value on a sense of being needed, and rewards participants with the satisfaction of a job well done; that centers around the strength, grace, and nobility of the equine athlete; and continues to feature so many of the old-fashioned virtues that our amateur-turned-professional sports have long since lost.

Sally O'Connor has here assembled and edited into polished form a most valuable collection of instructional articles about eventing—all written by people who are so familiar with and enthusiastic about their subjects that the reader, particularly the newcomer who seeks to learn more about the sport, is sure to finish chapter after chapter all the more inspired and better informed.

History of Eventing in the United States

Alexander Mackay-Smith

International Editor,
The Chronicle of the Horse

Alexander Mackay-Smith on Yachtstrain at the Blue Ridge (Va.) Horse Trials, 1967

Alexander Mackay-Smith needs little introduction to anyone connected with horses. He has served as the Editor of the weekly journal, The Chronicle of the Horse, and is now the International Editor of the same magazine.

His deep understanding and knowledge of horses has been keenly sought after by many organizations, and he is a founding member of both the U.S. Pony Clubs, and the U.S. Combined Training Association. Who could do a better job of writing the history of combined training in this country than Alex?

His warm support and interest in young riders from the very beginning has inspired several of our top event riders, including his own stepdaughter, Caroline Treviranus. A lifelong association with foxhunting has led him to contribute to many books on the lore of that sport, and articles by the dozen on foxhunting, racing, and eventing have left his typewriter for magazines all over the world.

As one who has watched the tremendous growth enjoyed by combined training in the United States, Alex has chronicled for us the various stages of development of the sport from its early days through the early 1980s, into the position of respect it holds today.

Early History: The U.S. Army Teams (1912–1949)

The sport of eventing traces its origins to the cavalries of the world. America was settled by immigrants who were protected and aided by countless cavalrymen and their horses. A strong tradition of the partnership between man and horse carries over to this day, in a country where the horse was all important in the development of a young nation.

The advent of the automobile and the airplane in the 20th century brought about the mechanization of the armed forces, rendering the horse obsolete for modern-day army use. But the age-old partnership between man and beast remained as the new "machine age" shortened work days and increased the amount of individual leisure time. People turned once more to the horse as a source of enjoyment, and fox hunting, racing, and showing all became major sports.

Before 1949 virtually all combined training, or eventing, took place under the auspices of the U.S. Cavalry. Once a friendly series of tests between fellow officers, the Three-Day Event, or *Concours Complet* ("complete test"), was designed to discover the perfect cavalry charger—one that was fast, brave, enduring, and obedient to the end.

Competition in the first Olympic Three-Day Event, held in 1912 at Stockholm, Sweden, was limited to cavalry officers. The United States sent a team of four, including Capt. Guy V. Henry, who was later appointed President of the FEI (Federation Equestre Internationale) and Chief of the U.S. Cavalry. The U.S. team finished in third place to win the team bronze medal.

Capt. Henry, influenced by his European experiences and friendships, decided that American riders should be given a chance to assimilate European equestrian expertise. He began sending young cavalry officers to the great schools of Europe, such as Saumur, in France, and Pinerolo, in Italy. Subsequent U.S. teams consisted largely

The U.S. Army three-day event team at the 1947 Olympic Trials, Chicago. Left to right: Col. Frank Henry, Cpt. Jonathan Burton, Lt. Bob Banner, Col. Earl Thomson, Col. F. F. Wing

The U.S. Army jumping and three-day event teams, 1948. Left to right, standing: LtC. Frank Henry, Col. Fuddy Wing, Col. Tommy Thompson, Col. A. A. Freenson, LtC. Henry Ellis. Kneeling: LtC. Charles Anderson, LtC. Charles Symnask, Cpt. Jack Russell, Cpt. Jonathan Burton

of officers who had had the advantages of studying at these schools.

The United States sent a four-man team to the 1920 Olympic Games at Antwerp, which was ignominiously eliminated. But at the 1924 Olympic Games in Paris, France, Maj. Sloan Doak on Pathfinder won the individual bronze medal for the United States. At the Amsterdam Olympics in 1928, our team made little impression among the 17 competing nations, but at Los Angeles in 1932 the U.S. team won the gold medal. Capt. Earl F. Thomson, on the mare Jenny Camp, finished second to win the individual silver medal. Thomson's teammates included Capt. Edwin Y. Argo on Honolulu Tomboy and Capt. Harry D. Chamberlin on Pleasant Smiles. Capt. Chamberlin later gained fame as the chief architect of the famous instruction program at the U.S. Cavalry School at Fort Riley, Kansas. His two books, *Training Hunters, Jumpers and Hacks* and *Riding and Schooling Horses*, won a permanent place in equestrian literature and are still used as models for the training of riding horses to this day.

The 1936 Olympic Games, held in Berlin on the eve of World War II, were designed as a showcase for Hitler's Germany. A total of 19 nations and 50 riders competed in the Military Three-Day Event. 14 of those nations sent a full team of three riders, all of whom were required to finish in order for their team to win a medal. For a while it appeared that the U.S. would repeat its 1932 victory. But the infamous Pond Jump in the speed and endurance test produced more than its share of catastrophes—including a fall for Capt. John Willems on Slippery Slim. Unfortunately, Slippery Slim broke his leg and had to be destroyed, and the U.S. team was eliminated. However, Capt. Earl Thomson again won the individual silver medal on Jenny Camp. No horse has since won two consecutive individual three-day Olympic medals.

The next Olympic Games took place in London in 1948, after the war. 16 nations (with 15 full teams) took part and the U.S. Army Team won another team gold medal. Capt. Frank S. Henry on Swing Low won the individual silver; teammate Capt. Charles H. Anderson on Reno Palisade finished fourth; and Capt. Earl Thomson on Reno Rhythm finished 21st.

Civilians Take Over—The Transitional Years (1950–1960)

By the war's end, trucks and jeeps had replaced horses in the U.S. Cavalry. The Three-Day Event of the Olympic Games passed from military to civilian hands, and civilian riders became candidates for participation on the U.S. team. At this time, however, few civilians were well-versed in the intricacies of the sport. Naturally enough, the U.S. Cavalry riders became the coaches and advisers of the newly formed United States Equestrian Team (USET), which was created in 1950, with Col. John W. Wofford as president, to fill the void left by the disbanding of the U.S. Cavalry School. The USET would be self-supporting,

relying on tax deductible gifts to raise funds for sending teams to all three Olympic disciplines—Dressage, Jumping, and the Three-Day Event. In 1952, Whitney Stone was elected president of the USET and served in that capacity until the Olympic Games of 1972, assisted by Brig.-Gen. Franklin F. Wing, a former cavalry rider who was executive vice president of the USET.

The first civilian Three-Day Event in the U.S. took place in September 1949, in conjunction with the Bryn Mawr (Pa.) Horse Show. It was won, not surprisingly, by a U.S. Army officer, Lt. Col. W. Randolph Tayloe on The Flying Dutchman (owned by George P. Greenhalgh, Sr.).

The demise of the traditional cavalries did not diminish participation in the Olympic Three-Day Event. In Helsinki in 1952, a record number of 21 nations, 20 teams, and 61 individuals showed up for the so called "Military Event." The U.S. team, ably coached by Col. John W. Wofford, won the team bronze medal. Team members included J.E.B. Wofford, Col. Wofford's son, on Benny Grimes, Charles Huff on Cassavellanus, and Walter Staley on Craigwood Park. In addition to coaching the team, Col. Wofford lent both Benny Grimes and Cassavellanus to the team for the competition.

Apart from the quadrennial Olympic Games, there were few opportunities for U.S. riders to gain much-needed practical experience by riding in actual competition. The need for competition at all levels—up to and including the international levels—became urgently apparent.

In response to this need, the first continuous one-day event in the United States was organized in 1953 by Margaret Lindsley Warden, the equestrian correspondent of the *Nashville Tennessean*. The event took place at Warner Park, just outside Nashville, and the organizers were guided by the expert advice of Major Jonathan R. Burton, a former cavalry officer then stationed at Fort Knox in Kentucky. (Burton had trained with the military three-day event team and later went on to compete in the 1956 Olympic Games in Stockholm.) In 1954, team selection trials for the

Then-Cpt. Jonathan Burton competing in a jumping derby in Dublin, Ireland, 1949. Maj.-Gen. Burton has been instrumental in building a foundation for eventing in the U.S., and he won the Wofford Trophy in 1981

upcoming Pan American Games were held over the course built at Warner Park.

1954 was a milestone year for American eventing. A group of eventing enthusiasts, headed by Mrs. Dean Bedford, Howard Fair, and Alexander Mackay-Smith, founded the United States Pony Clubs, Inc., largely following British and Canadian models. Through the U.S. Pony Clubs, young riders received their first introduc-tion to the world of eventing and combined training and were provided with sound instruc-tion in basic riding and stable management skills.

Yet throughout the 1950s, the few eventing competitors had little or no organized training. Most serious competitors were either ex-cavalry officers, or, as one of them wisecracked, "refu-gees from other sports." Col. Wofford died in 1955, leaving the fledgling USET without an ex-perienced coach. Mrs. Wofford donated a per-petual memorial trophy in his memory to be awarded to the top U.S. rider.

The Pan American Games of 1955 were the first to include any equestrian competition. Wal-ter Staley won the individual gold medal for the U.S. aboard Mud Dauber, while Frank Duffy on

Passach finished eighth. J.E.B. Wofford and Cassavellanus were eliminated, so the U.S. team did not place.

Gradually combined training began to attract riders as an alternative to the show ring. Eventing offered a unique challenge to the serious horse person, since the sport emphasized all-around ability and the scoring system was based on performance alone. In the show ring, horses and riders are judged on the basis of subjective opinion. It is often difficult to understand the opinions of individual judges in the ring and even more frustrating to determine the basis of their opinions after the class is over. In the dressage phase of combined training, the judge dictates the marks to a secretary and comments on each movement; the resulting sheet is turned over to the competitor at the conclusion of the event. The jumping tests (cross-country and stadium) are matters of fact rather than opinion.

A team was later assembled for the 1956 Olympic Games in Stockholm, but misfortune again plagued the U.S. riders. Walter Staley on Mud Dauber, Major Jonathan R. Burton on Huntingfield, and Frank Duffy on Drop Dead all were eliminated on the cross-country course. Obviously the transition from military to civilian teams had left a great deal to be desired. Better training grounds for young riders and horses were clearly needed.

To encourage further growth in the sport, Alexander Mackay-Smith, a member of the USET Executive Committee, suggested the appointment of H. Stewart Treviranus as Technical Adviser for combined training. (Treviranus, a graduate of the British Cavalry School at Weedon, had competed for Canada in the 1952 Olympic Three-Day Event at Helsinki.) He lent his talents to organizing several events in the eastern U.S., including, in 1956, the Blue Ridge Horse Trials in Clarke County, Va.—the second oldest continuous event in the country. The honors for the oldest continuous event go to the Tennesseans Horse Trials in Nashville.

Then-Cpt. Jonathan Burton riding in international dressage competition, Wiesbaden, Germany, 1949.

In 1957, Gen. Tupper Cole headed a three-week combined training instruction center at South Woodstock, Vt. with Stewart Treviranus as his assistant. This intensive three-week training session, later headed by Treviranus and relocated to the Virginia Combined Training Center in Middleburg, Va., was held annually for the next two decades. Many graduates of the Center later achieved distinction in competition, including Rick Eckhardt, Don Sachey, and Caroline Treviranus, Stewart's daughter, who all went on to represent the U.S. in international competition. Many riders turned from horse shows to combined training, relishing the challenge it offered and the readily understandable results.

By the late 1950's the major event in the U.S. was the Wofford Trophy Competition. Fittingly, the event was won in 1957 and 1958 by horses owned by Mrs. J. W. Wofford, Tingling and Passach, both ridden by the Wofford barn manager, Jonas Irbinskas. After these competitions, the qualifications for the Wofford Cup changed and the trophy went to the highest-placed U.S. rider at the Pan American Games and the Olympic Games in the years these events were held.

In 1959 the United States hosted the Pan American Games in Chicago, where the Canadians won the team gold medal. But the individual gold went to U.S. rider Michael Page, riding John Galvin's little horse, Grasshopper. In 1956, under his former name, Copper Coin, Grasshopper competed on the Irish team at the Olympics in Stockholm. The individual silver medal in Chicago went to a young rider who would make history for the U.S. three-day event team—J. Michael Plumb, on the USET's Markham.

The Great Years of Development
(1960–1970)

By the spring of 1959, the USET had established a grass roots enthusiasm for combined training. With the rapid growth of equestrian sports, the USET felt the need to restrict its efforts to the fielding of international teams in all *three* equestrian disciplines. To continue the work begun by Stewart Treviranus, Alexander Mackay-Smith wrote to over 100 combined training enthusiasts, asking them to attend a meeting during the Pan American Games in Chicago. This meeting resulted in the formation of the United States Combined Training Association (USCTA), an organization that would drastically affect the growth of eventing in America. Philip Hofmann, father of Carol Hofmann (a member of the USET jumping squad) was elected president, and Alexander Mackay-Smith was elected secretary. Four years later, the presidency went to Edward Harris, who had spearheaded the founding of the Morven Park International Equestrian Institute in Leesburg, Va.—a school devoted to the education of instructors in the equestrian arts, modeled on the great schools of Europe and England. J. Gibson Semmes took over the presidency of the USCTA in 1959 and held that post for the rest of the 1960s, while the sport grew steadily in the number of events offered and in the number of riders competing.

The U.S. Combined Training Association has been a major factor in promoting combined training in the United States. The organization works closely with the American Horse Shows Association (AHSA), the organization designated by the Federation Equestre Internationale (FEI) as the equestrian federation in the United States. Many of the USCTA's officers serve on the combined training committee of the AHSA. The USCTA also works with the USET to organize selection trials for team members who will represent the U.S. in major competitions, such as the Olympics.

The 1960 Olympic Games were held in Rome. Col. Earl Thomson, who had retired from active competition, was appointed coach of the U.S. team. J. Michael Plumb, beginning his Olympic career, placed 15th on the USET's Markham, and Michael Page on Grasshopper finished 17th. Although the third U.S. rider, David Lowry on Sea Tiger, also finished, the U.S. team

Two USET riders, past and present at the Lexington (Ky.) World Championships, 1978—Kevin Freeman and Derek di Grazia

did not win a medal. Australia made a surprisingly strong showing to clinch the team gold and the individual gold and silver medals. The French team took home the team bronze medal, aided largely by the efforts of French rider Jack Le Goff, who finished sixth on Image. In one of the ironies of international competition, Jack Le Goff and J. Michael Plumb, who were fellow competitors that year in Rome, would develop a highly successful coach/rider relationship years later, when Le Goff became the coach of the U.S. three-day event team.

At this time the United States lacked a coach to train civilian riders at the same level of expertise as their army counterparts. In 1961, Stefan von Visy (a member of Hungary's Olympic three day event team in 1936) was appointed full-time coach of the USET three-day event squad, with training operations based at the USET headquarters in Gladstone, N.J.

In 1963 the U.S. decisively won the team gold medal at the Pan American Games in São Paulo, Brazil. Michael Page on Grasshopper won the individual gold medal, and Kevin Freeman—the first west coast rider to figure significantly in international competition—won the individual silver on Reno Pal. The individual bronze went to Carlos Moratorio of Argentina on Chalan, the same horse who would later represent the U.S. in 1967.

The 1964 Olympic Games took place in Tokyo, where 12 nations sent teams for the three-day event. The Italians won the team gold medal, and the United States brought home the team silver medal. Michael Page on Grasshopper captured fourth place honors, while Kevin Freeman and Gallopade finished 12th. Sadly, the horse Michael Plumb should have ridden—Markham—became uncontrollable on the flight overseas and had to be destroyed en route. In response to this unfortunate emergency, Bill Haggard of Nashville, Tenn., generously offered his horse Bold Minstrel (who had been a member of the U.S. gold medal winning jumping team at the last Pan American Games) to Michael Plumb. Bold Minstrel was flown to Tokyo by special plane the next day; the pair finished a remarkable 15th and clinched the team silver medal for the U.S.

At the Tokyo Olympics, women participated in the three-day event for the first time. The sole woman entry, Lana DuPont, was a member of the U.S. team. Although she fell, she finished the event, thereby making Olympic history. Of course, women had previously and convincingly demonstrated their ability to compete on equal terms with men in many of Europe's toughest and most prestigious competitions: The well-known English rider, Sheila Willcox, had won the European Championships at Copenhagen in 1957 and had also won at Badminton in 1957, 1958, and 1959.

In the mid-sixties the calendar of international three-day events continued to grow. In addition to the Olympic Games, the European Championships, and the Pan American Games, a new competition was added when the FEI proposed a quadrennial World Championship, to take place two years after each Olympic Games. The USET sent a team to Burghley, England—site of the first World Championships—in 1966. Disappointingly, the U.S. team failed to finish, probably because the horses arrived only a few days before the event. It was not altogether surprising that the relatively inexperienced young rider, J. A. B. Smith, was eliminated on Bean Platter, but consternation reigned when J. Michael Plumb on Foster met the same fate. Kevin Freeman, on M'Lord Connelly, had a fall at fence 5, leaving the old reliable Gallopade with Rick Eckhardt up to finish with a clear but slow cross-country round. With two imported horses and two American horses, the U.S. team clearly had not yet caught up with the Europeans.

But the story changed at the 1967 Pan American Games in Winnipeg, Canada. The U.S. Team included J. Michael Plumb on Plain Sailing, an English part-thoroughbred donated to the USET by Raymond Firestone; Michael Page on Mrs. Mathias Plum's Irish-bred, Foster; Jim Wofford on his mother's Kilkenny, another Irish-bred horse; and Rick Eckhardt on the only American-bred horse, The Stranger. The U.S. team was the only group to finish and convincingly captured the team gold medal.

Despite this happy victory, the U.S. system for producing top horses clearly had a long way to go. Imported English and Irish horses were the mainstay of the team. Moreover, few top-level competitions existed in the United States where domestic riders and horses could gain valuable competitive experience. While the events being held throughout the country steadily gained in sophistication, the standards of most U.S. competitions remained far below Olympic levels.

On the domestic front, the Wofford Cup remained the most prestigious honor in eventing, and Michael Page and Michael Plumb vied for the trophy for the next few years. Page was awarded the trophy in 1959, in recognition of his victory at the Pan American Games. Plumb captured the trophy in 1960 as the highest-placed American in the Rome Olympics. Page regained the trophy in 1961 by winning the Myopia Hunt Club event in South Hamilton, Mass., riding Syphon. But Plumb's win at the Pebble Beach Three-Day Event in 1962 brought him the Wofford Cup once again. With each Michael holding two legs on the cup, Page finally retired the Cup permanently, with his gold medal victory in the 1963 Pan American Games on Grasshopper.

In response to Page's victory, the USET offered a new cup in 1964, designated as the National Open Three-Day Event Championship Trophy, to be awarded annually at a specific competition. Kevin Freeman won the new trophy at Gladstone, N.J. in 1964 on Royal Beaver; in 1965, Charles D. Plumb (father of J. Michael Plumb) took home the trophy riding the English import M'Lord Connelly, a former Badminton winner, in the Meadowbrook Hounds event on Long Island. Kevin Freeman regained the trophy

Major John Lynch, center, with students at the Morven Park Institute, 1973 (Photo by E. C. Rainey II)

on the USET's Royal Imp at Gladstone in 1966 and Jim Wofford captured the Championship Trophy on Kilkenny at Myopia in 1967.

As a warm-up for the upcoming Olympic Games in Mexico, the USET sent a group of horses and riders to compete at the prestigious Badminton Three-Day Event in England during the spring of 1968. The team included several new horses and riders: Bill Haggard, who had purchased Chalan from Argentina; Sara Lord on Evening Mail; Charlotte Robson on Royal Imp; and Rick Eckhardt on Thunder Road; these last three all being American-bred horses. However, the more experienced part of the American contingent placed respectably at Badminton: Plain Sailing, ridden by Michael Plumb, finished 9th; Jim Wofford on Kilkenny finished 13th; and Michael Page on Foster finished 20th. The American team did not distinguish itself particularly,

but the competitive experience gained at Badminton would soon pay off at the upcoming Olympic Games in Mexico.

At the 1968 summer Olympics, the entire U.S. team rode imported horses: Foster from Ireland, Plain Sailing from England; Kilkenny from Ireland; and Chalan from Argentina. The U.S. coach was also imported. Stefan von Visy had left the USET, so Maj. J. Lynch from England took a three-month leave of absence from his post as director of the Morven Park International Equestrian Institute (in Leesburg, Va.) to prepare the U.S. team for the Olympic Games. Major Lynch was no stranger to international competition, having coached the British bronze medal team of the 1936 Berlin Olympics, and the Irish silver medal winning team at the European championships in 1961.

The number of participants in the three-day event at the Mexican Olympics had dwindled to 13 nations and 12 full teams. The site for the event was a golf course at Avandaro, some ninety miles from Mexico City—a place infamous for the afternoon rains which flooded the valley with great regularity. On the speed and endurance day, horses and riders found themselves floundering in head-high streams as they struggled around the course in a downpour.

Despite these adverse conditions, Michael Page won the individual bronze medal on Foster, who fortunately overcame his aversion to water. Kilkenny (under Jim Wofford) turned in perhaps the greatest cross-country round in the history of the Olympic Games but lost his shot at an almost certain medal when he slipped and fell in the final stadium jumping phase. Riding as anchor man (after Kevin Freeman had been eliminated on Chalan), Michael Plumb on Plain Sailing made sure to finish, despite the chaotic flooding. Riding a safe but slow round, Plumb assured the silver team medal for the United States. Great Britain retained its supremacy by clinching the team gold but it was Jack Le Goff's student, Adj. Chef J. J. Guyon on Pitou, who took home the individual gold medal to France.

The Golden Era (1970–1980)

Two men came into the forefront around 1970 who were to influence eventing in North America as no others had before—Neil Ayer and Jack Le Goff.

Neil Ayer, M.F.H. of the Myopia Hunt in Hamilton, Mass., an avid polo player and event organizer, took over as president of the USCTA late in 1970. He brought untrammeled enthusiasm, organizing genius and unbridled energy to the sport. Through his strong leadership and boundless support, he provided a central thrust for the development and growth of the sport. Solutions for many problems that had seemed insoluble before were found during his tenure.

Jack Le Goff had compiled a brilliant competitive record representing his native France in international three-day competition. He had coached many successful teams, including the 1968 French Olympic Team. In 1970 Whitney Stone (president of the USET) persuaded him to become the coach of the USET Three-Day Event Team. He not only proved to be a brilliant coach but he also took great interest in the grass roots of combined training, frequently attending minor as well as major events. He gave clinics open to the public in various parts of the country and became involved in Pony Club competitions. He broadened the team's accessibility by designating certain events as selection trials for the USET. Former competitors could no longer be assured of a certain place on the team; all riders and horses had to produce results immediately before any major competition. Under Jack Le Goff's leadership, general enthusiasm for combined training has grown by leaps and bounds in the United States.

Upon his arrival in America he selected a group of young, unproven riders to work for an extended period of time under his tutelage at the USET headquarters at Gladstone. Among them was the young and then-unknown Bruce Davidson. Le Goff's first goal was to produce a team to compete in the 1972 Olympic Games at Munich,

James Wofford on The Regent winning the National Championships at Fair Hill, Md., 1971

Germany. He had only two scant years in which to mold a winning team.

In 1970, two American riders entered the second World Championships (held at Punchestown, Ireland) as individuals. Mason Phelps on Rowen had to withdraw during the endurance competition, but Jim Wofford and his great Kilkenny managed to improve their dressage score by some 30 points from the results in Mexico and, in spite of a fall cross-country, Kilkenny was the only horse to finish with maximum bonus points on Phase D. As a result, the combination won the individual bronze medal.

Due to an outbreak of Venezuelan Equine Encephalomyelitis along the Texas border, no American team was sent to the 1971 Pan American Games held at Cali, Colombia.

Meanwhile, Jack Le Goff was concentrating on finding the best horse and rider combinations to take to the 1972 Olympic Games in Munich, Germany. He had few horses to draw on: Plain Sailing, the most experienced horse, was assigned to the least experienced rider, Bruce Davidson; while Jim Wofford could rely on Kilkenny. Michael Plumb and Kevin Freeman, both riders of vast experience, were to ride the least experienced horses, the American-breds, Free and Easy and Good Mixture.

The Munich Olympics attracted full teams from 18 nations for the three-day event, and a total of 73 riders began the competition, a field equalled previously only in Rome in 1960.

Kevin Freeman, participating in his third Olympic competition, rode a well-paced round on Good Mixture, finishing in fifth place overall. Bruce Davidson, Le Goff's star pupil, finished eighth. Michael Plumb fell with Free and Easy, but finished in 20th place, and Jim Wofford, who also fell, struggled on to a 30th place finish. Great Britain retained its eventing superiority by winning a second gold team medal with Richard Meade on Laurieston taking the individual gold. The United States team under Jack Le Goff's direction won the team silver medal—the third team silver in a row for the USET.

Le Goff then set his sights on the World Championships to be held at Burghley, England in 1974, the next major international three-day event. He set to work searching for new talent by organizing a series of screening trials. He spared no effort in his quest for excellence, both in the skill of the rider, and in the athletic ability of the horse.

Whitney Stone, who had served as president of the USET since 1952, stepped down after the 1972 Olympics in Munich. He was succeeded by one of the USET's most famous riders, William Steinkraus, who had long served as captain of the USET jumping squad, was a veteran of five Olympic Games, and the winner of the individual gold medal at the 1968 Mexican Olympics.

New events were added to the calendar, and the numbers of participants grew steadily as courses improved and the USCTA standards for recognized events were upheld. By 1973, Neil Ayer decided that America was ready for the "big time." Ayer arranged to hold an internationally-recognized FEI event, a CCI—Concours Complet International—in October. The location was the Ayer farm, Ledyard, in South Hamilton, Mass. With the able assistance of the local pony clubs, the members of the Myopia Hunt and the Myopia polo players, Neil Ayer set out to organize the best of three-day events. Invitations were sent out to England, Ireland, France, and Germany. Germany declined, but three entries came from Ireland, three from France and a grand total of thirteen riders made the trek from Great Britain. The British group included Mary Gordon-Watson, Bridget Parker, and Lorna Sutherland, plus a member of Britain's 1972 Olympic gold medal team, Mark Phillips. Ledyard was a hard-fought event, where places changed down to the last fence in the stadium jumping test, making the competition an exciting duel to the very end. Sue Hatherly from Great Britain, riding one of the 1972 Olympic Australian horses, Harley, eventually won the event; and Michael Plumb won both second place on West Country, and third on Johnny O. Mary Gordon-Watson, on her world champion, Cornishman V, finished fourth, due to two rails down in the last test. Bruce Davidson finished 5th on Plain Sailing and Chris Collins of Great Britain on Centurion was 6th. The event was well-publicized and the crowds exceeded any who had previously gathered to watch a combined training event in America.

South Hamilton, Mass. was to become even more important to combined training. In 1974 the USET Three-Day Event Team headquarters moved from its base at Gladstone, N.J., to property near Neil Ayer's Ledyard Farm, thanks to the generous donation of the old Clark estate by Forrester A. Clark.

The World Championships

The 1974 World Championship Three-Day Event was held in Burghley, England. As a guest nation the United States was allowed six competitors, four to be entered as the official team, and two to ride as individuals. Le Goff's search for new talent—both riders and horses—had by then been well-rewarded. Proven riders Michael Plumb and Bruce Davidson were chosen to ride, along with newcomers Denny Emerson and Beth Perkins from Vermont, and Don Sachey and Caroline Treviranus from Virginia. Three of the horses selected had already competed internationally. Good Mixture, ridden by Kevin Freeman in Munich, was now partnered with Michael Plumb; Plain Sailing, the old reliable who had given Bruce Davidson his start in Olympic competition, was ridden this time by another relatively inexperienced rider, Don Sachey. Beth Perkins' horse, Furtive, had competed under Australian colors in 1968. Under Le Goff's coaching Denny Emerson's part-Morgan, Victor Dakin, improved so much in dressage that this combination had also been selected. Bruce Davidson had flown to England earlier that year and had finished third on his Irish Cap at the im-

portant spring three-day event at Badminton. On the strength of this performance and Bruce's rapidly growing experience at home and abroad, Le Goff chose Irish Cap, a relatively inexperienced horse of great potential, to go to Burghley. Caroline Treviranus rode her Canadian-bred mare, Cajun, a horse that had received the USCTA award for the leading horse and leading mare in the country in 1973. Beth Perkins and Caroline Treviranus were the first women to represent the United States in international Three-Day competition since Lana DuPont's debut ten years before in Tokyo. Le Goff decided to form his team from the four men, while the two women competed as individuals.

On their home ground the British exuded an aura of confidence. With gold medals in two successive Olympic Games and a previous World Championship victory, England was a heavy favorite. The United States had a reputation for finishing second.

After the dressage phase, the Germans held the lead, but the U.S. contingent followed closely. Bruce Davidson stood in second place, Beth Perkins held fifth, Caroline Treviranus was sixth and Michael Plumb was 16th.

A large contingent of enthusiastic U.S. supporters had flown over to follow the fortunes of the American riders. Sporting red, white and blue rosettes, they cheered as the USET horses galloped by during the cross-country phase. Bruce Davidson went clean on Irish Cap, as did Michael Plumb on Good Mixture, who negotiated the speed and endurance test at nearly racing pace to pull up to within .25 points of Davidson and Irish Cap. Denny Emerson produced a third clear round, but Don Sachey and Plain Sailing fell late in the course. Beth Perkins and Furtive went clear, but Caroline Treviranus and Cajun had a bad fall at fence 23, where the mare stepped on her rider, breaking Caroline's collarbone. She nevertheless remounted and went clear over the nine remaining gigantic fences. At the end of the day the United States team was in front, and the highest-placed English horse, Columbus, had suffered from a slipped achilles tendon and was unable to continue.

Tremendous excitement hung over the stadium jumping grounds as the American supporters cheered their team on through each successive round. They knew that Hugh Thomas of Great Britain could conceivably overtake either Bruce Davidson or Michael Plumb if either American made any mistake. But both Irish Cap and Good Mixture jumped clear rounds and the American team won the first team gold medal in world competition since the U.S. Army team's triumph in 1948. Bruce Davidson became the first American World Champion, with Michael Plumb a mere fraction behind in second place. Beth Perkins and Furtive finished a highly creditable sixth, while Don Sachey was 21st.

By winning the team gold medal the United States automatically became the host country for the 1978 World Championships.

The U.S. gold medal three-day team at the 1974 World Championships, Burghley, England. Left to right: J. Michael Plumb on Good Mixture, Denny Emerson on Victor Dakin, Don Sachey on Plain Sailing, and Bruce Davidson on Irish Cap

Because of rain, the 1975 Badminton event in April was cancelled. As a result, the most important three-day event of 1975 became the Ledyard Farm CCI in June, since it attracted representatives from the countries that had finished first, second, and third at Burghley—the United States, Great Britain, and West Germany. Holland also sent two riders. The presence of Princess Anne and her husband, Mark Phillips, attracted much interest from the public and press alike, giving the sport of combined training a great deal of exposure throughout the country.

Ledyard was again a hard-fought competition, with less than ten points separating the first four horses by the end of the second day of competition. Beth Perkins on Furtive held the lead going into the final phase, with Bruce Davidson on the USET's Golden Griffin close behind. Former Ledyard winners Sue Hatherly and Harley were standing third, with young Tad Coffin, another Le Goff protégé, standing fourth on Bally Cor. A freak fall on a tight turn cost Beth Perkins the winner's trophy. Bruce Davidson finished first, Sue Hatherly was second on Harley, and Bruce also finished third on Royal Cor. Tad Coffin and Bally Cor remained in 4th place.

For the Americans, the only other major event in 1975 was the Pan American Games held in Mexico City in October. Le Goff chose a young team to represent the United States, in order to give the younger riders some much-needed international experience. Led by Bruce Davidson on Golden Griffin, the team consisted of Tad Coffin on Bally Cor, Beth Perkins on Furtive, and—due largely to her excellent showing at Ledyard, where she had placed sixth—Mary Anne Tauskey on Marcus Aurelius, a tough little part-Connemara who had been purchased in England.

The American team had a good lead after the dressage phase and went on to take the first three places at the end of the speed and endurance. Disgraceful harassment from Mexican soldiers stationed along the roads and tracks phases and a serious altercation with officials during the cross-country phase marred an otherwise splendid result. Golden Griffin, who was stiff on the final day from a fall cross-country that had been caused by one of the Mexican officials, had two fences down in stadium, thus exchanging places with Tad Coffin and Bally Cor who won the individual gold medal. The American team won the team gold medal and the individual gold and silver medals, repeating their performance at Burghley. 1974 and 1975 were truly golden years for Jack Le Goff and his riders.

The Montreal Olympics

The record of the two previous years placed an undue amount of pressure on Le Goff and his team, who were clear favorites in the 1976 Montreal Olympics Games, held in the little skiing village of Bromont.

Only 13 countries managed to send riders to Bromont, where 12 full teams and 49 individuals were in competition.

A series of selection trials in the spring of 1976 led to a final training session with Le Goff prior to the summer Olympics. He again opted for a mixture of experience and youth. Michael Plumb, riding in his fifth consecutive Olympics over a 16-year span in international competition, was partnered by a very green horse, Better and Better, because Good Mixture, his first choice, suffered from weakened tendons. Bruce Davidson's Irish Cap had nearly died the previous year from a lung infection but he seemed recovered by Bromont and Le Goff chose the World Champion for his team. Tad Coffin was again partnered with the gallant Bally Cor; by this time the pair had become one of those rare combinations where the horse and rider complement each other exactly. Mary Anne Tauskey and her small but impressive Marcus Aurelius completed the squad of four; sadly, Denny Emerson's Victor

Bronze medalist Karl Schultz of West Germany on Madrigal at the 1976 Olympics, Montreal, Canada

Dakin had strained a ligament just before the competition.

West German Karl Schultz on Madrigal rode one of the best dressage tests ever seen in Olympic competition to take the lead after the dressage. With his great flair for dressage, Bruce Davidson was second, and Tad Coffin and Bally Cor were sixth, with Michael Plumb and Better and Better immediately following them, in seventh place. After dressage the United States took the lead from West Germany, with Great Britain third.

The somewhat controversial cross-country course took its toll on the horses during the second day of the competition. Karl Schultz re-tained his lead on Madrigal but other placings changed dramatically. Tad Coffin and Bally Cor moved up into second place, while Michael Plumb and Better and Better had the second fastest time of the day to come within one point of Tad and Bally. Although Bruce Davidson and Irish Cap had an unfortunate fall at the water obstacle, the United States had held their lead, with Great Britain pulling into second place. Unfortunately, two of the British horses had been injured and were withdrawn overnight, thus eliminating Great Britain's team from the competition.

An excited crowd of over 20,000 watched the final phase. Tad Coffin and Michael Plumb were standing second and third respectively, with Karl Schultz just five points ahead of them. Tad and Bally Cor jumped a flawless round but Mike and Better and Better failed to clear the water jump and incurred ten faults. Karl Schultz and Madrigal had only to jump clean to win the gold medal for Germany but Madrigal pulled not one but two rails down, catapulting Tad Coffin and Bally Cor into victory, with Michael Plumb and Better and Better winning yet another silver medal.

The U.S. team's gold medal victory marked another incredible win in a string of unparalleled accomplishments for American riders. In three major competitions in three years, Jack Le Goff had piloted his squad into three successive gold medals, and had also been responsible for three individual gold and three individual silver medals. Little wonder he is credited with bringing about a second French Revolution with a Midas Touch.

Steady Growth at Home

With all the excitement of the international competitions, sparked by the phenomenal successes enjoyed by the top riders, the grass roots of combined training were steadily developing a firm base for the sport. By the end of 1976, 176 competitions at different levels—with over 12,000 competitors—had taken place around the country. By comparison, in 1972 after the Munich Olympics, only 65 U.S. competitions with 3,731 competitors had been held.

The Wofford family, so involved in the sport from the very beginning, re-dedicated the Wofford Trophy that had been retired in 1963 by Michael Page, with the provision that it be awarded to the "non-riding member of the USCTA who has done the most to further the sport of Combined Training." Fittingly, Neil Ayer was the first recipient of the Wofford Trophy.

Once Neil Ayer had decided to run a major international event he naturally wanted to find the best possible officials and experts available. He contacted Col. Frank Weldon, the director of the Badminton Three Day Event in England, to act as a Technical Delegate, and Colonel Weldon recommended Eileen Thomas to organize the scoring and time scheduling. Eileen's streamlined

The U.S. three-day team proudly accepts the gold medal at the 1976 Olympics, Montreal, Canada. Left to right: Mary Anne Tauskey, Bruce Davidson, J. Michael Plumb, Tad Coffin

efficiency smoothed so many rough spots that she was asked to score three more major events —Joker's Hill in Canada, Ledyard in 1973, and Essex in 1974. By this time Neil Ayer had recognized that Eileen could be of tremendous value in easing the USCTA through its growing pains.

Eileen accepted the job as Secretary of the USCTA in 1974 and after the World Championships, held in Burghley, England, moved across the Atlantic to take up residence in Massachusetts.

Widely experienced in all the details of running three day events of world class, Eileen lent her expertise to organisers of small home town horse trials, serving as scorer and secretary for many new events. Her cheerful outlook and her deep knowledge of the sport has helped the USCTA increase in size and efficiency year by year. In recognition of her ability the USCTA promoted her to the position of Executive Director in 1981.

The National Open Championships attracted more and more contestants each year. Bruce Davidson won with Golden Griffin in 1975 and Denny Emerson with Victor Dakin in 1976. The list of winners began to look like a roster of the Olympic riders, due to Le Goff's talent in finding and training the top riders.

Meanwhile, competition among the junior riders matched the growth of the sport. The National Junior Championships, which took place at a designated three-day event at the Preliminary level, had attracted only a handful of competitors in the late 1960s. By the 70's, however, it was not unusual to find upwards of 60 juniors eager to win the Harry T. Peters Trophy. Most of these juniors had learned their basic skills in their local branches of the U.S. Pony Clubs before going on to participate in local and national events. Such riders as Bea Perkins, who was Junior Champion on Little Flyer in 1972, Ralph Hill in 1973, Laurie Penfield in 1975, Story Jenks in 1976 and Bea Perkins again in 1978 (this time on County Frost), went on to become international riders. Tad Coffin and Caroline Treviranus were both Pony Club A riders who graduated to the international scene. The opportunities for training young riders improved each year.

After each Olympic Games, Le Goff set in motion a four-year plan. In each post-Olympic year he organized a series of screening trials throughout the country where he scouted for promising riders. The cream of these were invited to an intensive training session with Le Goff and the very best were invited to stay on for future training. This constant search for talent continues to this day and the young riders selected are given the opportunity to compete both at home and abroad under the watchful eye of the USET coach.

Giving further impetus to the junior riders was the North American Junior Team Championship competition between the United States and Canada, which was first held (in Canada) in 1974. The Canadians also hosted the next competition in 1975, the Americans hosted the next two and then the competition began alternating annually between the two countries. The USCTA Areas and the Canadian Combined Training Association's zones began to hold their own regional selection trials and to pick coaches for the junior teams, thus giving the junior riders a taste of international competition at the Preliminary level. The Junior team from USCTA Area II was the first American team to win in 1976, coached by Jim Wofford. The Area I team, coached by Tad Coffin, took home the title in 1977, 1978, and 1979. Offering junior riders a chance at their own competition created an intense interest among the ranks of the Pony Club riders.

The most exciting event of 1977 was held in October at Ledyard Farm and was again designated as a CCI. Riders from England and Europe made the trip in hopes of taking the title away from the Americans on their home ground. Besides the usual excitement of the competition, additional interest was sparked by the presence of MGM film crews, who were busy recording the action for "International Velvet." Tatum O'Neal and her co-stars were surrounded by a sea of riders and spectators as they acted out their roles. Drenched by a wicked nor'easter, the Ledyard Three-Day Event of 1977 attracted thousands of spectators, TV cameras, and a large contingent of national and local press. Michael Plumb, riding the ex-Australian horse Laurenson, purchased by Mr. and Mrs. Ronald Marra at the close of the Montreal Olympic Games, won the Ledyard 1977 event, also designated as the National Open Championships that year. The same pair also became the Leading Horse and Rider of the Year. As further proof of his superb skills, Plumb also finished second in the Ledyard event on his Olympic mount, Better and Better. Lucinda Prior-Palmer of Great Britain was the leading foreign rider, finishing in third place on Killaire. The Ledyard Event had become one of the premier international events and the European riders had developed a great respect for the courses Neil Ayer had designed there, considering them to be equal to any in the world.

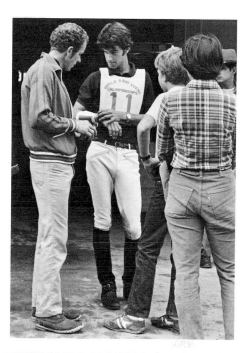

Right: The oldest and youngest USET riders at Lexington 1978—J. Michael Plumb (left) and Mike Huber (right)

Below: The USET three-day world championship team poses after the 1978 Chesterland (Pa.) selection trials. Left to right: Assistant coach Denny Emerson, Jim Wofford on Carawich, Tad Coffin on Bally Cor, Bruce Davidson on Might Tango, and J. Michael Plumb on Laurenson

Davidson and Might Tango emerged as the new World Champions, with an unprecedented double gold for Bruce. John Watson of Ireland on Cambridge Blue was the individual silver medalist, and Helmut Rethemeier of West Germany on Ladalco was the bronze finalist. Canada won the team gold, West Germany the silver and the U.S. the bronze.

Right: 3 USET riders scrutinize dressage rides at the Lexington (Ky.) World Championships, 1978. Left to right: Mike Huber, Story Jenks, Ralph Hill

Below: Capacity crowd at dressage day, Lexington (Ky.) World Championships 1978

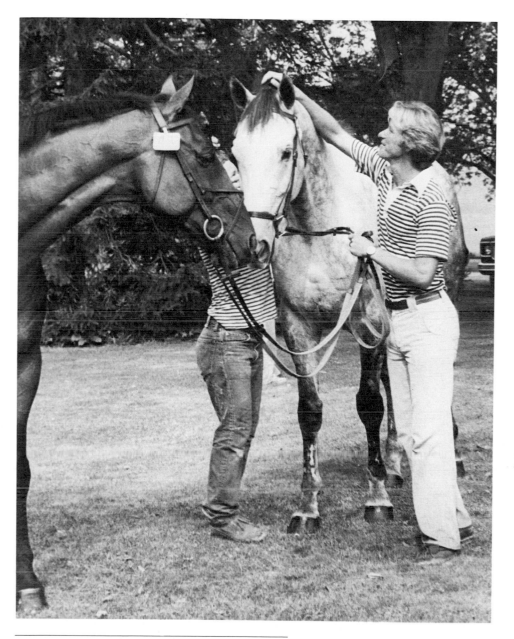

Two-time world champion Bruce Davidson poses with his winning horses—Irish Cap (left) and Might Tango

Caroline Treviranus, riding in her second World Championships was fifth after the endurance phase and had a chance at a medal. But her horse fell on the stadium course, catapulting her to the ground where a heavy rail struck her temple. She was evacuated by a U.S. Army helicopter to a hospital in Lexington, Ky., where she lay in a coma for two weeks. Fortunately the strong constitution of an event rider stood her in good stead and she regained consciousness after a heart-rending period and is riding in competition again today. Her accident sparked a renewed interest in safety, resulting in a new AHSA rule requiring all hats for jumping competitions to be secured by a proper chin harness.

As a climax to the year, Bea Perkins won the National Junior Championships for the second time, and Michael Plumb won the National Open Championships for the third time on yet another great horse, Better and Better.

Jack Fritz, who has served on just about every committee involved with combined training, has written the AHSA Combined Training Rule Book and has supported the sport in countless ways, was the second recipient of the newly dedicated Wofford Trophy in 1978.

Jack Fritz, winner of the Wofford Trophy, 1978, and one of eventing's most dedicated enthusiasts (Photo by Judith J. McClung)

The Pre-Olympic Year and the Olympic Year 1979–1980

The controversies stirred up by the results in Kentucky swirled throughout the international eventing community. Several suggestions for reducing the severity of the speed and endurance phases were offered by many concerned riders and coaches. Jack Le Goff called for eliminating the roads and tracks phases, arguing that it proved nothing and took too big a toll of the horses who then had to run and jump. Others argued for reducing speeds, while still others suggested lengthening the compulsory halt before Phase D. The FEI finally made two slight changes in the rules: the speed for roads and tracks was reduced from 240 mpm to 220 mpm, and the length of the steeplechase phase was limited. The general consensus was that to eliminate the roads and tracks phases would change the sport drastically.

With the 1980 Olympics on the horizon, the expense involved in preparing a U.S. team that could compete at the level became a major concern. As more and more major competitions are added to the calendar, more and more riders find

that they are in desperate need of good sound horses. The expense of eventing at the international level is astronomical. Without sponsorship or state funds, producing and competing an international horse becomes almost prohibitively expensive.

The USET, a non-profit organization largely dependent on private contributions, has funded the teams that have represented the United States but the organization cannot manage alone. Corporate sponsorship, well established in Great Britain, for the most part has been lacking in America. But gradually the big corporations have begun to recognize the attraction of the sport. For Ledyard in 1977, Insilco (the international jewellers) offered both a trophy and prize money. In early 1981, Almaden (wines) became a major, on-going sponsor for USET competitions, including the Chesterland (Pa.) Three-Day Event. Later that year, Rolex (watches) sponsored the Rolex Kentucky Three-Day Event, as well as the three spring selection trials for the 1982 World Championships at Blue Ridge (Va.), Ship's Quarters (Md.), and Lexington (Ky.).

The Pan American Games of 1979 were to be held in Puerto Rico and would not include a Three-Day Event, so the USET decided to send horses and riders to England to compete at the Badminton Three-Day Event. With the Olympic year coming up, it was vital that the Americans have a chance to participate in competitions abroad. Jack Le Goff believes that there is no substitution for the experience of international competition.

Jim Wofford and Carawich and Derek di Grazia with Thriller II were given USET grants for the trip; Karen Lende with March Brown, Karen Sachey with High Kite, and Wash Bishop with Jones also made the journey with the coach. Unfortunately, Derek di Grazia's Thriller II injured a leg prior to the event and was unable to compete. Jones was eliminated in a still-controversial decision after the dressage test. Karen Sachey, who had only one stop cross-country, was eliminated by the triple combination in the sta-

dium round. Karen Lende finished in tenth place on March Brown, with four rails down in the stadium round and Jim Wofford and Carawich finished fourth overall, also a victim of the stadium course.

On the home front, the National Open Championship was won by Denny Emerson on the New Zealand-bred York; USCTA Area I again won the North American Junior Team Championships; Nina Fout won the Junior National Title on Rimrock; and Karen Ehmann from Oregon won the newest trophy—the Linda Moore Trophy for the leading junior rider in the country. Karen is yet another young rider to emerge from the ranks of the U.S. Pony Clubs.

In 1979 Whitney Stone, who had guided the infant USET through all its growing pains ably and with much enthusiasm, was awarded the Wofford Trophy as a token of respect for his great organizational achievement and sound leadership.

If Badminton is the major spring attraction in England, the Three-Day Event at Burghley is the autumn drawing card. The USET awarded a grant to Torrance Watkins to travel to Europe with Red's Door and Poltroon for their first big competition. Poltroon, a small pinto mare, is somewhat of an anomaly in the event world, which is accustomed to large horses. Poltroon's quickness, agility, and heart make her able to compete on terms with the best in the world. The little mare attracted the attention of the vast British crowds, not only by her odd coloring, but also by her sparkling performances. Torrance finished second, just one point behind Andrew Hoy of Australia—to the consternation of the British, who regard Burghley as their own event. Jack Le Goff was delighted to discover a talented new pair.

Alexander Mackay-Smith was awarded the Wofford Trophy for 1980, in recognition of his contributions as co-founder of both the U.S. Pony Clubs and the U.S. Combined Training Association and for his early efforts to encourage combined training in this country. Through his position as editor and more recently as international editor of the weekly magazine, *The Chronicle of the Horse*, he has been a prime factor in developing interest in and support for eventing in the United States and Canada.

Although the Olympic Games are supposed to be above politics, the world situation in 1980—particularly the crisis in Iran and the Russian occupation of Afghanistan—led to a boycott of the Olympic Games held in Moscow. Most of the major eventing countries opted to bypass the Three-Day Event in Moscow. As an alternative the French offered to host a major Three-Day Event at Fontainebleau. Twelve nations sent riders; eleven full teams competed.

The usual series of selection trials proved once and for all that Torrance Watkins and Poltroon were the pair to beat in America. Second in the Ship's Quarters (Md.) Horse Trials, the pair won the next two selection trials at Blue Ridge and Kentucky. Jack Le Goff, with his eyes forever on the future, decided to take riders to compete not only at Fontainebleau but also at the annual Three-Day Event at Luhmuhlen, Germany, to get a look at the terrain to be used for the next World Championships in 1982.

A total of twelve horses and riders made the trip to Europe with Le Goff: Michael Plumb and Laurenson; Jim Wofford and Carawich; Torrance Watkins and Poltroon; and Michael Huber with Gold Chip made up the team of four at Fontainebleau, while Wash Bishop on Taxi and Karen Stives on The Saint competed as individuals. Fortune again withheld her favors from the American team. Michael Plumb and Laurenson were again eliminated cross-country, while Gold Chip suffered a fracture on course and could not compete in the stadium round. The remaining two U.S. team members, however, upheld the American reputation: Jim Wofford on Carawich won the individual silver medal and Torrance Watkins on Poltroon finished third, to take the individual bronze medal. Karen Stives finished in 34th place on The Saint. The French won the team gold medals and young Nils Haagensen of Denmark, who had won the European Championship the previous year, took the individual gold medal, riding Monaco.

The second-string American team, with less experienced horses, went on to the competition in Luhmuhlen, Germany. Michael Plumb again led the U.S. squad, this time riding his old friend Better and Better. The remaining American riders were Derek di Grazia with Thriller II, Ralph Hill and Jump Shot, Grant Schneidman on Leonidas, Karen Sachey on Alpine, and Kim Walnes on The Gray Goose.

Luhmuhlen was classified as a CCI and was not an official FEI international team competition. Nevertheless, unofficial teams were named from four nations, namely Great Britain, Switzerland, the United States, and West Germany. Individual riders from Canada and Holland also competed. Michael Plumb vindicated himself by taking first place and Derek di Grazia overcame his streak of bad luck to finish fifth. Grant Schneidman, riding in his first international event, placed eighth overall, assuring the United States of a team victory, albeit an unofficial one. Kim Walnes was 22nd and Karen Sachey finished 32nd. Jump Shot (Ralph Hill's horse) pulled a muscle and was unable to complete the stadium phase.

The results of both Fontainebleau and Luhmuhlen were both encouraging and disappointing, but some invaluable experience was gained by the U.S. riders.

Since most of the Advanced level horses had competed in Europe, the entries in the U.S. National Open Championships were somewhat reduced. Jim Wofford on the USET's Alex won the competition, held at Chesterland in Unionville, (Pa.). Poltroon and Torrance Watkins won a total of five annual trophies between them, including the leading horse and rider awards. Nancy Bliss on Cobblestone won the National Junior title along with the Linda Moore Trophy for the leading junior rider of the year. The number of competitions reflected the enormous growth of eventing during the 1970s.

Maj.-Gen. Jonathan Burton was the fifth winner of the Wofford Trophy in 1981. In addition to being a former member of the U.S. Team, as organizer of some of the first events ever held, he was instrumental in the foundation of eventing as a popular sport in the United States. For 30 years Jack Burton has been an active and positive force furthering the development of combined training in the U.S.

Looking Back—Looking Forward (1951)

Since the Three-Day Event has been included in the Olympic Games it is interesting to note that only two countries, France and the United States, have sent teams to every single Olympics.

Whereas twenty years ago there were only a few combined training events in the United States, attracting only a handful of riders, by 1980 there were 171 events with over 15,000 starters. Although they are primarily concentrated on the eastern seaboard, registered and unregistered events are now held all over the United States, with new ones being organized every year.

The widespread availability of Pony Club training and the increased number of events at all levels has afforded every opportunity for the talented horse and rider to climb the ladder. Since winning the silver team medal at the Tokyo Olympic Games in 1964, the United States has become a top international contender in combined training. There is every reason to believe that we will continue to occupy a top position in the future.

James Wofford presents the 1981 Wofford trophy to Maj.-Gen. Jonathan Burton (Photo by Irene Cromer)

The Pre-Training Level Course at Lang Farm (Cheney, Wash.)

Pete Costello
(Photo by Ed Lawrence)

Pete Costello began his course-building career in the East, although he is known primarily as a West Coast course designer. He built a course near Norfolk, Va. when he was still in the U.S. Navy and built another course at Sweet Briar College in Sweet Briar, Va. On his return to Oregon he was asked by Kevin Freeman to help construct some training fences before the 1976 Olympic selection trials and from then on he has been building courses all over the West.

Like many of the major course builders, Pete developed a feel for what is appropriate at each level, and since most of the western riders to date have been competing at the lower levels, Pete has become one of the most experienced course designers for the Pre-Training and Training level events.

He commutes between the East and West Coasts and can often be found in the East, helping to construct major courses, or observing the competition at any major event. With his truck camper and his dogs, Pete is perhaps the most traveled course builder on the continent.

Pete Costello, Designer

I believe that a Pre-Training course should be built so that everyone should get around. I do not think that the emphasis should be on competition at this level. I think that the Pre-Training level should just be an introduction to the sport, which is geared toward giving horses and riders experience more than awards.

A Pre-Training course should be easy enough so that anyone on a horse or pony can get around it. People who have foxhunted all their lives and who can get around a very basic hunter course should have no trouble competing at the Pre-Training level.

A course at the Pre-Training level should include almost everything that the higher levels include, but on a smaller scale: banks, drops, ups and downs, water (if at all possible), brush fences, oxers, verticals, and logs—all little inviting jumps that say "come jump me," and that the rider does not have to worry about. The course should be somewhat over a mile in length, and I do not think that any particular fitness should be required. The riders should get a taste of galloping between fences; you do not want to put a lot of little fences too close together. I will not include any 24-foot in and outs, but I will put in some fences that are related to each other. I like to run a Pre-Training course alongside a Training level course, and a Training level course beside a Preliminary one, so the riders can see that it is not such a big step to move up a division.

The course

Lang Farm is in Cheney, Wa., just outside Spokane, and is the property of Dr. Henry Lang, a cardiologist. Dr. Lang took up riding at the age of 54 because his daughter rode. Since there were no events for him to go to in the immediate vicinity and the demands of his profession prevented him from traveling far away, Dr. Lang purchased some country property with the idea of building a house and designing and constructing a cross-country course, in order to start a new event. Richard Newton had visited the site and drew up some preliminary plans for courses; I based my plans on his and added some of my own ideas. Oddly enough, when Richard walked over the ground it was very wet, but for most of the year the ground is very dry. The total precipitation in Spokane is four inches or so per year. It does not rain very often, and I could use a great deal more of the land when it was dry.

This is one of the two events in the West that offer really good footing. The other one is in Flagstaff, Az. The soil here is a sandy loam, both in the open and in the woods, and it remains soft; you cannot hear the horses coming along. The ground does not get hard, and it does not get mushy. Much of the course runs through rolling barley fields. There are some pine woods, and an island of pine trees in the middle of one barley field. It is one of the most perfect sites I have ever seen for the lower levels. I think it would be possible to add a Preliminary course, but no higher, because there just is not enough room.

For the dressage ring you can just go out and pick a spot—there is plenty of level ground, and the same applies to the stadium course. Last year we set up the stadium course on a slight rise so the riders had some incline to deal with on the course.

Most of the property is of a yellow hue, with the barley fields and sandy soil. The pine trees are dark green and brown, and the house has been built as an earth shelter in tones that blend into the scenery. I built the course out of local materials to try to blend it in with the landscape.

The first fence consists of bales of barley, baled in the field with a pine rail over the top. It is simple and inviting, with a bigger fence just like it right next to it for the Training level. The facing frontage of these fences averages about 20 feet across because that is the practical length to get out of the local pine trees. Placing the fence alongside the Training level fence makes it look quite long and imposing. Most of the fences on the course were this wide, although some in the woods were narrower.

The course then ran into the woods and over a vertical gate made of pine rails. I placed the gate about three strides into the woods so that the horses would already be in the shade by the time they approached the fence, and their eyes would have adjusted to the change of light. From there they galloped by a couple of the Training level fences and came to a bank.

I cut back a natural hill and piled three pine logs on top of each other to revet the ground, making a simple bank up. Again there is a larger version of the bank right alongside, using bigger logs, for the Training level.

The next fence was the first question for the rider. It was a simple stacked cord of wood but I added rails sloping from left to right on the top, to make it more

challenging. The fence is sited on the crown of a hill and, as the riders approach, it looks like a huge, huge fence, but when they get up to it it is nothing.

From there the course winds out into the barley field again and I put an oxer at the top of a slight hill. Each time the course went out into the barley field we had cut a path for the horses to follow, and we made that path curve and bend so that it was not just simply a case of getting out into the field and galloping hell bent for leather down a straight track; it made them keep some semblance of control.

After the oxer they came on downhill to the island of trees in the middle of the barley field. It is natural to bend a horse around this clump of trees. Here I offered them a type of L fence—not a true L, but a fence that would give them the feeling of an L fence. I built a true L for the Training level competitors and put the Pre-Training fence on the outside of that. Training riders had to jump a big fat log, and then turn and jump out over the end of the other fence. Although the Pre-Training fences were not actually connected, the Training level fence was, so this gave the riders the feel of jumping an L. The Pre-Training riders actually had three or four strides before the second part.

The next fence was not made entirely out of material from the property. It was a standard steeplechase type of fence with a brush box two feet high, with some flimsy brush in it that the horses could brush through. It caused quite a bit of trouble. It was not at all solid but rather flimsy and it stood in the middle of the field after the island of trees and had a Training level fence next to it. I have no idea why it should have caused any problems, but it did both years it was there.

After this fence the riders had a good gallop across the barley field into the woods again. We built an oxer between two trees, banging rails high and low and making a frame. Again this was sited after they had come into the shade, probably about eight strides into the woods.

I found a natural gully in the woods and built a version of a coffin fence there. I put a fence of stacked pine rails about 2' high just before the lip of the gully (I put the Training level stack of rails right on the lip) and a fence on the far side of the gully. If you measured straight across there was probably about thirty feet between the two fences, but taking the gully into consideration, it was more like fifty feet. There was not much of a gully but it gave the feeling of jumping down into something. It rode very well indeed; a couple of people got a little concerned and stopped the first time, but on the whole the horses just jumped right on through.

Then came the waterloo for many riders. There have been a great many theories as to why this fence caused so much grief. I had put a big fat log over a small ditch with a trickle of water running through it. The ditch was

not revetted because it had good established turf on both sides, yet only about seven horses managed to jump it clean. You could see the jump from all the way across the field. The first four horses jumped it with no problem at all, but the fifth girl fell off when her horse stopped and she fell on her shoulder. After that there were six eliminations in a row.

There were 55 entries in the division and I believe seven of those people had evented before. In fact, out of all the organizing committees—everyone on every committee—only one person had even seen an event before. I think the psychological factors began to mount up. The fence judge at this particular fence, who was the one person who had been to an event before, allowed the riders to keep trying once they had refused out. She sat there and let the riders back up and so the next rider would be coming along and look over at the fence and there would be two or three other horses piled up there, milling around. The riders would come galloping along, turn towards the fence, and many of the horses looked down into the ditch and refused. But by the time I got back to the fence and got things straightened out, the fence's reputation had been established and it became a psychological problem. Half the horses in the division were eliminated there.

On every course I have built since then I have tried to include a similar fence. I have built fences before that were just the same; I do not know what happened. For the second year, I changed the obstacle somewhat. I did not want to take the fence out

of the course and make a drastic change, which would be tantamount to admitting publicly that it was a mistake, but I raised the log to get the horses to look up instead of into the ditch, and I put a ground line in front of it. I also added another jump four strides in front of it. I took two big logs and put another log across them, just as I had at the ditch, so essentially I built the exact same fence four strides out. Many of the competitors jumped the first log fine and still stopped at the second.

I have heard many theories but no one has come up with a good one. Jack Burton was almost killed there. He was conducting an educational seminar on eventing and he could not get the horses over this fence. He was acting as a wing, standing on one side to help a horse over when he got knocked down and trampled. There were hoofprints on his overcoat! I am still at a loss to explain what went wrong; this should be a good Pre-Training ditch with a log over it. You have to include these types of fences in courses to prepare riders for the higher levels.

After that, the riders came to a fence that consisted of two pine poles with a drop on the far side. It was a natural wide drop and I added sloping rails on either side, to entice them over. From there the course swung back to the barley field again and out into the open.

The Training level course followed another loop around to give those riders more distance, but the Pre-Training people

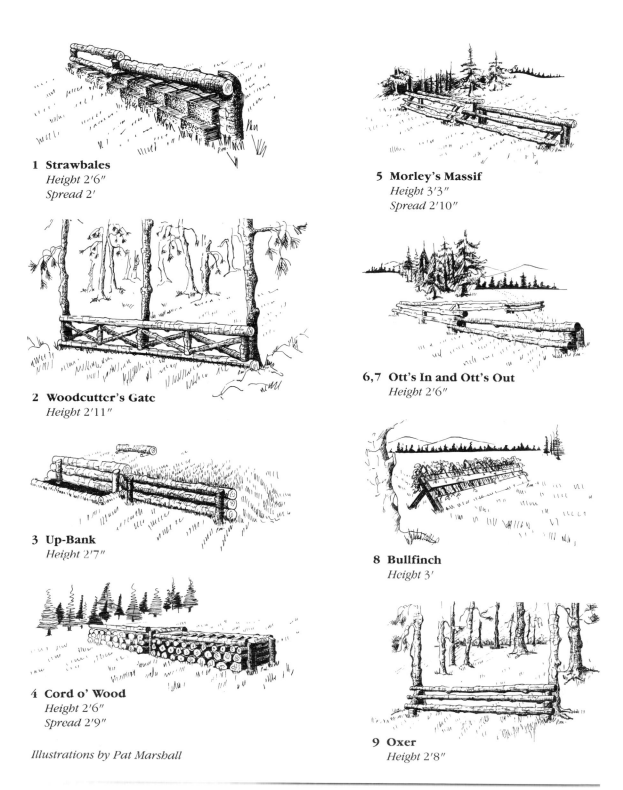

1 Strawbales
Height 2'6"
Spread 2'

2 Woodcutter's Gate
Height 2'11"

3 Up-Bank
Height 2'7"

4 Cord o' Wood
Height 2'6"
Spread 2'9"

Illustrations by Pat Marshall

5 Morley's Massif
Height 3'3"
Spread 2'10"

6,7 Ott's In and Ott's Out
Height 2'6"

8 Bullfinch
Height 3'

9 Oxer
Height 2'8"

*jumped a Tidworth next. I think
this is a useful jump because it
looks like the jumps you see in
the books on eventing and yet it
is nothing to jump.*

*I put a tiger trap next, to lead
them back over the same ditch.
The water at this point had dried
up and there was not much of a
ditch left. I put a shark's-tooth
type of tiger trap over it. It did
cause some problems, perhaps
more at the Training level than at
Pre-Training, mostly (I believe)
because of the name of the fence.*

*The final fence was a triple
bar, which was raised for the
Training level.*

*This course was designed for
riders who do not get to many
events. The standard of riding
has improved a little over the
past two years, but the event is
still the only one in the immediate vicinity. (There are some a
good distance away.) The people
who ride in this event do not
event a great deal; this event is
the one they prepare for all year.
It has a little bit of everything
and it is a nice friendly place to
go for the weekend.*

Leslie Ratti, Rider

When I walked the course I
thought that it looked very
straightforward, with nothing
particularly complicated about it.
The footing was soft and excellent, both in the fields and
through the woods. Some places
in the woods were a bit tricky,
and there were a few rocks and
uneven places. I remember
thinking to myself that I had to
stay in the middle of the track to
avoid some of the ruts. I
watched some of the Training
level riders jump around their
fences.

On Course

The first fence was inviting
and jumped very well. The time
allowed for the course was very
generous so I kept my eye on the
watch and decided that I could
go very easily to see if I could
stay close to the optimum time.
The second fence was just inside
the woods—an upright gate. The
mare had time to adjust to the
dark, so she jumped it well. After
that we went along past one of
the Training level fences and my
mare thought that she was meant
to jump that too, so I had to turn
her away from it. We got around
it and jumped the bank up. Some
riders seemed to lose some of
their momentum here. I almost
lost our forward movement going up the hill after the bank.
The log pile on top of the hill
looked big but I pushed on.
Koos gave an enormous leap and
I nearly fell off because she
jumped from a standstill and I
was behind the motion. I got
myself back together going
down the hill toward the L. I had
decided to stay over to the right
on the approach. I got her lined
up, trotted over the first element,
and went on in a smooth line
over the second part. A lot of
horses had problems here because their riders' approach was
not organized.

The bullfinch, which came
next, caused a lot of trouble.
Koos started to back off when
she saw it but I kept my leg on
and tried to build up the speed.
She jumped right over the brush
instead of through it! The fence
had some high and low spots in
it and was airy; a lot of the
horses were not used to fences
like this. The horses that had
some mileage did better here
than the green ones did. I remember smiling to myself all the
way across the field after that
fence because the mare had
jumped about four feet in the air
to clear the brush.

We galloped on at a leisurely
pace to the halfway marker. I remembered to look at my watch,
and we went back into the
woods again. It was dark but not
so dark that it was ominous. By
this time Koos was going really
well and the next fence was easily the best fence on the whole
course—it was a fun fence. I had
to keep my wits about me after it
because the track went to the left
and uphill and the inclination
was to go straight on down another track. The next fence was
fun also; there was a small fence
before a drop into a ditch and
another log on the far side. I
tried to keep the mare in balance
and to keep up the momentum
and go with the horse. It turned
out to be no problem. We then
went on through the woods and
down the hill to the ditch filled
with water. I had watched this
fence being jumped the previous
year when everyone had such a
terrible time with it and I remember thinking to myself, "I would

10,11 Gulley Down and Gulley Up
Height 1'10", 2'

12,13 Log and Rivermere
Log: height 1'6"
Rivermere: Spread 2'9"

14 Log
Height 2'1"
Drop 2'3"

really like to do this eventing."
At that time I had never seen an event before.

There were two ways of getting to this jump—one downhill on a slight angle, or you could bring the horse down the slope earlier and make a flat approach. I concentrated on the first fence and got that one right and the second one almost made an in and out. The mare hesitated so I

15 Tidworth
Maximum height 3'
Minimum height 1'6"

16 Tiger Trap
Height 2'6"
Spread 3'8"

17 Triple Bar
Height 3'1"
Spread 4'2"

reached around and smacked her with the whip and she hopped over. All the spectators cheered, which gave me a boost, and I gave the mare a pat and galloped on out of the woods. I felt terrific.

The third to the last fence was easy. At this point I was anticipating the tiger trap. Unfortunately, I have this habit of looking down into the ditches, which makes the horse hesitate. If I can keep my eyes out of ditches I'm all right. We got over the ditch in good fashion, and I was laughing

to myself as we went on to the Tidworth and the long gallop to the triple bar. Because I had been so conscious of the time allowed, I had gone very slowly cross-country but, as it turned out, I was just within the optimum time.

The stadium phase has never given us any trouble since Koos has had lots of miles over stadium fences. We jumped a clean stadium round but had .75 time penalties. However, the rider who tied for first with us in dressage had time penalties on cross-country and stadium, so we won the division.

Next year I plan to move up to Training level and will try to get to at least four events if I can take the time off from my job.

The Training Level Course (Heritage Park, Johnson Co., Kans.)

Richard Newton

Richard Newton left his native England in the early 1960s to become farm manager for the Potomac Horse Center in Maryland. There he built and designed Potomac's well-known cross-country course, site of the 1973 Junior National Championships. As Richard gained a reputation for building sound and safe courses, his course-building hobby turned into a full-time occupation. Today Richard has had a hand in building and designing many of the country's leading cross-country courses, including those at the Blue Ridge (Va.) and Ledyard (Mass.) events.

Richard Newton, Designer

The Site

When I reached the park I could see why Gary had been so enthusiastic about it. The land was like much of the farmland on the East Coast. It was not tremendously hilly, but there were some nice rolling hills, with quite a few trees and wooded areas, plus some existing fence lines that could be incorporated into the course design. It was not all wide open flat land as I had expected. Between the small hills and valleys, and the gullies that had been eroded by water runoff (which had since been allowed to fill with grass), I had a wide choice of sites for obstacles. The terrain was considerably more challenging than I had expected.

Most of the trees were osage orange, or hedge, as they are called out there. The wood of those trees is so hard that I know I broke ten teeth off my chain saw trying to cut through one tree in a fence line (although the barbed wire embedded in it did not help). Many of the trees had grown into or around the wire fences, which had obviously been there for years. I could definitely use both the fence lines and the little rises and dips in the fields.

As you crossed what appeared to be very flat fields, you came across hummocks and soft ditches—all very useable.

My job was to inspect this property and to see first of all if it was suitable for a cross-country course. Secondly, I was to decide what level of competition could possibly be held there. There had been some talk of starting an annual senior riders competition at the Preliminary level—much like the National Young Rider Championships— and Gary Goodwin had mentioned to me that Heritage Park might be an ideal site for such a competition, since it was geographically in the middle of the country. When I inspected the site, I kept thinking in the back of my mind that I might eventually need a place to put a steeplechase course and that I might need room for roads and tracks. I would need to reserve areas for this and plan everything else around those areas. The course designs I did come up with lend themselves to future expansion.

Training Level

My first objective when designing a Training level course is to provide an enjoyable experience for the horse and rider; second, I want to get all or most of the horses around clean (even though I know full well that I will not); and third, I want the course to be a learning experience. Perhaps for a lot of riders this course might be their introduction to the sport.

I like to have every obstacle be straightforward and very solid with direct approaches. The approach can be uphill or downhill but I do not like to ask a Training level horse to come upon a fence suddenly and be taken by surprise, or to jump where it looks as if the horse will be jumping off into space. I do not mind if, as you come into an obstacle, it looks as if you are going to drop away into a great abyss— as long as there is an obvious place to touch down when you get there. Very often you see slides built with a rail at the top, but that type of fence does not interest me. I think that what we need to do is to educate the horses and riders at the Training level so they can move up to the Preliminary level.

The Training level course I built in Kansas came in for some criticism because it lacked combination fences. Before the actual competition, some people were of the opinion that the course was far too easy and that no one would have any trouble getting around it. They were amazed by the final statistics on refusals and eliminations.

It is very difficult to go into a new area of the country, where you know absolutely nothing about the capability of the riders, and to come up with a course that is going to test them yet not frighten them. At the same time, the riders need to have some fun so they will come back the next year and move up a level. What I

tried to do was to lay out the Training level course as close as possible to the Preliminary course, so the riders would not only look at their own fences but could see what the other division was jumping. Eventually I also designed and built a Pre-Training course at Heritage Park and I laid that out along the same track for the same reason. Obviously this overall plan also made it easier to move the jump judges and spectators around the different courses.

The Course

The first fence was made of two old horse-drawn wagons. I placed them back to back and— since I had a great deal of timber left after I had cleared out those osage orange tree lines—I simply piled this wood over the wagons. This served as the first fence for both the Training and Preliminary levels. From there on I separated the courses because I wanted to use a tougher second fence for the Preliminary division than I was allowed to use for Training level. Both second fences were designed along the same lines. I found a slight step (of perhaps 9 inches) down from one field into another, through an overgrown hedgerow. I just fitted rails into the existing trees. The Preliminary fence caused no trouble but the Training level fence caused some, perhaps because the horses were not galloping on as yet, and changed their minds and backed off at the last moment.

I wanted to build a trakehner for the third fence, but I did not

want to leave too much air under it for the Training level, although I did not mind some air underneath for the Preliminary level. This was a fence that could be shared by the two divisions—a factor of paramount importance for course designers to keep in mind when trying to keep costs down (and building a brand-new cross-country course anywhere these days is expensive). I built this trakehner on an angle so that the Preliminary people had a choice of approaching the fence at a 45 degree angle and at the last moment either going inside or outside a clump of trees, then straight on to the succeeding fence; or, if they wanted to take it straight, they had to ride almost a figure "S" between obstacles. The Training level riders approached the fence straight on. I tried to set up different approaches for the shared fence so the Preliminary people would not think the course was beneath them, and so the Training level people would not think they were jumping a course that was too hard for them.

I had to build a ramp up to the take-off for the trakehner because the ditch itself was not deep enough. I also put a rail over the ditch. The spread from the back of the ditch to the front of the revetting was 4'6", and with the rail in the middle it appeared to be about 3' high. It was something that most of the Training level riders had not seen before and they started to have problems here. There was one refusal and one fall.

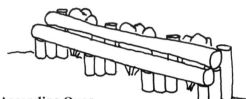

1 Log Wagon
Height 3'
Spread 3'6"

2 Ascending Oxer
Height 3'

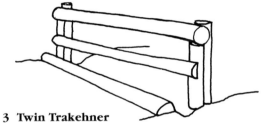

3 Twin Trakehner
Height 2'9"
Spread 4'6"

4 Lamb Creep
Height 3'3"
Spread 4'7"

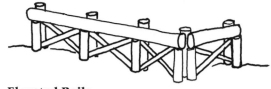

5 Elevated Rails
Height 2'9"

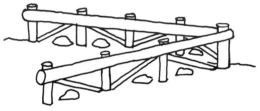

6 The L
Height 3'3"

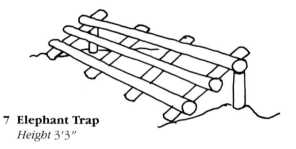

7 Elephant Trap
Height 3'3"

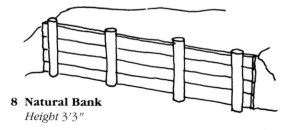

8 Natural Bank
Height 3'3"

Illustrations by Jean Hammond

For the next fence (4) I built a very solid lamb creep—the first solid fence they had seen. The fence line was very airy, with only a few trees in it, and I conceived the idea of putting a lamb creep here because there had been an old sheep shelter there at one time or another. It was a solid fence that they could land on and jump off if they wanted to.

The fifth fence was the first one I had fun with. I had no idea of the capability of the Training/Preliminary level riders and if I had built what I had originally intended, I was scared that the competition might have ended right there. Originally I wanted to have a double-ditch coffin starting with a jump across a small post and rails on top of a small slope; then a short downhill approach to a straightforward 4' wide ditch (which would not be revetted, but would have the take-off side capped with a half-round telephone pole). Then they would jump onto a grassy bank on the other side with 18 feet to another 4' ditch; then 17 feet to another post and rail. This year (in 1981) I just used the second ditch and the second post and rails (the C and D elements of the entire complex) and everyone seemed to get through with hardly any trouble at all. Some riders approached the combination a bit too aggressively and it appeared as if the distance between the ditch and the vertical might have been a little short for them. However, I believe that if we put two more elements in front of the ones we gave them this year, it is going to make the horses back off that much more.

It seems to me that the more elements there are, the shorter the horse's strides will become between elements, and the less momentum (impulsion) the horses will have. If you have two fences they attack the combination; if you have three, the horses are a bit slower between the second and third elements; and if you have four, they really lose their momentum between the third and fourth.

This fence (5) was actually a post and rail on top of a rise. The Preliminary level fence had an overgrown ditch about 17 feet in front of it that I had dug out, but on the Training level side there was just a small swale in front of the fence. I did not particularly want a ditch in front of a vertical for the Training level horses and riders; I just wanted to give them the feeling of riding over some uneven ground before jumping the rail. The Training level horses would jump that this year, and if they moved up a level next year, they would have had something in their background to prepare them for the type of fence they would ultimately be dealing with at the Preliminary level.

The next fence on the Training level course was a simple L fence that the rider had to steer through very carefully to avoid the blackthorn locust trees on either side. There is no kidding around with blackthorn locusts—even the thorns have thorns. They are incredibly nasty. The fence was not a true L—it had a more

open angle, which did not give the rider the option of jumping the corner. It could be bounced, or the horse could take one or as many strides as needed. The fence was 3' high and there was plenty of room to do whatever the rider wanted. It was the first time that the riders had been asked to jump two fences in quick succession and I wanted to give them a choice. I did not dictate that they must jump the first one in a certain place and the second one in another specified place. I feel very strongly that in the lower levels you need to make a fence wide enough and long enough so that everyone can choose his own line through it. If the rider makes the wrong decision and has a stop or refusal, then it is his own fault.

The next fence (7—an elephant trap over a ditch) was a straightforward galloping fence for the riders after giving them the steering problem of the L.

The eighth fence was just a simple step up from one level to another. This year the fence rode so easily that no one took any notice of it, so next year I am going to add a ditch at the base to make the horses stand off more, and—about 19 feet from the bank—I shall add a post and rail. This was something I would have liked to have done when the course was first built, but I was afraid that if I built it to Preliminary level standards, no Training level horse would get through; and if I built it for Training level standards, it would be just another fence in the way for the Preliminary riders. I let everyone jump the simple bank just as it was.

From there the Training level course ran up a hill into a wide open field with absolutely nothing to attach a fence to. I built a Montreal oxer just over the top of the hill. I call it a Montreal oxer because the first time I saw a fence like it was in Montreal at the 1976 Olympic Games. Instead of building it with both the front and back rails at a slope, I built this fence with vertical back rails. Training level dimensions are so small that if I were to make both elements lean in an oxer like this, the top would be too narrow or both elements would be almost vertical. If you want the front rails to lean at any angle then the back ones have to be vertical.

The organizers of the event questioned some of the riders as they came off the course. All riders naturally think about how the course went for them personally, so the comments ranged from bad to good. The one fact that I really remember was that most people said that this ascending oxer was the one fence they could really gallop at and that they got an exhilarating feeling of flying out over it. The oxer was placed on top of the hill and it loomed up on the skyline as they came up the slope, but when the horses actually got up to the fence, the field stretched away in front of them. It was the high point on the course.

From that point the Training level riders went down to a drop fence. I had envisioned placing a big curved log in front of the drop here, but I could not find a big enough log, so I came up with a couple of willow trees instead. There was a big drop on the landing side, which you could not see until you came up to it. I had thought that there might be more trouble here because this was the first time the ground really dropped away on the far side, but the gully into which they were jumping was readily visible from ten strides away. I thought that the riders might have some problems in steering a good line because the willow trees were curved. I was concerned that they would be concentrating on steering and would not come in with enough impulsion to coax their horses to jump over the trees and land on ground that was falling away from them. The fence stopped one horse completely, but otherwise rode well.

We were fortunate enough to be able to build a water jump. It seems to me that water jumps make or break a cross-country course. I would rather have water and use it well than use a muddy puddle that does not prove anything. Luckily at Heritage Park there was an area next to a pond that was a little bit damp and swampy because cattle had been walking around in it. We went in there with a big tractor, dug out a big basin, and filled it with about 165 tons of rock to solidify the footing. The base was clay, which is great for holding water but is not a great surface for holding up horses. First we put down some crushed stone (three-inch rock), and covered this with some smaller gravel (¾-inch rock) to form a base. This works well because one kind of rock adheres to the other. We did not have any footing problems but it did take a lot of money to build the jump. However, it will be there forever. We built a dam from the pond to the new jump and pumped the water up from the existing pond into the rectangular dug-out area depression.

The Preliminary level horses had to jump over a log into the water and they also had to jump out. By the time we put the rock in and then put the water in up to the depth we wanted, the fence out was only a small step up. The revetting of the bank was no more than 2' high. As it turned out, I moved the whole fence up from where I had originally planned it so that the Preliminary had a tree right in the middle of the jump out, whereas the Training level riders just had to go to the side of the tree.

I heard some criticism to the effect that the fence was too easy for the Training level because there was no jump into the water, not even a log. Some people thought that the fence might have jumped better if there had been something to jump over into the water. I honestly did not know what to design for that group of riders; I did not know if they had ever seen a proper water jump before, and I wanted to give them the benefit of the doubt. As it turned out I believe the critics were right—it was too easy. From now on we will be able to use a log on the inside. Out of the 15 Training level horses there was one refusal, one would-be refusal, and one elimination at this fence.

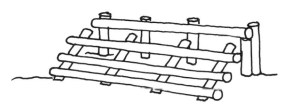

9 Oxer Massif
Height 3'3"
Base spread 4'7"
Top spread 3'11"

11 The Water
Height revetting 2'

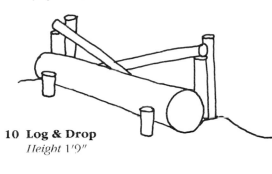

10 Log & Drop
Height 1'9"

12 Ditch & Rails
Height 3'3"
Spread 3'6"

The water was about 6" deep. I honestly feel that water does not need to be deep; in fact, the rule about the water being up to 20" deep is absolutely ridiculous. A horse jumping into 20" of water is going to stop dead. We built an overflow drain when we put the dam in so we could control the level of the water.

This was the first water jump that I was able to build when I had a transit, or theodolite—an instrument that surveyors use for leveling. It makes a big difference in construction if you have an instrument to shoot gradients through. You feel very silly when you do all the revetting on a water fence, and then when you put the water in you realize that your railroad ties are unlevel. It is much nicer when you put the water in to have it come out level

with the lines of the revetting. At Radnor (Pa.) this year I had a transit, and being able to set it up on the side of the hill and know just exactly how much earth to cut out for the step jump made construction a lot easier.

After the water I found another old worn cow track right in front of a fence line that I dug out deeper to make a ditch, which I framed with a telephone pole on the take-off side. I do not like to have a ditch, especially at the lower levels, without having something to delineate the front. Training and Pre-Training horses need some help getting off the ground. If you put a telephone pole on the front of the ditch the horses realize that there is more to the jump than just the rails sticking up out of the ground. If they stop they can do it without sliding into the ditch. At Prelimi-

nary level and up it is not necessary. I did not want a very challenging jump right after the water, but there were no problems at all here. For another year I plan to add some rails and some cedar to make more of a hedge or bullfinch here. I did not know what the water was going to do to the horses. I did know that many of the competitors had been competing over courses without water.

At this point the Training level course veered off from the Preliminary one and went on over a Giant's Table. I had built a small bench in the front to serve as a take-off rail and chairs on the end to serve as wings. The course then crossed a field that originally was terraced to keep it from eroding during water run-off, so it was full of undulations.

The terracing had been allowed to grass over and the field had a series of mild steps about 30 or 40 feet apart, not the type of terrain you would put a fence on. Bearing in mind that I might need to be able to reverse the course in future years, I designed a moveable fence that could be dragged out and set anywhere on the course. I was not too certain about the distance of the course; the organizers were thinking about spectator parking, and this particular field was used as a hay field so we could not build a permanent fence here. I built a feed trough with rails on the back, filled it with straw, and pulled it out to the field. We placed the trough in a small dip in the ground so that as the riders approached it looked tiny, but as they got close to it the fence was a lot bigger.

The final fence was meant to be fun more than anything. It was a double picture frame, for the sole reason that the trees were already growing in the fence line and all I had to do was to fill in and around them. I thought perhaps the jump was a bit too airy this year and plan to fill it in with cedar trees another time.

I was happy with this course. Out of the fifteen obstacles the problems were distributed evenly, between fences 2, 3, 4, 5, 6, 7, 10, 11, and 14. The course did its job. The competitors were a strong cross-section of the lower levels; riders came from eleven different states. The organizers did a good job of building the course—not one horse or rider was hurt, and not one fence was broken all day. The weather conditions unfortunately were miserable—cold, wet and windy.

Although it worked well, I would not be happy about running exactly the same course for a second year. The competitors now have a rough idea of what to expect and have time to prepare themselves and their horses. I do not want to overface the horses but I do wish to challenge them and let the riders have fun. I think that if the riders drive all the way from say, Colorado, and have to jump exactly the same course year after year they are going to be disappointed. I built the course with an eye to the future, with alterations and additions already in mind.

The course is built in a circle, around a central hub of a wheel. The spokes go off at various angles and I plan to do many variations on the basic design. I was somewhat limited the first year because some of the areas had been ploughed up for crops, but that will no longer happen since the land has been acquired by the park system and it will be grassed over again. The footing is consistently good. The area that is used for hay will have been mowed in time for the event. I think that we have built the foundation for a first-class competition here, and that there is certainly room to expand this course to Preliminary three-day status.

Donna Littleton, Rider

The Course

This course was one long gallop—there were no rest periods on it. The jumps were all different and they asked a lot of questions. They also were very well built.

On Course

Quicksilver weaved in and out and didn't pay attention going into the first fence the way he usually does but we got over it well.

The second fence, the vertical rails, rode fine. At the third one I yelled at him and hit him with the stick because he is a bit sticky at ditches. He did hesitate but then he jumped. I told myself to look straight ahead and not to look into the ditch—I always wonder if he will fall underneath me at that kind of fence.

He galloped to the 4th fence, the lamb creep, and jumped it really big. At fence #5, the vertical rails on a slight hill, I placed him in there at the take-off point with a half-halt, but he put in an extra stride and had to twist over the fence.

I had planned to jump fence #6A and B—the L—straight in, take a couple of strides, turn, and then jump the second part. This worked fine.

Quicksilver was sticky over the next fence, but we went "hell bent for election" up to the bank and that was good.

13 Giants' Table
Height 3'3"
Spread 3'9"

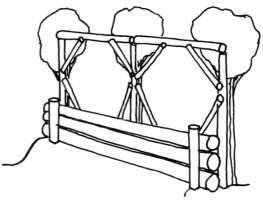

15 Picture Frame
Height logs 3'
Spread top rail 12'

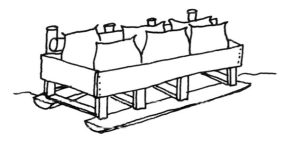

14 Feed Trough
Height 3'3"

The oxer on the hill was probably the most fun fence on the course.

Then I had to rattle him to get his attention because he was looking at the crowd and he took a huge jump at the next fence.

He took the drop (10) fine. I looked up and waited for him to come up under me, which he did.

I knew that he would take his time at the water and I was running out of steam, so I let him plop into it and trot through and out of it.

The ditch and rails afterwards rode real well and after that we flew the rest of the way home.

Quicksilver jumped the last two fences really well. I could feel him tiring so I made sure he was paying attention to them, and we finished with no problems.

Part One
The
Event Horse

1 *Selecting the Event Horse*

by Edmund Coffin

Individual Gold
Medalist, Three-Day Event,
1976 Olympics, Montreal

Edmund–Tad–Coffin

At age 20, Edmund—Tad—Coffin became the youngest gold medalist in history at the 1976 Montreal Olympic Games. Teamed with the great mare Bally Cor, Tad rode a superb dressage test, a flawless cross-country round, and a clean round in the stadium to win the gold medal.

One of the first protegés of USET coach Jack Le Goff, Tad was selected for training with the team and spent two years learning his trade. His partnership with Bally Cor has gone into the history of eventing as one of those rare successful combinations that become virtually unbeatable.

Today Tad coaches aspiring young eventers in his native New England and is also training young horses in preparation for a return to the international scene. His knowledge of combined training and his ability to pass on that knowledge to his students have benefited countless junior event riders. His young riders team from Area I (New England) won the North American title two years in succession. Eventing seems to develop itself through riders like Tad, who are eager to pass on their hard-won skills to a new crop of younger riders.

No rider can expect to begin an eventing career at the Olympic Games. Eventing involves learning many different skills and, as with all complex sports, one must begin at the lowest level and gradually work up. Not everyone has the time or the ability to reach the international levels but eventing is a sport that can offer realistic goals and challenges at all levels.

The First Horse

When looking for a horse one of my pupils can compete with at the Training level (and possibly at the Preliminary level), there are two routes to pursue—choosing the experienced horse or the "green" horse. For the rider who is just starting to event, I would choose the experienced horse, which, ideally, has had a successful record. This horse need neither be a top-class horse nor one with extensive experience, but simply a horse that has had good basic schooling on the flat so that his dressage is not a problem. In other words, the horse should be able to move in an orderly frame, should be basically well-balanced and should have successfully competed over a number of cross-country courses without having been eliminated and/or having too many falls. If a horse starts falling at Training level, trouble surely lies ahead. As for breeding, I would prefer that the horse be a half- or cross-bred rather than a Thoroughbred.

Soundness is one of the prime considerations when buying a horse. There is absolutely no point in looking at any horse that does not have four very good legs—without any bows (even if it's an old one), weak ankles, or big knees, etc. In any case, the horse should *always* be vetted before purchasing, no matter how sound he appears.

Disposition ranks very high on my priority list. I would rather put one of my pupils on a horse that has to be pushed on a bit than one which has to be slowed down constantly. Even at Training level, horses can become quite strong. The old saying that "it is easier to fire them up than to quiet them down" still holds true. For the rider who has little or no competitive experience, it is best to have a horse that is bold and talented over fences, yet needs to be ridden. When I say that the horse should be a good jumper, I don't mean that he has to be brilliant over 4-foot fences. Such ability is impressive, but not necessary; cleverness is a more important talent.

When trying the horse, I watch carefully to see how he handles himself coming into obstacles and combinations with distances that are both long and short. It's best to let the rider just sit there and watch how the horse takes care of himself. I'm rather keen on the horse that has a healthy sense of self-preservation, so he can handle it if he finds himself in a tough spot, without twisting or hanging a leg.

If it is impossible to find a horse with eventing experience, I would then look for a horse that has hunted. A horse that has followed hounds in a bold, yet mannerly fashion and can easily handle different types of terrain (mud, water, uneven ground, hills) already has a lot going for him as a potential event horse.

If this type of horse is also unavailable, then and only then—for a "green" rider—would I resort to a horse that has only had show experience. I always try to avoid putting an inexperienced rider on an inexperienced horse. This happens all too frequently. Such combinations may work, but training both horse and rider is a slow process and much time may be wasted. In many cases the flavor of eventing is lost, and confidence is nipped in the bud. A novice rider learns a lot faster and has more fun on a horse that "knows his stuff", even when the rider doesn't.

I don't worry if the horse has a little age on him. That's sometimes all to the better, especially if the horse has had some good mileage—anywhere up to twelve is fine. You then still have two, three, or four years to work with this "first" event horse. Many horses, if they are at all able and are properly ridden, can compete in Preliminary horse trials. But don't expect this horse to go on to a Preliminary three-day event. He might, if you have a talented horse and run into good luck all along the way, but remember that the main purpose of a first event horse is to introduce the novice rider to eventing, to bring the rider along and give him or her confidence.

The Second Horse

After a successful year or two at the Pre-Training or Training levels, when the rider decides that he or she is ready to go on a bit further, the rider will need a horse with a little more quality— preferably one that is older and has had some good experience at the Preliminary or Intermediate levels. The horse doesn't necessarily have to be a winner, yet he should be able to take the rider around larger courses safely. Most importantly, I want my riders to get out there and learn, have fun, and accumulate the experience and mileage for a couple of years at the Preliminary level (both at one-day horse trials and at three-day events).

Many competitors don't understand that competing at the Pre-Training or Training level and at the Intermediate and Advanced levels are almost two different sports. The demands made on both horse and rider at the upper levels are quite different.

The Third Horse

A serious rider aspiring to the Advanced level may need a scopier horse (unless, of course, the rider has had the rare good fortune to have found one already.) Again, in order to gain experience at these levels, I would look for the older

horse that has had some high-level experience, but not necessarily one that has been a winner. This horse's strong point should be cross-country. He may not be a top horse, perhaps because his dressage or show jumping is not up to par, but this is OK. If you can find such a horse, you can count yourself among the fortunate ones, as they are hard to come by.

If this kind of horse is unavailable, then there are two routes that can be taken. One is to buy a horse with the potential to take the rider to the Advanced level; the other is to find a horse with potential to *win* at that level. Here we have two entirely different situations. You can buy a race car that will get you to the Indianapolis 500, but you can't always buy one that will win the race.

What kind of horse, then, are we looking for? Preferably a Thoroughbred cross, seven-eighths or three-quarters bred. At the upper levels I'd steer away from Quarter Horses, Morgans, and Arabs. Quarter Horses don't usually have the stamina and the speed to go the distances. I wouldn't discount Appaloosas, because sometimes they can do the job. Again, I would have to stress soundness—no leg problems. Even a bow "way back when" can cause trouble. If you plan to shoot for the Advanced level and put in all that ground work, time, money, energy, and hope— only to find that the horse, who seemed all tuned and ready to go, had developed a soundness problem from an old injury—what could be more disappointing!

Next comes temperament. Basically, I prefer a horse that is "a nice guy" with an even disposition and a kind eye. A few bucks on a cold day and being a little bit strong is O.K., but stay away from the "nuts" of this world. They'll just waste your time. Our potential Advanced horse need not be a huge striding horse, or one that just floats, but he must be a better than average mover. Avoid the kind of horse that hits the ground hard because by the time you put the mileage into him to reach the top, the horse won't stay sound. Bear in mind that we are looking for a horse that can compete at the Advanced

Mary Anne Tauskey on The Sheik, an English Thoroughbred, donated to the USET by Mr. and Mrs. Vincent B. Murphy, Jr.

level, not necessarily win there. If this horse has shown that he can perform a nice steady dressage test in a Training level event, so much better. Steadiness is a most important dressage quality.

I would hope that this horse has already had some cross-country experience and has handled at least Training level courses with ease. The horse should have some speed and stamina and should be an able jumper. By this I mean that he should be able to jump a 4'6" to 4'11" square oxer. If a horse can't do this when he is fresh out of the stable, he is not going to be able to handle a 3'11" high, 6' wide table when he's tired at the end of a cross-country course.

This is not all. Many horses can jump a good big fence and still not be able to get themselves out of tight situations. So I would have to say

that "cleverness" is one of the most important ingredients in a three-day event horse. Bally Cor had her limit in jumping, but she was exceptionally clever, which was a very strong point in our favor. A lot of competitors have gone far on horses that don't appear to have enormous talent, yet are careful and clever.

When trying a horse, you can test for cleverness by setting up various combinations. First I would try the horse over either two square oxers or over some other combinations with quite tight distances, 21 ft. or perhaps a bit less. If the horse has had some jumping mileage, I'd put it through a couple of bounces, trotting first a bounce set at 9 feet, then cantering through a second bounce set at 15 ft. (which could subsequently be tightened to 12 or 13 feet). The fences should ultimately be set at 3'6" to 3'9". A bounce taken at a canter over obstacles set at 3'9" will immediately tell you whether or not the horse gets off the ground quickly. This is an invaluable quality to look for. On cross-country, many difficult situations have been salvaged by a clever horse that can either leave out a stride or get airborne a stride early!

All the time a horse is being tried, keep an eye on his ears. I like a horse that "puts his ears on a fence." No matter what the rider is doing, the horse should still focus on the obstacle. The horse is doing the jumping, not the rider, so the horse had better darn well pay attention to what he's about.

That's what it takes for a three-day event horse—one that is sound, has a good temperament, is a good, steady mover, has speed and stamina, can jump 4'9", and is very clever. With good fortune, this horse should take you to the Advanced level.

Tad Coffin gives victorious "thumbs-up" sign after winning the 1976 Olympic gold medal on Bally Cor in Montreal, Canada.

The "Phenomenal" Horse

Perhaps now you say, "Aha! I want to ride in international events and beat Mike Plumb and Bruce Davidson." That is a different situation altogether. The horse required to do this must be phenomenal! Ever since the Montreal Olympics I've felt there would soon be a new standard for event horses at this level, and that sooner or later the horse that wins the dressage would win the whole event straight through. It happened this way at Ledyard in 1977 with Mike Plumb on both Laurenson and Better and Better; and it will most likely happen one of these years at the Olympics.

The potential top international horse must be an exceptional mover; not only must he float across the ground, but he must have a very big stride with a great deal of natural engagement and good hock action. Karl Schultz's ride on Madrigal in Bromont was one of the outstanding international dressage tests of all time and was an example of this. Karl pushed Madrigal to the limit of his capabilities and achieved extraordinary results.

But the most magnificent mover in the world needs a good temperament to cope with crowds, noises, flags, clapping and cameras. If you have to compensate or cover up for a nervous or "hot" horse, you simply won't be able to get 100% out of him in a dressage test.

Our horse that is truly exceptional on the flat must also be very clever and wise over fences. This horse should give you the feeling that he can run right on down to any fence, and leave the ground anywhere—long, short, or right smack in the middle—and get to the other side with no problems. Stopping should never enter his mind under 99% of the circumstances.

If you can find this kind of horse, you will have found an exceptional animal. I've been looking for a good while and have come up with three horses that may qualify. Out of the three, if one works out, I'll be lucky—very, very lucky.

2 *Basic Training for the Young Event Horse*

Jack Le Goff

Coach, United States
Three-Day Event Team

Jack Le Goff

A tall, elegant Frenchman, Jack Le Goff has devoted himself to the sport of three-day eventing for the past thirty years. Le Goff spent many years as riding master at Cadre Noir, the famous riding academy in Saumur, France. Later Le Goff rode in the 1960 Rome Olympics as a member of the French three-day event team. As his skills developed his reputation as a coach kept pace and he later became the coach of the French Olympic three-day event team, as well as coach of the French junior teams.

In 1969 he was persuaded to move to America to become three-day event coach for the USET. Under his leadership since then the USET teams have reaped a golden harvest in world competition, winning the team gold medals at the World Championships in 1974, the Pan American Games in 1975, the Montreal Olympics in 1976 and the individual gold medals at the World Championships of 1974 and 1978, the Pan American Games in 1975 and the Olympic Games in 1976.

Le Goff has influenced the sport of eventing in America as no other single man has done and, thanks to him, the sport has undergone a tremendous upsurge of popularity during the 1970's. Originally a sport that attracted a few determined elitists, eventing has become the fastest growing equestrian sport in the country.

As a teacher and trainer Jack Le Goff has no equal. He believes that his ideas and methods are constantly growing and improving and the sport is continually evolving.

For The USCTA Book of Eventing, *Le Goff has generously consented to share his ideas on bringing a young horse through its first stages of training up to the point where it is ready to compete as a serious international event horse.*

Eventing is a sport that continues to evolve, to change and to grow; that is part of the fascination for me. I am still learning after thirty years and that is the real reason I have not as yet tried to write a book on eventing. I feel that I am still learning, still widening my range of understanding of training the horse and my conception of the sport. Nothing is fixed and rigid. Over the years I have accumulated a great deal of experience and I am more than happy to share my knowledge. My own teachers often made a mystery of the methods they used and as a pupil I suffered from that mystique. I am not about to create any mysteries. I am perfectly happy to share in one form or another what I do know very well.

Any thoughts I have on training the horse have to be prefaced by stating that I believe eventing for all practical purposes is divided into three different sports. The Pre-Training and Training levels are for everyone, for all horses. Any rider should be able to canter around a Training level course on a backyard pony or someone's reliable old hunter; any rider who wants some fun should be able to go out to compete and enjoy the challenge. The second category of the sport comes at the Preliminary, Intermediate, and Advanced level horse trials. These levels are for the busy rider with a full-time job, who wants a challenge but lacks the time required to devote to full-time training. A great many horses can compete in horse trials. A horse that is a good jumper and a good dressage horse, but that perhaps lacks the endurance and speed required for the international levels, can still be successful here. The half-bred horse that is a good mover can shine, even at the Advanced level. Most horses can gallop a two- or three-mile cross-country course at 520 meters per minute or even at 550 meters per minute; 570 meters per minute might be slightly beyond its capability but if the horse has a good dressage score it can afford a few time penalties cross-country and still do well.

The three-day event, however, is an entirely different sport—and at the international level, an entirely different game. You cannot bring a horse up to the international three-day event level without giving it the chance to understand what is ahead on the cross-country, for that is what the whole sport is about at that level.

Selecting the horse

What do you look for when selecting a horse you hope will make an international three-day event horse? What criteria do you base your selection on? The major requirement for an event horse is that it be able to run and jump—in addition, it must have that extra quality you call "heart" or courage. This is something you cannot teach a horse; horses either have courage or they don't.

You begin by selecting a horse on the basis of conformation and breeding. The horse must show evidence that it will be a good jumper and fast enough to cope with the steeplechase and the cross-country speeds, so that it does not have to use all its energy just to run. In other words you must look for quality. But all the conformation, all the breeding, all the ability in the world are of no use if the horse has its heart in the wrong place—and that you will not truly know until you test the horse. Sometimes you can tell very early on if a horse does not have the heart. If, by its attitude towards jumping or by its behavior, it shows a lack of cooperation, then you know it is not going to do the job; it will use any excuse to avoid work. You should write off a horse like that immediately. Then there are some horses that do everything you ask them to, and you still will not know if they are international horses until you ask them to compete at the international level. You can tell if a horse is *not* going to make it but you cannot always tell if a horse is going to make it. All you can do is to make sure that the horse receives the best possible education.

Bally Cor, whose great heart exemplifies the courage of the event horse

Bally Cor, the gold medal winner at the Montreal Olympics in 1976, is a prime example of a horse with heart. She was not a great mover, nor did she jump with all that much scope. When I first had her at the team I did not honestly think that she would make an international horse. I thought she would be a good horse to use in the education of young riders but she did not strike me as having the potential to be a top international horse. Yet she won the Olympic gold medal because she had that extra special little thing that is called heart.

In contrast. I recently bought two young horses in England with the proper credentials to become international horses—Blue Stone, who is in training with me now, and one other. The other horse was a beautiful horse who had won several conformation classes and had superb breeding—he was by the same sire as Hugh Thomas's international horse, Playamar, but he had no heart. When we began to school the horse cross-country he would stop and look at water, or he would wheel away from the starting box. He had all the ability but none of the desire.

If a young horse has been lightly raced as a three-year-old, or even hunted, his education already has had a promising start. I prefer to begin with a four- or five-year-old that has been broken and ridden. Hunting teaches a horse to be clever and to handle itself on uneven ground; racing will tell you something about its breeding and aggressiveness. Temperament is very important. Aggressiveness in a horse is a good quality provided the horse is aggressive in the sense of being self-confident. I do not agree with the old-fashioned belief that a good competition horse necessarily has to be a mean horse, or a tough horse to handle. Toughness in a horse can work for you and against you; above all the horse must be sensible. I think that horses can display heart and courage and be bold and honest without being mean. A horse should be kind and still have these qualities—that is what I mean by good temperament.

Here, then, is your raw material—a horse that has a good disposition, moves well, and has some jumping ability, along with breeding that leads you to believe the horse can handle speed work and endurance. This prospect should be four or five years old and should have been lunged and ridden, perhaps hunted or raced. Now you begin its formal education as an event horse.

Jack Le Goff and USET rider Bea Perkins di Grazia discuss a cross-country plan

Work on the flat

I believe that the basic education of a horse should be the same, whether it is destined to be a show jumper or an event horse, a steeplechaser, or a hunter—I start with work on the flat. Some people seem to have the wrong conception of flat work or dressage; they say, "at such and such a point I teach the horse shoulder-in, I teach half-pass, I teach turn on the haunches, I do this, I do that . . ." It does not matter what you do with the horse, or when; it all depends upon *how* you do it.

Dressage is really quite simple. The horse must accept the bit in its mouth. The horse must also accept the rider's leg and it has to remain steady in the rider's hand and be willing to go forward, come back, and turn. Once these basics

have been learned, it is just a matter of teaching the horse various gymnastic exercises.

I cannot specify how long you need to work a horse in dressage, since this varies with each horse. I do believe that horses need to learn the lateral work to improve their way of going forward and to improve their way of coming back and their suppleness. Horses must also learn to perform the requirements of the dressage tests, however long that takes. But there is no magic formula for this. I cannot recommend a timetable—I shy away from doing that as each horse is different. It is useless, for example, to

Jack Le Goff stresses the importance of fluid forward movement in training session with Nanci Lindroth and Auchinbreck

start to teach the shoulder-in when a horse is not even moving away from the leg.

Instinct is especially important in the training of any horse. My own ideas have developed through my own experience over many years. One thing I have learned is that you do not want to push event horses to too high a level of dressage. In the upper levels of dressage, the *haute école*, one demands complete obedience and the horses must obey the will of the rider instantly. By insisting on such performance, one takes away the initiative of the horse. The dressage horse must submit itself completely to the will of the rider, and all the horse's force must be in total control, so that it is not allowed to think for itself. Such training is not good for an event horse, who must be free to make some degree of decision for itself at times.

When I was in France training for the Rome

Olympics I was working with two horses. One of them won all the horse trials I entered—he was very good at dressage. Everyone said "My! That horse is really something!" When he was injured and I could not jump him for a while, I continued his dressage training. I trained him to do passage, piaffe, and flying changes—all the movements of the *haute école*. At the same time I had another horse, a mare, who was terrible in the dressage ring, but she had the heart and the blood to make a great event horse. When I put the first horse back into eventing after the advanced dressage training, he was not half the horse he had been before; he was always waiting for me to command every step. The mare, on the other hand, went on to compete in the Rome Olympic Games.

In the dressage training you must have some guidelines. You need someone with enough experience to help you get the work done. There is no instant dressage, like instant coffee, and that is what people have to understand. Dressage takes time.

Before I start jumping fences I want to have some control over the horse. I begin by riding forward so that the horse will go from my leg and I keep a quiet contact so that it learns to accept the bit in its mouth. I do not demand as much from the young horse as from the fully schooled horse. I am not teaching the actual school movements at the beginning; I am just doing the exercises. I teach the young horse to yield from my leg and I start teaching the shoulder-in quite early on, but then I have the experience to know where and when to start. I want the horse to go forward, to slow down or halt and to turn. When the horse can do this then it is just a matter of teaching the horse the various gymnastic exercises.

Teaching the Horse to Jump

Once I have control on the flat I start teaching the horse to jump. I often free school the horse over fences in the ring and, if I have a Hitchcock pen available, I will let the horse loose to jump in that. I also lunge the horse over jumps without a rider. In the beginning, I want the horse to be able to jump freely, without the burden of the rider's weight.

After that I let the horse go over cavaletti with a rider. In teaching the horse how to jump, I always do all the beginning work at the trot. I do not go out and jump the green horse over solid fences to start with. Instead, I use cavaletti and rails that will fall if the horse knocks them. If the horse makes any mistake over rails that will fall you can get away with it, but if the horse makes a mistake over a solid fence early in its training, it can easily be frightened.

After the cavaletti work I let the horse start to jump single fences, still out of a trot, until I know

that the horse understands what it is doing. I take great pains to avoid refusals at this point. I try to manage the lessons so that the horse never even imagines that it can stop anywhere—ever. I believe that you should be careful not to put a young horse in a position where it can stop. If the horse begins to think that it has the option to stop if something is not quite right, you are in deep trouble. You can force a horse over a show fence because the rails will come down if the horse doesn't make it. But if you force a horse over a cross-country fence, and get in trouble, the fence will not come down—the horse or the rider may come down and can get hurt.

I was told by my own teacher that only a refusal is shameful; a fall is not. If a horse never thinks of stopping, and by chance it has a fall, the next time that horse jumps it will simply be careful not to fall. On the other hand, if it believes that it can stop, it will. The stop will not prevent the fall, but a fall can teach the horse to avoid another fall. I am very careful about what I ask a youngster to jump. I want to be sure that when I ask the horse to jump it will go by itself, or that I can make it go. I want above all to avoid a stop.

If a show jumper refuses a fence it incurs three faults, but for an event horse a refusal costs 20 points, which is much more costly. Of course a horse may refuse at some point in his career, but in the early training all sorts of precautions should be taken to avoid a stop.

I had a horse called Alex at the team for seven years who was recently retired. He was not a great international horse, and he never went to the Olympic Games, but he was a good soldier and carried a great many people. I had him at the same time as I had Bally Cor and she had just that much more ability than he did. But that horse, Alex, never stopped in his entire life, not at home schooling over cavaletti, not at a cross pole, not at any kind of fence. I can truthfully say that I have never seen him stop in seven years. I cannot say the same about too many horses.

If my preliminary schooling on the flat has been thorough I can ask the horse to jump small

fences without getting into trouble, because I am able to steer the horse and it is responsive enough to my leg that I can ride into a fence without the horse stopping or running out. I have to establish the control on the flat so that I have control over small jumps.

Once the horse has the idea of jumping single, easy show jumping fences, then I will take it outside and jump some easy natural cross-country fences. I begin by riding out with an older experienced horse. I do everything I can to pump air into the tires of the horse and make it keen. As we go along and I think that perhaps I can take the horse in front and jump a log without stopping I will go ahead of the lead horse, but if I have doubts, or if I get into trouble I turn around and get someone to give me a lead at once so that the horse forgets about stopping right away.

The basic education of any horse is to learn to go on forward on the flat, to jump some single fences and to negotiate some simple cross-country jumps.

The next step is to take it away from home to some shows. I think it would be a terrible mistake to take a young horse out for its first competition to a horse trial. Why? It would mean getting up at five in the morning, trailering to the event, warming up for the dressage phase for about an hour and riding the dressage test; then, half an hour later, you would start to warm up for the cross-country and jump practice fences for half an hour before jumping a course of twelve to fifteen cross-country fences. Then you put the horse away only to bring it out again and jump another thirty fences or so and go, in the show jumping. I don't care how good a horse is and I don't care how good a rider may be, this is punishment for a young horse. If I were a young

The dynamic jumping ability of the well-schooled event horse—shown here by Red's Door's tremendous leap over the imposing double brush at Ledyard (Mass.), with Torrance Watkins Fleischmann aboard

horse, I would hate to go to an event—it would be asking too much too soon.

My philosophy with a young horse is that once it is going reasonably well on the flat and can jump some simple fences it is then ready for some small schooling shows. I take it to a dressage schooling show and enter one or two classes at Training or First level. I nurse the horse along for its first experience away from home. Similarly I will also take the horse to a horse show and enter it in some baby green classes over fences with the jumps at two and a half feet. I use these shows as an introduction to the world away from home.

The horse has to learn to go into the warm-up area where there are perhaps thirty horses milling around amidst much confusion. This experience is like sending a child away from home to school for the first time.

If I start a four-year-old horse in September, I spend the winter teaching it the basic things it needs to know and at the beginning of its five-year-old year I will take it to dressage and horse shows. Only at the end of that year will I be thinking about taking the horse to a couple of Pre-Training events.

Provided the horse has behaved well at the dressage schooling shows and horse shows, I will take it to a couple of good Pre-Training horse trials, since most Training level courses are too difficult for a young horse at the very start of its competitive career.

I used to start my horses at the Training level but nowadays the courses at that level are becoming more difficult all the time to a point where it is beginning to be ridiculous. The difficulty of the courses at the upper levels has not increased so much over the past years, but every level from Preliminary on down is powering up. Training level courses now are similar to Preliminary courses five years ago; the degree of difficulty has not increased gradually.

Once the horse has competed in a couple of Pre-Training horse trials without difficulty I would probably move it up to Training level. A horse that is normally prepared and normally ridden should be able to gallop around any Training level course since the whole focus of Training level is to provide training for the young horse. Sometimes an accident happens, of course . . . some bit of bad luck; the rider or horse can make mistakes, but a horse that is ready should be able to get around clean. If the horse does *not* get around clean it should be because it was not ready, or because of an obvious mistake. It should not be because the course was unsuitable to the level of competition—the majority of horses should be able to get around a well-conceived Training level course.

In general the horse should spend roughly one year at each level, but I feel strongly that the horse should spend more time at the Preliminary level than at any other. At the Preliminary level the horse will begin to see the type of obstacle and combination that it will see on a larger more difficult scale at the Advanced level. My philosophy of teaching the horse to jump cross-country is to teach it to jump single fences and very easy combinations with simple striding. After that the horse must learn to face more complicated combinations with more complex striding, but still with fairly low Preliminary heights. This will teach the horse how to be clever. After that the horse should face fences at the international heights and spreads and, if all goes well, it should be ready to move up to the Intermediate or Advanced level.

Galloping

In addition to the dressage, gymnastic jumping, and cross-country schooling at the lower levels, the horse must at some point learn how to gallop. A horse does not need conditioning gallops for the lower levels of competition. Pre-Training and Training levels courses are ridden at speeds of 350 to 450 meters per minute and are from one to one and a half miles long. Any horse that

Bea Perkins di Grazia demonstrates perfect galloping form on County Frost

is ridden every day for an hour or more should be fit enough to do that.

If you do any galloping in the early stages of training, you are not necessarily galloping to make the horse fit, but to teach the horse how to gallop. You must teach the horse to gallop up and downhill and to cadence its respiration with the galloping rhythm. The horse should learn how to relax in its stride so that it can handle uneven terrain. Any event horse should have a weekly schedule with a variety of work so that it learns all it has to and will be fit enough. But it is not until you are going to compete over a tough Preliminary course of upwards of two miles at a speed of 520 meters per minute that you need to do any serious conditioning. Nonetheless, you must teach the horse to gallop steadily so it can find its balance and rhythm.

For the horse's second year of competition you might start out with one Training level competition, and then, providing all goes well, move on up to Preliminary. What you do from here on depends on what your ultimate goals are. If you are an amateur rider, or a junior rider wanting to compete in the Young Rider Championships, then I think your plan should be to compete in a Preliminary three-day event at the end of the year. If your goal is to make this horse into a horse that can compete in international competition, then your aim should be to get this horse to as many cross-country fences at the Preliminary level as you can. The horse needs to jump as many combinations and fences as possible to gain the mileage and experience it needs.

I do not care whether the horse places well or not in the lower levels of competition. If the horse does well, it is a bonus and I am delighted, but I am not after ribbons at the lower levels; I am much more interested in how the horse reacts to the competition. How does it behave? Does it jump poorly? Is it reluctant to leave the other horses? Does it get scared by certain types of fences? If so, then I am not happy, because something is wrong with the training. I do not mind if the horse performs poorly in dressage, since I can always train a horse to the point where it can perform passably well in the dressage. I am much more concerned with cross-country at the lower levels because I know this phase counts most in a proper three-day event. I am interested in how well the horse analyzes what it is supposed to be doing. Can it cope physically and mentally with the cross-country problems? Again, my job is to give the young horse the confidence and experience required to meet any cross-country challenge. After all, I am not training dressage horses or show jumpers; my goal is to train international event horses by giving them the necessary skills they will need for all three phases, especially cross-country.

If you plan your horse's first year in the Preliminary division to include two Preliminary three-day events, you will be restricted in the number of horse trials that you may enter that year. The horse must have a break after the first three-day event. Then you have to condition the horse all over again and probably enter one more horse trial before the other three-day event—by this time the season is over. That schedule works for the seasoned horse. But I would rather take a young horse to as many horse trials as possible at the Preliminary level and forget about the three-day events. I usually take my young horses to ten horse trials per year. The following year, when I feel they have enough mileage, I will take them to one or two three-day events at the Preliminary level. The more mileage the horse gets on different types of courses the better off it will be.

Since the young horse needs exposure to competition, you should view early competitions as schooling for the horse. You do not have to win every time; you do not need to "put your foot on the accelerator" each time out. I advise riders to compete in horse trials and get as much mileage as possible that first Preliminary year, so that the horse will be ready to start seriously in the big time the next year. If you want a horse to have a great success in a certain year, you must give it as much experience and exposure as possible in the *previous* year.

The heart of the endurance test is the cross-country; any horse can do the roads and tracks and steeplechase. Where horses get into difficulty is on the cross-country because they do not know how to handle the fences. Even if the horse has the heart and the talent and the rider rides properly, the horse can still get into trouble if it has not had enough exposure to different types of fences, especially ones that pose tight distance problems. The horse must be able to recognize the problems because it has seen similar problems before, and knows that it will get through the maze of poles in front by simply going forward. Only experience gained by entering as many horse trials as possible will give the horse such confidence. The horse will not learn this if you enter three-day events as soon as the horse reaches the Preliminary level.

The two young horses at the team at this time, Blue Stone and Grey Tudor, were educated entirely according to this philosophy. They went to horse shows and dressage shows, then competed

Jack Le Goff gives Bally Cor a reassuring pat. Tad and Bally Cor are two of Le Goff's most famous pupils

at the Pre-Training and Training levels, then they progressed to Preliminary. They competed in a great many Preliminary horse trials before competing in the Preliminary Three-Day Event at Essex, N.J. in 1981. They were rested, brought back up in the fall, and finished the year by running in the Intermediate Three-Day Event at Radnor, Pa. in October. In 1982 they will compete in the selection trials for the World Championships. These two horses have gained most of their cross-country education in Preliminary horse trials.

I hesitate to say this, but my feeling is that once the horse has gained enough experience at the Preliminary level and has successfully completed a Preliminary three-day event, you can almost skip the Intermediate level. I do think the Intermediate level is important for young riders on their way up; it is important for the kids to feel the pressure of riding over an Intermediate level course before they ride over an Advanced one for the first time. But a well-educated horse usually needs only one or two Intermediate competitions before it is ready to move up.

If I had to educate the horses and riders together it would be very difficult. When I first came to America I had to educate the riders; now I have riders who are capable of competing at the international levels and I find myself educating the horses. Once I have trained the horses I am able to pick riders who can ride those horses.

Once the horse has had its basic education, all you have to do is to give it the proper conditioning. Competing in a major international three-day event is the culmination of all your schooling to date. The horse's performance is the final product of this education.

I cannot set out a specific program for a hypothetical horse. I need to have the necessary information to plug into my computer first—what competition are you aiming for? What will the terrain be like? When did the horse compete last? Has it been out of work for any reason? There are so many variables I cannot give any specific information without having the answers to these questions.

I believe in conditioning a horse based on a set of principles known as interval training and I can set training guidelines for a horse accordingly, but the program for any two horses will not be the same. Most of the time horses will not be trained in the same place and same climate. My principles will have to be adjusted according to the needs of each horse. I can only tell you that you have to train a particular horse for a particular competition.

The overall education of each event horse must contain certain elements: the flat work, the gymnastic jumping, and the cross-country experience. The combination of these skills mixed in the correct dosage and administered at the correct times, makes up the prescription I use to produce an international event horse.

3 Caring for the Event Horse— At Home and at the Event

Jeanne Kane

Stable Manager, United States Three-Day Event Team

Jeanne Kane (Photo by Warren Patriquin)

Jeanne Kane has been the head groom of the U.S. Equestrian Team's three-day horses for the past three years. She has always been passionately involved with horses, and began her career as a student at the Potomac Horse Center in Gaithersburg, Maryland, where she passed her Horsemasters examination and stayed on to take charge of the entire stables. Her cheerful competence led Betty Howett (then Director of the Center) to recommend Jeanne to the team.

Jeanne has sole command of the USET stables in South Hamilton, Mass. Her practical approach to the care and well-being of the team horses is reflected in the glow of good health of each horse. Jeanne believes that event horses are workers, not just show animals, and her program for grooming and safety might well be emulated in every barn in the country.

An event horse is an athlete and can only perform to the height of its ability when brought to a competition in top form. The fit horse—muscles bulging with power, eyes alert and eager, coat reflecting every light— is the end result of a total program of proper training and care. Eventing begins at home in the stable.

The daily routine in any stable needs to be well organized and intelligently planned. Too many times an accident involving horses is the result of carelessness and lack of thought, "There is no such thing as an intelligent accident." The safety of the horse and the safety of the people working in and around the barn must be a prime concern in organizing the daily schedule.

All equipment, tools, tack, and medications should be kept in designated places, carefully se-cured so that, in the case of an emergency, everyone knows just where things are.

Each barn will set up its own daily routine, but as much as possible horses need to have a set schedule. Feed should be given at approximately the same time each day. The horse should preferably be fed at least three times a day, since the horse's small stomach will digest a small feed more efficiently. Each horse needs to be properly groomed daily, and should be brushed off before work and then have a thorough strapping preferably after it has been worked. However, after the horse has been ridden it is best to put it away in the stall for a short time so that it can

The well-organized USET tack room in South Hamilton, Mass.

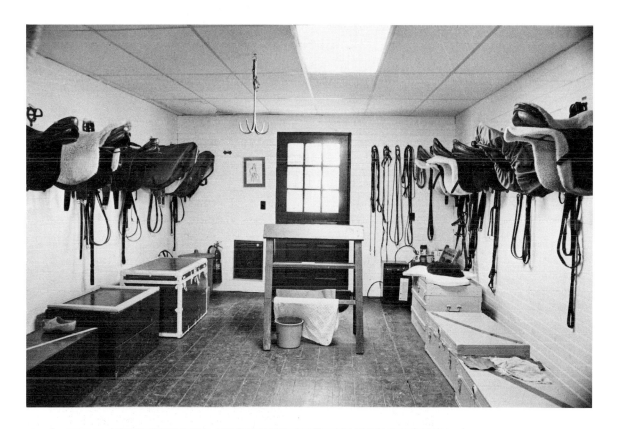

relax and digest the lessons of that day before being bothered by the grooming procedure. Of course, any routine can get mixed up if the blacksmith or veterinarian comes by, but if possible one should try to keep to a routine as much as possible.

The event horse should be fed quality feed and hay. There is no point in feeding inferior grain, as the horse will lose condition and not be able to perform. You should buy the highest quality hay and grain you can find. Most horses need hay in haynets to prevent waste; hay fed from the floor tends to get tracked into the bedding and spoiled. Lots of fresh water should be available to the horse 24 hours a day, even when the horse is turned out. A salt lick or block should also be available at all times. The type of bedding used in the stalls will again depend upon what is available locally, but it should be picked out and kept fresh no matter whether it is straw, shavings, or something else. An event horse has a busy schedule and faces many demands, so the stable routine should be geared to relaxation. The horse should have a window to look out of, or barring that, it should be able to see the other horses in the barn, and not be shut away out of sight.

The horses go better if they have time off every day, a turn-out period. Here again, safety is a main concern. In most cases the horse should be turned out alone, so there is no danger of it getting kicked, but it should be in sight of other horses so that it does not try to jump out. Young horses starting training can be turned out together provided they do not have hind shoes. If the horse has just completed a three-day event and has been at the competition for perhaps a whole week without turn-out, it should be worked before being turned loose and perhaps hand-grazed until it settles. If a horse has been kept in for one reason or another, perhaps an injury, a tranquilizer may be used upon the advice of a qualified veterinarian.

The horses at the USET stables in South Hamilton, Mass. are fed three and sometimes four

times a day. In winter their diet includes sweet feed, oats, and barley. They are fed a cooked bran mash once a week on the evening before their rest day. (The oats and barley are boiled and simmered slowly and bran is mixed in.) Each horse gets carrots every day to perk up its appetite, and is fed a supplement called Source®. For the horse that tends to be on the thin side, beet pulp is added to the feed to keep weight on.

The annual veterinary care for the team horses includes preventive shots for eastern and western encephalitis, tetanus, rhinopneumonitis, and flu. Their teeth are floated twice a year. These routine measures ensure that they remain in good health. Since the horses at the team are generally turned out only at home in well-cared-for pastures they are wormed three times a year. If a horse is turned out with a great many other

Left: USET headquarters in South Hamilton, Mass.

Right: Screw-in studs afford better traction on the cross-country course

horses it is probably wise to worm all the horses more frequently to avoid parasites. The kind of worm medicines used should be rotated so that all the various types of parasites are taken care of.

In the winter months when the horses are in work but not competing, everything is allowed to return to a natural state. Whiskers are allowed to grow long, the grease in the coat builds up to protect against the cold and the horses do not get bathed, just brushed off and checked for injuries. Their back shoes are pulled off to allow the feet to grow out.

As the horses come back into serious work the grooming routine changes. Each horse is groomed for at least 45 minutes. The person who cares for the horse, whether it is the rider or a groom, must know the horse inside out and be alert to any change in attitude or habits. In the morning you should come into the barn, look at the horse and check to see if it is acting in a nor-

mal fashion. You should know your horse well enough to pick up on anything that is different. The legs should be checked each morning and after each gallop and again at night.

Prevention is better than cure, but the use of galloping boots is not really necessary at the lower levels. At the Pre-Training level the horse should be allowed to be as natural as possible, with shaggy legs. If the Pre-Training level horse knocks itself going cross-country it should learn a lesson and be more careful. But by the time the horse is competing at the Training and Preliminary levels, bell boots and front galloping boots, provided they are properly fitted, can be of great value. Be sure that any particular piece of equipment your horse wears is really needed and be sure that it fits properly. Ill-fitting tack can do more harm than good . . . just because you see one of the team horses wearing a particular piece of tack you should not rush out and buy it for your horse. Horses were born to walk, trot, and canter and at the lower levels their legs should be left alone. So many times at the lower levels you see Pony Club kids going cross-country in polo wraps. People are getting carried away and using too much equipment. When the team first came out in figure-eight nosebands everyone went out and bought figure-eight nosebands, and now everyone has flash nosebands, and seat savers and polo wraps with their colors so that, when you go to an event, it looks like a rainbow.

Screw-in studs for traction can be used at the Training level. At the Pre-Training level the horses should learn to take care of themselves. But nowadays at the Training level it is perhaps time to start putting studs on the front and even the back shoes. When you get to the higher levels you will definitely need to use them and it is just as well to practice taking them in and out. They definitely do make a difference just as cleats make a difference to a football player.

Road studs are basic equipment, and can be put in all around. If the footing is deep and muddy then medium studs should be used on the outside of the hind feet, and if the footing is truly dreadful we put medium studs on both sides behind. When studs are in, however, keep off hard surfaces. For the roads and tracks and steeplechase phases you should use just road studs, then change to medium studs (if necessary) during the ten-minute break. One very important point to remember—*never* leave studs in overnight.

Preparing an event horse is a year-round production. It takes at least six months to prepare the horse for the riding part of any event and you are not going to get the horse there unless you care for him. Communication between the horse, the rider, and the groom is vital, particularly if the rider and the groom are not the same person. If the rider has to have a groom care for the horse because he or she does not have the time, then the rider must take time out to hand-walk the horse and get to know it away from the riding arenas. The groom should keep the rider informed of any changes in the horse, such as whether it seems off its feed, or has a slight swelling on one leg.

Two other essential people in the horse's life are the veterinarian and the blacksmith; both are as involved in the preparation of the event horse as anyone. Routine care by the vet and careful attention to the horse's way of going and the condition of its feet are as necessary as good grooming and feeding. Each event horse has a support team working to help in various ways to prepare for the competitions. Any dedicated, organized, and sensitive competitor will not only see that the horse is physically fit and mentally happy, but will also want to give the horse a chance to show that it is not just an athlete but also a showman.

First and foremost an event horse is a working horse, so he does not need to be showy, just workmanlike. The event horse must be tough enough to gallop through mud and brush, over stones, roots, and uneven ground, uphill and down. It does not need unnecessary showiness, but should reflect the pride and concern of its rider and groom.

The well turned-out horse in competition has been prepared well ahead of time. All the trimming and tidying up have been taken care of well in advance of the competition. Preparing the horse is a matter of work done gradually over a period of time; you cannot snatch it out of the field and expect to have it looking neat and tidy in a day or two.

Start with the head. The first decision is whether you want to trim off the whiskers or not. Some people feel that whiskers play a sensory role that is as important to the horse as it is to the cat; however, a smooth muzzle does appear neater. The clippers should run lightly over the muzzle, leaving it trim and neat. After the initial clip it is necessary to keep reclipping the whiskers to avoid unsightly stubble.

To make the underneath part of the horse's head look neater you can run the clippers on either side of the jawbone and underneath the

The well-groomed event horse ready for the cross-country ride

chin. Move the clippers very lightly over the sides of the head to remove any "cat" whiskers, but never clip the little hairs under the eyes.

If the horse is turned out regularly it is best to leave the hair inside the ears untouched for protection from insect bites. You can still trim the outside edge of the ears with the clippers or scissors and make quite a difference in the appearance of the ear. If the horse is kept in then it is possible to clip all the hair out of the ear, but it is best to stuff a piece of cotton in the ear first (so all the loose hairs will not fall down inside the ear).

At the Team headquarters all the horses have

J. Michael Plumb with Better and Better—perfectly turned out for dressage

clipped "bridle paths." The mane is clipped, usually just a little bit wider than the width of the bridle; sometimes, if the horse's conformation warrants it, a longer path is clipped. It is important to keep this area clipped regularly as there is nothing more unsightly than a clump of prickles standing straight up on top of the horse's head.

Except at the lower levels, where you may want to leave the horse's legs "fuzzy" for protection, the horse's legs need to be clipped also. Clip off any hair on the cannon bone and fetlock, being careful not to strip it. If the horse wears bell boots they can chafe. The hair around the coronet band can be clipped off by running the clippers upwards; for an event horse you might consider leaving this hair intact to protect the coronary band.

The mane needs to be neatly pulled so that it

can lie flat and it should be kept clean. The length of the mane will vary with each individual horse, but generally a comb and a half's length is a good guide to use—if you pull it any shorter, it is likely to stand up on end. Some people have the knack of mane pulling, others never quite master the art. There are a few pointers which can make the end result more rewarding. If you start out with a long mane, be sure to pull it over a two- or three-day period—do not try to pull it all at once. Work by pulling the hairs underneath, pulling only three or four of them at a time. Do this along the whole length of the neck and keep doing it until the mane has reached the desired shortness. Do some more the next day. It is most important to go along the whole mane and not to pull it one section at a time. Thinning gradually and evenly is less painful for the horse and will give you more even, consistent results.

You will find that some hairs in the mane still are not quite even. Press your arm down along the mane and the uneven hairs will be obvious. They can easily be snapped off with the finger tips. After the mane has grown out a bit and you wish to re-shorten it, if it is too thin to use a comb, you can snap the ends in a similar manner. A razor blade thinner can also be used to taper the mane from below.

The horse's mane and tail are much like the hair on a person's head—the hair gets dirty and itches, and needs to be shampooed regularly. You can wash the mane and tail every one to three weeks, depending upon the time of year, the amount of work the horse is doing, and how sweaty or muddy the horse gets. After shampooing apply a creme rinse, or better yet, Show Sheen®, which helps separate the hairs and makes a tail look fuller and more flowing.

The tail should be trimmed in much the same way as the mane, by pulling out a few hairs at a time, over a period of two or three days. The idea is to pull the hairs on the side of the tail while leaving those on the top of the tailbone long and flat. A comb, rubber gloves, and the edge of a pair of thinning scissors are needed to

do a good job. The hair should be grasped between the fingers and the edge of the scissors or a metal file. The comb works best when the hair is long if you are pulling the tail for the first time, and the scissors or the file are easier to use when the hairs start growing out again. A word of caution—never shave the sides of the tail with clippers in order to get the pulled tail effect; this will make the hairs stick straight out and look awful, the way cutting the horse's mane with scissors would. Gradually thin out the hairs on either side of the tail but do not go on until these areas are completely bald. The hair that is left should be even and thin and should lie flat. How far down the tail you continue is a matter of personal preference, but 6 or 7 inches down the dock is a good distance. Visually, the narrowness of the pulled tail should flow into the fuller main part of the tail.

Ideally, if a tail is pulled properly it should not need a tail bandage. All that should be needed is to dampen the top of the tail and brush downwards. However, only about one tail in fifty will be suitable on its own; all others will need a bandage to encourage the hairs to lie flat.

Track or elastic bandages on the tail may be used but great care must be taken with the elastic bandage. Bandages should be applied firmly enough to stay on but not so tightly as to stop the circulation of blood to the tail bone. A too-tight bandage can also make the hair fall out and the skin peel off. If the bandage is properly applied, however, there is no need for worry.

First you should dampen the hair, then lift up the tail and let it rest on your shoulder. With a firmly rolled bandage start as high up as close to the base as possible, leaving four inches of bandage free. Make the first turn around the tail and bring the four inches of bandage down over the top of the tail, then continue to wrap down the length of the tail bone. Be careful to keep wrapping with even pressure, keeping the bandage very close to the tail. The distance between each turn of the bandage should be even. When you reach the end of the tail bone, continue wrap ping back up and down. When you reach the end of the bandage, tuck the end into one of the layers or tie the tapes around the wrapped tail.

For the average competitor who does not have time to fiddle with tail bandages every day, putting a tail bandage on for five or six hours a day one or two days before a competition will suffice. In between, a wet brush applied to the top of the tail will help keep the pulled hairs lying flat. Never leave a tail bandage on overnight.

Many stables (including the USET) never allow a brush or curry comb to touch a horse's tail. If three or four hairs are ripped out of the tail each day, multiply that by a month and 120 hairs are missing. It is difficult to cultivate a decent tail that way. Each tangle should be separated carefully by hand. For the average rider this need not be done every time the horse is ridden, just on certain occasions. It is not a monumental task, as the hairs of a clean tail (especially one shampooed with Show Sheen®) will be easy to separate.

As a finishing touch to a well-pulled tail the bottom should be "banged" off straight. To do this properly, lift the horse's tail (by putting your arm under it) to the height at which the horse normally carries the tail when moving. Then, with a pair of scissors, "bang" off the bottom hairs evenly. The most flattering length will vary from one horse to another, but a good length is usually about halfway between the fetlock and hock.

Besides the usual sponging or hosing off when the horse is warm, it should have a good overall shampoo every now and then. This will make the horse feel better and look better, but you must be careful not to overbathe the horse because this can cause negative results such as dry skin and strip too much of the natural oil from the coat, leaving it lusterless.

Shampoo the horse well with a rubber curry or a body brush. This improves the circulation and lifts out all the dirt. Apply Show Sheen® to the full part of the tail, avoiding the pulled area because this would make it too slippery to hold

the tail bandage. Rinse well, scrape the horse dry, dry the legs well, brush the mane over flat, and apply the tail bandage. As soon as the horse's coat has dried, give it a good grooming with a clean brush.

Although the team horses are groomed perhaps more than the average horse, every horse

---

Major Medical Kit

Cotton—absorbent, sheet and Kendall
Vet-wrap®, Ace® bandages, standing bandages
Plastic wrap, Antiphlogistine *(poultice)*
Tape—masking, adhesive
Scissors, Safety Pins
Gel Cast
Spider Bandage *(for knee injuries)*
Instant ice medical pack
Epsom Salts
DMSO, Azium
Mineral Oil, Colic Medicine
Calamine Lotion (for skin irritations)
Naquazone *(for soft tissue filling, stocked-up legs from hitting fence)*
Cooling astringent
Topazone®, antiseptic
Phisohex®, iodine-based shampoo *(for cuts)*
Antibiotic eye ointment
Bute tablets
Syringe *(for washing out wounds)*
Desetin ointment *(for boot chafes)*
Telfa pads, sterile gauze
Q-tips *(for puncture wounds)*
Stethoscope
Dose syringe
Balling gun
Sponges
Thermometer
Vaseline®
Electrolytes
AHSA Drug Rule Book *(handy references – so some vets can be advised on forbidden medications for competition)*

---

that is being worked should get at least 20 minutes of grooming beforehand and about a half-hour groom when it comes in. Most of this time should be spent with the curry comb and body brush, applied with lots of elbow grease. It only takes about five minutes more to pick out the feet, dampen the mane over to one side, wipe the eyes and nose, and apply hoof dressing if necessary.

Grooming for Competition

Most event horses are done up in "hunter" or "button" braids. The average number of braids is about 15-20. A well-braided mane enhances the

Ralph Hill admires Sergeant Gilbert, braided for the vet inspection

appearance of the horse and can give a graceful clean look to the top line. Some horses with poor necks can be helped by skillful cosmetic braiding. An undeveloped or ewe neck can be helped by using "button braids," which are nobbier and are placed higher on the neck, giving it a more substantial look.

It helps to dampen a mane before you braid it and, if the hair is unmanageable, a little hair-setting gel is useful. Each braid should be about ½-1 inch apart. The line between each braid should be absolutely straight, and the three parts of each braid must be of equal thickness—this is a point many people overlook, but it is important in the overall results. Be sure the braids are very tight and that they are braided close to the neck so they will lie flat.

Some Vaseline or Baby Oil applied to the muzzle and around the eyes can help keep gnats away and at the same time darken the area, which makes the eyes look more prominent. Apply the oil just around the eyes, over and under the eyelids. Since this will tend to attract dirt, it should be done just before a competition.

Hoof dressing or hoof-black adds a final touch to the picture and should be applied just before the horse goes into the ring.

The finishing touches that are required just before the horse is "on" in the dressage ring include a quick wipe all over with a damp towel to remove dust and sweat that have accumulated during the warm-up period. Hoof dressing can be touched up and the horse can receive a quick spray of fly repellent. The groom should also wipe off the rider's boots to perfect the picture.

At a Three-Day Event

The experienced event horse knows just what is going on at a three-day event; it knows dressage day, and it knows that the cross-country day follows. The groom needs to have everything prepared in advance so that only the essentials will have to be done at the event. Much of the preparation can be done at home where a great deal of thought can be given as to just what will need to be done—where and when, and what equipment must be assembled to carry the horse and rider through the entire competition. Lists should be written well in advance to ensure that all the tack and equipment is in good repair and in order.

If the groom is well organized the work around the stall can be done in the least amount of time possible to give the horse time to relax. The less fuss around the horse the better. The horse should be groomed and fed as much as possible on the same schedule as at home, its legs should be checked and it should be left alone. People do not need to stand around the barn

Stud Box
Tap *(for screwing in studs)*
Road studs
Bullet studs
Block studs
Toothbrush
Vaseline®, Baby oil
Cotton balls
Nail, hoof pick
Wrench *(for tightening studs)*

talking to their friends; the horses are already nervous and there is enough confusion with competitors feeding their horses at different times and working in their stalls. One thing a groom can do is to take the horse out on a lead shank and let it graze away from all the commotion in the barn. There is a great deal of tension at any event, a whole bubble of intensity over the grounds, and it helps if the horse can get out of that atmosphere. Grass is a natural laxative for horses and since they are used to being turned out at home, you must try to replace the turn-out period with hand-walking and grazing.

The horse must be presented for the vet inspection looking as fit as it can. A good shampooing before the trip to the event and a thorough grooming will bring up the highlights in the horse's coat. The tail must flow nicely from a well-pulled top, and the horse should be presented in the bridle. Braiding is optional. A last-minute wipe off with a damp cloth before the horse trots up for the panel is in order, as is a last-minute application of hoof dressing. The horse can then return to the stall and the mane unbraided. The horse may be taken for a walk or given a last dressage school at this point. Everything will depend upon the rider's timetable and the rider and groom must have a notice board with all the times of the various phases written on it in large letters. Be sure you know exactly

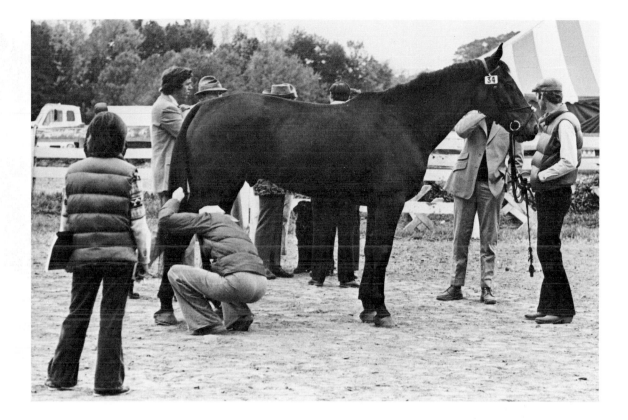

The vet inspection, or vet check

what the rider expects and when, so that you will be ready in plenty of time without being rushed.

For the dressage ride of a three-day event (as in a horse trials), the horse must look clean and neat. Braiding is optional for the lower levels, but the tail should be trimmed and well-separated. Many trainers prefer riders *not* to braid at a lower level horse trial; they feel the young rider's time is better spent walking the cross-country course than braiding the horse's mane to perfection. After the dressage ride, the horse should be led out to relax, and braids, if any, should be removed.

It is on the cross-country day that the horse, rider, and groom must become an efficient and super-organized team. Everything needed should be ready and in place the night before the endurance phase.

The stall as always should be bedded and banked at the sides to prevent any drafts on the horse and to give it a little extra protection.

Be sure that the horse has plenty of fresh water and that the haynet is hung high enough to prevent the horse from getting a leg caught in it. The evening feed should be a hearty one and should include carrots and apples to encourage the horse to clean it up. A late-night check and an additional small feed helps the horse prepare for the task ahead. As a matter of course the legs must be checked for any changes.

After the horse is settled, the rider's gear needs to be assembled: spurs, hat, helmet, gloves, shirt, etc., and all the stitching on the bridle, breastplate, martingale, galloping boots,

Steeplechase Kit

Spare pair of reins
Sponge
Towel
Small sponge *(to wash out horse's mouth)*
Elastoplast®
Easy-boot®

Equipment For Vet Box

Spare shoes and pads to fit horse
Extra bridle, cheek pieces, reins, bit, and
noseband
Extra breastplate, martingale, girth, and
stirrups
Halter and lead shank
Hole punch
Extra galloping boots
Extra galloping bandages
Scissors
Buckets for water
Sponges, sweat scraper
Vetrolin® or liniment
Buckets (with lids) filled with water
Large and small sponges
Electrolytes
Container for ice
Fishnet sheet
Wool cooler
Rainsheet
Towels
Drink for rider
Small medical kit

saddle, girth and overgirth, must be double-checked. If you find any problems make a substitution.

If the horse runs in bandages, you will need vet wrap, cottons, tape and scissors. If studs are used in the shoes, make sure the stud box is fully equipped and that the studs are clean so they may be screwed in more easily the next morning.

The equipment that has to be transported to the vet box the next morning must be assembled in addition to anything you may need to take out to the end of the steeplechase phase. Plan your strategy carefully and make sure that your helpers know exactly what is expected.

The routine in the vet box needs to be carefully planned. Nowadays the situation in the vet box is getting out of hand. It often seems as if

Vet box equipment set up at the event

The horse needs to be walked around, washed off, and have ice applied where necessary if it is hot. If the horse is fit and the weather conditions are good there is no need to get into a flap—this can put the horse in a flap also. When the weather is hot the grooms should be all the more cool, to keep the horse calm. Two efficient people are better than ten muddled ones.

Cross-country day starts early. The horse should have a small feed that morning not less than three-and-a-half hours before it goes cross-country. If the horse does not go until late in the day, the regular morning feed can be given. Skip the hay altogether as the horse will run better without a full stomach. Unless it is very hot, remove the horse's water two hours before the starting time. Check the horse over quickly and then leave it alone until it is time to get it ready. If the horse does not start until the afternoon, take it out for a quiet hand-walk.

Be sure to have enough starting time schedules on hand so that all the help will know what to do when—including, of course, the rider.

Take the equipment for the vet box down as early as possible and stake out a good spot (preferably near a treeline) and set up away from the general confusion. Find out where the blacksmith, the vets, and the water and ice will be located. Lay out a waterproof tarpaulin and organize all the equipment on it. Place all the extra tack together. If you have a small trunk you will find it very handy for transporting equipment to the vet box. Fill your water buckets (one with some brace such as Vetrolin® or Absorbine® in it) from the water containers you have brought and set them in the sun to take the chill off. Later place the buckets away from your equipment so that you won't soak everything when you wash the horse down. Be sure to refill your water containers before you go back to the stable because there will be no time to do this between the ten-minute break and the end of cross-country. Water pressure is usually quite low at events so this can be a tedious procedure.

The vets will be busy examining the horses in

there are swarms of people around a single horse, taking off boots, washing the horse, getting ice, and doing all sorts of unnecessary things. There should be two people for each horse, and perhaps a third person to stand back and dry off the boots and hand things to the others. Only two people are needed per horse— one to handle the horse and one to work—and these two should keep cool, calm, and collected.

Medicated spray for cuts
Peroxide
Cotton, gauze
Elastoplast®
Tape
Thermometer
Electrolytes
Liniment
Set of bandages
Sheet cotton
Ace bandages
Vaseline

the vet box so have a small medical kit there to handle minor problems. (See small medical kit list.)

Have Vaseline available to rub on the horse's hind legs to help it slide over any fence where it might otherwise hang a leg. A hole punch is essential in case any tack needs some extra work.

Before leaving the vet box, be sure all your equipment is covered with another tarpaulin in case of rain.

Carefully brief the help you have enlisted. It is useful to have someone go to the end of the steeplechase phase to check for lost shoes, broken tack, minor injury, etc., but it is taking a chance to have the same person try to get to the end of steeplechase and back to the vet box on time. If you have enough help it is better to send one person to the end of Phase B and the rest to the vet box.

Check to make sure that your rider's posted times are correct. Consult the rider for any changes, so that your list is current. Some riders who have done a number of three-day events sometimes do not show up until a short time before weighing in—this makes it even more imperative for the groom to have everything well organized.

All the items that may be needed at the end of steeplechase—a spare pair of reins, a towel, a small sponge and an Easy-boot® in case of a lost shoe—can be kept in a small bucket for easy transportation. As soon as the horse has gone out on Phase A (Roads and Tracks), dispatch your helper to meet the horse as it completes Phase B (Steeplechase). But make sure the helper knows where the neutral areas are where the groom may handle the horse and speak to the rider.

Give the horse a light grooming; the whole idea is to keep everything as low-key and relaxed as possible. Experienced horses know what is coming and become nervous. Fiddling with them for too long will only tire them at a time when energy is a big consideration.

Put on the bridle and plait in one small braid at the poll with a shoelace through it so that the bridle can be firmly secured to prevent it coming off over the horse's head if the rider should fall. Check the horse's legs and put on the bell boots before putting the studs into the shoes. Then put on the galloping boots or bandages. Be sure to check the galloping boots several times after the horse leaves the barn, as some horses may stock up in the barn and the boots may have to be tightened later. Finish tacking up and make sure the rider's number is handy.

Before leaving the barn be sure that the stall has deep fresh bedding and that the water bucket and haynet are filled. Lay out some poultice, paper and bandages, and a bucket of water for the horse's return. Have your medical kit ready.

If the groom has been asked to lead the horse to the weighing area, be sure to stay off the hard road if the horse is wearing studs because this is jarring to the legs. Follow the rider to the start and hold the horse while the rider weighs in. Check the tack, make sure the girth and overgirth are tight and recheck the galloping boots. Give the rider a leg up if necessary and watch the horse start.

The horse will usually finish Phase A early before starting on the steeplechase and, as soon as

Left: A properly-fitted figure 8 noseband

Right: Karen Ehmann checks stop watch before starting cross-country on Go Between

the horse finishes Phase B, it is automatically on Phase C. The groom should be right beyond the finish flags as the horse slows down coming off the steeplechase phase and should take a quick look at the shoes and tack, wipe off the reins, sponge off the horse's neck and between the hind legs. Should a shoe be missing (which happened to Better and Better at the Montreal Olympics) apply a piece of Elastoplast® around the heel and clamp on an Easy-boot® to protect the hoof until the horse reaches the blacksmith at the vet box. Try to get word back to the box so that whoever is there will have alerted the blacksmith.

The rider may or may not dismount during this time and all this need only take about a minute while the horse continues to walk on Phase C. Most riders walk for the first minute or two on Phase C to give the horse a chance to recover its breath.

While waiting for the horse to arrive in the vet box, check around to see how the cross-country course is riding, what the problem fences are on course, and if there are any hold ups. All this information will be invaluable to the competitor.

Your priorities are to make sure that the horse is well and able to continue, to check it over for any minor injury, to see that it gets refreshed and, most important, to ensure that the rider is back on the horse in time to start on Phase D.

As the horse trots into the box, hold the horse while the veterinarians inspect it and jog it out if required. Put a halter over the bridle, loosen the noseband and the girth, and sponge out the horse's mouth with water. Someone should give the rider a drink. Most riders leave the saddle on at this time. Take towels and tie them around the top of the horse's legs so water will not run down into the boots or bandages while you are sponging off the horse. Some riders like to have all the boots taken off and washed and dried at this time. If the weather is hot, apply ice (wrapped in a towel) along the jugular vein under the horse's neck and on the major veins inside the hind legs. You can also do this under the horse's jaw and between the ears if the horse

Debbie Hoyt waits while veterinarian monitors Aachen's heartbeat during the 10-minute break

does not object. A word of caution here—never do anything to a horse at an event, such as applying ice or tying towels around legs, that has not already been done at home.

Be sure to keep track of time as you continue to check the horse over for any cuts. Change the studs if necessary and put more Vaseline on the hind legs if needed. Keep the horse walking around slowly all the time, preferably in the shade.

About four-and-a-half minutes before the start of Phase D make sure that all tack is back on the horse and in order, tighten the girth and the noseband and replace the boots. The rider should be up and on the horse at 2½ minutes. As the horse starts to walk around, check the boots again, let the vet do a quick check of the pulse and respiration and, if given the O.K., send the rider out onto Phase D.

While the horse and rider are out on course, refill the water buckets. The horse will be back in a matter of minutes, hot and blowing. As the horse comes in, the rider must request permission to dismount from the clerk of the scales and will then weigh in. The groom may not touch the horse until this has happened and can then take the horse from the official who will be holding it. *Be sure not to talk to the rider until this time.* Keep the horse walking and as you do, take off the bridle and slip on the halter. Check the horse over for any wounds. Continue to walk the horse and, if the weather is very hot, hold ice under its jaw to help bring the temperature down.

As the horse recovers its breath you can stand still long enough to remove the boots and the saddle and to rub both the legs and the back to restore circulation. Wash the horse down with tepid water that has had some kind of brace added to it, and scrape the horse off with a sweat scraper. Keep walking and wash the horse's mouth out with a water-soaked sponge. If the horse is wearing large studs remove them and stuff the holes with cotton or screws. Continue walking the horse until it stops blowing hard and seems on the way back to normal, then request permission from the veterinarians to leave the cooling out area.

Above left: Grooms quickly sponge the horse's head after cross-country

Above right: Don Sachey applies ice to horse's jugular vein to help cool the horse down after a tough cross-country ride

Below: Grooms working to cool horse and check equipment during the 10-minute break

*Rider quickly dismounts after
cross-country*

After walking the horse quietly back to the barn, put it in the stall to relax. Give it some water with electrolytes added. If the horse refuses to drink, add electrolytes to its feed later. Heat up a poultice and have bandages, paper and cotton ready to use. About 15 minutes after returning to the barn, jog the horse again for soundness, then do up the legs in the poultice. Give the shoulders and hindquarter muscles a good massage with liniment.

When the horse has cooled thoroughly, go over it with a light brush, then put on a dry sweat sheet covered with a light sheet or rug, depending on the weather. Fold back the front (shoulder area) of the fishnet (sweat sheet) and top sheet and secure them with a roller; this will keep the horse's muscles warm but will help prevent the horse from breaking out in a sweat again later. It is a good idea to take the horse's temperature to be sure that it has come back to normal.

Leave the horse to rest for about two hours and, if all is well, give a small feed with added carrots and apples and half a quart of damp bran. Straighten up the stable area, clean the tack and organize any items that will be needed for the vet inspection in the morning.

Jane Cobb lets Might Tango graze to relax him during the pressures of a major competition

Later on take the horse out for a quiet walk and graze. Feed a big dinner again, including apples, carrots, electrolytes and damp bran. Check the water and hay net.

If the horse is going to develop any stiffness, this will show up several hours later. Check on the horse at about 9 or 10 p.m. and take it out for a short walk to loosen it up. Then put it away for a well-deserved rest.

You will need to check the horse early the next morning for any swelling or heat in the legs. Wash off the poultice thoroughly and give the horse a feed early on. The horse will benefit from being hand-walked for a half hour before it has to trot out in front of the vets and the Ground Jury. For this second vet inspection the horse must again be spotless and presented in its bridle.

Depending on the wishes of the rider, the horse can be left to be quiet until time for the show jumping. However, if the horse was not braided for the vet inspection, he should be now. All that then needs to be done for the show jumping is to give the horse a quick wipe off and to take a damp towel and hoof dressing to the warm-up area. The procedure before the show jumping is the same as for the dressage—a last minute tidying up before the rider enters the ring. If the weather is hot, bring a fishnet cooler to throw over the horse's back when it has finished the course or, if it is cold out, keep a wool cooler on hand so that the horse can be comfortable while waiting for the presentations.

When all the excitement is over, the horse should be put back into the stall, have its braids undone, and rest from his exertions while the grooms get reorganized for the trip home.

Grant Schneidman jogs The Flying Dutchman out for the vet check at Radnor (Pa.)

Let-down period

After the major exertion of a full three-day event, the horse needs to be let down gradually, with its feed and exercise being decreased slowly until it is ready for a period of simply being turned out with the hind shoes removed. This will take place over a period of two to three weeks. You cannot just turn a super-fit athlete out to grass— it will be sure to injure itself. A gradual let-down lets the horse unwind and it will then appreciate a well-earned rest.

After the rest, it is time to start again on your year-round program of care and training, the never-ending cycle for a successful event horse and rider.

A horse waits at the end of an event, wrapped for the van ride home

The Course for the American Continental Young Riders Championships, Wayne–DuPage, Illinois (1981)

The growth of eventing has brought in its wake new and exciting competitions at all levels. Championships now exist not only for the experienced international riders, but also for young riders and those at Training level. The new competition for the American Continental Young Riders Championships, run under the FEI Rules, has evolved from the friendly competition for the North American Junior Team Championships held between the U.S. and Canada.

The new rules for this competition came into effect in 1981. The 1981 Championships were won by the team from British Columbia. The highest-placed American was Daphne Bedford from Bluemont, Va., who finished in second place.

Daphne was representing Area II for the third consecutive year. In the 1980 competition, held in Red Deer, Canada, Daphne won the individual title with her indomitable little 15-hand Connemara, Kilts—one of the smallest horses in the competition.

Daphne believes that the Junior or Young Riders team competition is a first-rate idea, because it gives young

Richard Newton

riders the feel of team competition on an international basis. The Area II teams have been coached by members of the USET's Olympic and World Championship teams, and the young riders competing in these championships benefit from the instruction they receive first-hand from these experienced international riders.

Richard Newton, Designer

This was the first important course I had designed that I was not able to follow through with on the construction. I made the design and then returned to see what had been built. The Technical Delegate did make some changes to the fences and he was

completely correct in doing so because not all the fences had been built exactly as I had envisioned them.

The Site

The terrain for this course was very flat and not very interesting. Before I even went out to inspect the site in Illinois, I had asked for the programs from previous competitions with pictures of the existing fences. It became quickly apparent that there were several tree lines—heavily wooded lines set around the perimeter of the property—and the obstacles had been interspersed between the trees. The course just serpentined up one tree line, went around the end of the field, and back down the next tree line. I asked why the course had evolved this way and was told that the land was part of a game preserve and the course could not go through the fields because the organizers were not allowed to mow paths. However, if this property was to be used for eventing I knew some paths would have to be mowed to give the spectators more to see. If you are to popularize the sport in any area you have to attract the spectators, and if the course can be moved more into the open it will be a more attractive course. Also, if the course is going to run up and down the fence line it will not be tremendously challenging; each obstacle will look much like the previous one and all the ap-

proaches are going to be the same. The riders will always be jumping fences off a curve. We asked permission to cut some paths and discovered there was no problem, in fact, the owners of the property offered to do the mowing for us.

There had been a steeplechase course at this event before but I hoped to find a better area for this phase. We measured off Phase A for the first part of roads and tracks, and I found that I could fit the steeplechase (Phase B) within a given area and still come out with the correct distances. I was eager to design the course like the one at Radnor (Pa.), where the spectators can see the whole picture from one all-encompassing point. They can see horses on roads and tracks and the steeplechase rather than having the horses turn up in the vet box and just watching the cross-country (Phase D) with no knowledge of what went on beforehand. Putting the steeplechase in a central position also makes it much easier to plan the communications systems, the medical support, and so forth. The only drawback to the design was that there was no shade for the horses in the vet box before they went out on the crosscountry course.

The courses went around a big rectangle. There was a railway on one side, a swampy area on the second, a road on the third, and a wooded wet area on the fourth. Since I had an existing course to work with, I had to try to beef it up and to offer a different track from the one used in the previous years.

The Course

For the first fence I had hoped to use a curved S rail as the base for a flower bed to house the first and last fences, but it was not possible to build this in the middle of the field. I wound up by using some enormous timbers that someone had rescued from an old building and built a simple step fence adding some trees for decoration.

This was to be a course for the Young Riders Championships so I built a big maximum-sized oxer for the second fence. I wanted a course that would challenge the good riders but would also allow the less-experienced ones to get around even if they had to take more time. I tried as much as possible to offer longer, easier routes at the difficult fences. I wanted this second fence to be big and imposing so the riders would know that they were off to do a job and that this was not to be just a hack in the country.

The specifications allowed for the Young Riders competitions under the FEI Rules are bigger and more demanding than the ones for our regular Preliminary division, but this year the event organizers voted to stay with the specifications that had been used for this competition in previous years. The FEI ruling had been made too close to the date of the competition to allow them to adopt the larger dimensions, faster speeds, and greater distances. My feeling was that this was actually just the type of property on which to upgrade the competition because of the nature of the terrain. If horses could not run faster and jump

higher on this type of level ground, they would not be able to run fast and jump high anywhere.

The third fence was an option fence. I picked up on an existing fence that was built of a succession of old fence line posts in the ground and capped off with a round rail. It had a ditch in front of one section and a ditch behind the other. I thought that this was a good fence to offer at this point to prepare the riders for the next one, which had a ditch with a rail behind it. There was a sharp turn into this fence; the riders had to gallop along the fence line, and turn to the fence three strides away. In addition, there was a tree growing out of the middle of the fence so the riders had to decide whether to go to the left or the right of that. I thought we might start to sort out the sheep from the goats here—the weaker riders might have problems but the stronger ones would be able to ride on through. That is exactly why I put this fence there. Actually there were very few problems here, only one or two refusals.

I inserted a hayrack in the middle of the next field. I had to be careful not to interfere with the track of the course here as it turned toward the finish line. The course builders had added a line of straw bales underneath the hayrack, which made it easier than I had planned. For the fifth fence I had wanted something a bit more challenging.

The sixth fence was a turning point, like the one I built in

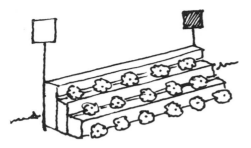

1 The Steps
Height 3'6"
Spread 4'

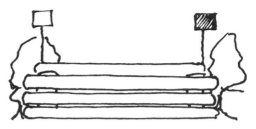

2 Oxer
Height 3'7"
Spread 4'7"

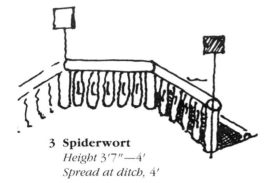

3 Spiderwort
Height 3'7"—4'
Spread at ditch, 4'

4 Richard's Revenge
Height 3'6"
Spread 4'3"

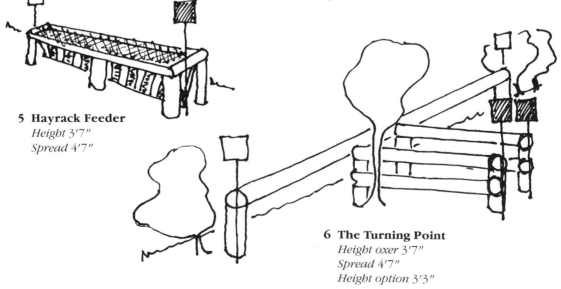

5 Hayrack Feeder
Height 3'7"
Spread 4'7"

6 The Turning Point
Height oxer 3'7"
Spread 4'7"
Height option 3'3"

Kansas. The choice was either to jump an oversized oxer, or to go around over two lower fences and take more time. I watched how the riders jumped this fence and I am happy to say that both options were used, about 50/50. In fact, on all the option fences I built for this course, every option was used. This made me feel good. I must add that some options were not really chosen in advance—sometimes the riders came down to the base of a fence without really knowing which way they wanted to go and the horse saw the way out.

From this point I moved on to the only hill on the course. Across the field was a formation that resembled an overgrown sand dune, probably about 15 feet high and 30 feet wide. It was very steep on both sides. Originally it had a railroad tie fence at the bottom and another railroad tie fence at the base of the far side, but I wanted to give the riders something more challenging. I remembered putting a post and rail at the bottom of a bank at Radnor, and Jim Wofford told me that whenever you put a post and rail at the bottom of a bank like that, the horses will all clear it—no matter what the height—because they will be concentrating on the top of the bank. This bank had a slight step on the way up so that when the horses jumped the post and rail they were able to land on this slight plateau and did not have to jump with straight legs into the bank.

After reaching the top of the bank the riders came down the far side to another choice. I had designed a very long, open letter Y here. The distance from the base of the bank to the tail of the Y was 24 feet; and if the rider took that route, then there was a 90° turn to the left-hand fork of the Y. This rail was much higher towards the end of the Y and much lower on the inside. On the right-hand side there was a dip in the ground, followed by a step up. I wanted to put a post and rail here, but with a much shorter face to the fence, which might invite some horses to run out. The rails were set at the base of the step, and unfortunately, the fence had been built in such a way that it was almost impossible to jump. As it was, there was nothing to keep the horses in the air and they were inevitably going to land on the middle stem of the Y. I remedied this by adding another rail at the same height beyond the step, to make it an oxer. This would keep the horse in the air longer by making them stretch out and then land on top of the step. Both options were chosen but the longer route without the oxer was preferred by most of the competitors. The faster route, with the oxer coming up out of the hole meant the horse had to be very quick and very much together—and I have to admit that not all of the horses were together coming down off the bank.

The course went on through a brushy area that had been cleared, but which had a number of trees scattered around. You had to pick your way through here, and then the track came back to the same bank. It looked as if there had once been a path cut through the bank, which left a gap that I filled with an upright gate. I could have just put a 3'7" gate in the gap, but since this was a championship competition, I wanted to give the riders more of a problem so I raised the height of this fence in order to make the other option viable. On the right-hand side of the gate, the bank was a solid, continuous part of the previous obstacle and I wanted to allow the horses to run over the bank and jump a rail off the back side out into space. I designed a rail that had two or three crooks or twists in it, connecting some trees. It was possible to jump off the bank at an angle right next to the gate—in fact you could almost step off—but it was hard to get the horse in there. If you took the straightforward galloping route, you had a bigger spread to jump and would spend more time in the air. I was pleased that the fence was jumped both ways. More horses went over the bank than I had originally expected, because we had raised the gate.

The course then turned back towards the hayrack. In a spot where the ground dropped away I put an L fence with the rails standing out from the slope. If the riders were bold enough and brave enough to jump the first rail at a slight angle, they would have no trouble in jumping the second one. If you jumped in straight, you had to be very careful about turning within the penalty zone. Most riders jumped the fence at an angle and did well. I did not feel that this was a fair question for the regular Preliminary level riders, so I added another section of the second fence farther down the line for them, which gave them more room to turn after the first element.

I built a simple oxer next, similar to a Montreal Oxer but with a square top. I came up with the idea of making the fence into a boathouse because it sat right beside a small pond. It was one of the existing obstacles on the original course that just needed to be solidified. It was built to maximum dimensions and was set up as a straightforward fly fence, because the next two or three fences were going to take some riding.

I found a sinkhole—a depression in the ground with a tree growing on the right-hand side of it. I had an idea of putting a single rail around the perimeter so that the rider would have to jump off the edge of the dip, down into the bottom, and out the other side. I wanted the rail to follow the contour of the terrain. This would make the rider concentrate on choosing the best take-off spot, because the drop would vary greatly. The rail was not particularly high—it was set at about 3'4" or 3'5". However, if you took the shortest route, close to the tree where the rail was lowest, there was a really big drop on the landing side. The farther you went around the sinkhole the less drop there was.

I went out to watch some of the riders take this fence and when I got to it I asked the fence judge if there had been any trouble. She said there had only been a couple of refusals. Right after I got there, three riders in a row came in and their horses put on the brakes at the last moment. Marie Davidson was one of the riders who had a stop here. She had won the dressage with a brilliant test but unfortunately her horse stopped here. I had built the fence in such a way that if the horse did stop, the rider could be clever and just slide around to the left-hand side and still jump it without losing too much time. But no one figured that out—if they had a stop, they would just turn around, go back, and try exactly the same point again.

This was one fence that was built incorrectly; the construction crew had put in four upright posts and connected them with four long rails. When you connect four posts with single rails on the edge of some uneven terrain like this, you wind up with a single high bar for the horses to jump and it makes it look as if they could just duck their heads and go underneath. We had to put more upright posts in between the original ones. We decided to wait until the fence had been constructed to see if it also needed a lower rail. I did not particularly want to add a lower rail because I was concerned about the horses getting a leg stuck between the two rails. It is possible to build a lower rail that will come off if a horse gets a leg caught on it, but I thought that the fence would be much more of a test with just one rail. If the

riders felt their horses needed something more solid to focus on, they could jump over one of the upright posts. As it turned out, the fence worked well—I was very happy with it.

The following fence was also quite a test—a sunken road crossing. The approach was parallel to the first element, a post and rail at 3'7". The rider had to turn and needed to have the horse really in hand because you had to take two strides to the rail, land on a 9'6" step, jump down into a sunken road, then up another step of 9'6" and out over another post and rail. This was one obstacle on the course that attracted the most spectators, although it was in a confined area overgrown by trees. The riders had to come in under control, turn, and then accelerate to make it through the entire complex. Many of the riders did very well here, but some of them allowed their horses to come in and slither to a stop. Once the horses had seen that there was somewhere to land, they would go through with no problem. Some of the horses had beautiful jumps coming up out of the second portion. I had sloped the second set of rails and had left a tree in the middle of the right-hand side.

From that point the course moved on to a drop fence. I beefed up an existing drop fence by placing a log and a rail behind it to build up the ground. The distance from the top of the log to the landing was about 5'3".

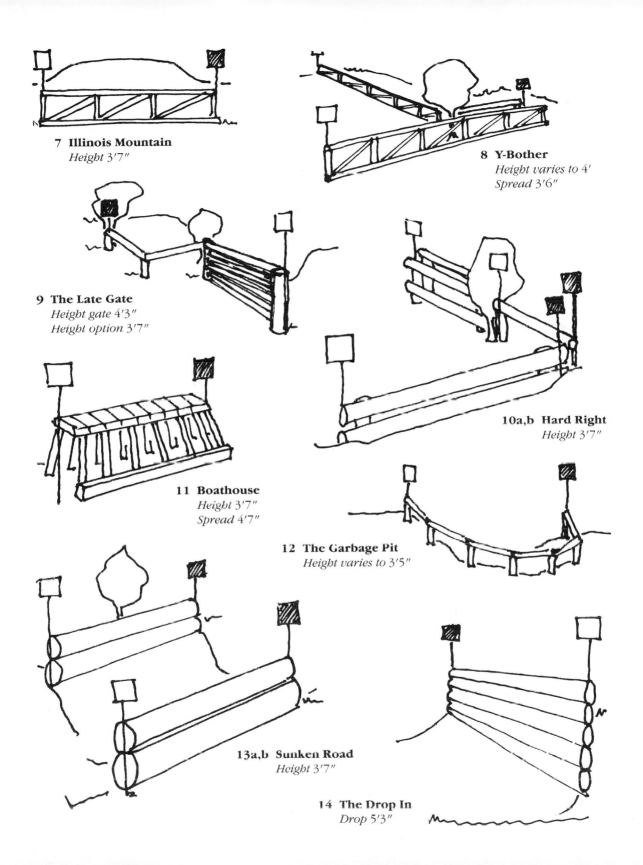

7 Illinois Mountain
Height 3′7″

8 Y-Bother
Height varies to 4′
Spread 3′6″

9 The Late Gate
Height gate 4′3″
Height option 3′7″

10a,b Hard Right
Height 3′7″

11 Boathouse
Height 3′7″
Spread 4′7″

12 The Garbage Pit
Height varies to 3′5″

13a,b Sunken Road
Height 3′7″

14 The Drop In
Drop 5′3″

The next fence was also part of the original course. It was a log pile at Training level height. To bring it up to Preliminary standards, I added some parallel rails above it. Bill Thomson designed a similar fence at Burghley in 1974. He had a pair of coops with trees on either side. This was exactly the same type of fence, but I added a rail in the middle of the face so that I did not create a false ground line. I did not want any horse catching a knee on the way up.

Originally the course had turned and gone through some woods here, but the distances were not working out well and the obstacles were not in a logical sequence. I looked at the plans and thought, "Do we send the riders into the woods for the next several minutes and lose sight of them, or do we send them back into the open?" I found a dip in the ground and placed a zigzag fence over it. Again, this was very similar to one of Bill Thomson's designs for Burghley, but not as difficult. I put the zigzag in the dip but the horses basically jumped off flat ground over the fence. The fence did look enormous. At Burghley, Bill Thomson had dug such a deep slope down to the fence that at the take-off, the horses were actually right down at the base of the fence, looking up at it. I put a take-off rail in front so the horses would not get down into the V and hook their knees coming up.

The wagons we used for the next fence were originally placed almost behind the zigzag. I did not feel that it was fair to ask the horses for a big effort over the zigzag and then follow it up with a sharp turn. We moved the wagons further on, to reward the horse that put in a nice fence over the zigzag by allowing it to gallop on.

After that there was a step up into a wooded area—another existing obstacle. I had a ditch dug in front of it and had some large rails extending above the bank. When this was originally built, the rails had a gap between them that was just large enough for a horse to catch his feet in, so I asked for the rails to be lowered about 3" to close the gaps. I think that lowering the fence solved the problem of getting a horse stuck in it, but we probably made it too easy as a result.

We built a bullfinch into one of the fence lines where the course cut back towards the finish field. When I discovered that we needed more distance on the track I then incorporated one of the existing fences—another log pile—and added some rails to it to make it an ascending oxer. It required the riders to ride on an S curve into it. I wanted to keep the horse's attention at this point, not just give them a fence that could be jumped without thinking. I had wanted to put some trees either into the oxer itself or in front of it, to avoid the appearance of having too many similar fences around the course but I did not want to create that much work for the builders.

The last fence was a huge stack of timbers—a wall—and on the back we put the logo from Arlington Farms, which had donated a considerable amount of sponsorship money for the championships.

In retrospect, I would have liked this course to be somewhat tougher than it was. I did think that the weather would have an effect on the horses, because at the time of the competition it was very hot and humid. The ground was very hard and the terrain was so flat that I tried to place the obstacles in a way that would encourage the riders to turn into them and out of them, as a way to slow them down. I did not want them racing through as if they had a straight three mile gallop with nothing in the way. I used all the ditches and gullies I could find; and the one thing I would have loved to have been able to do was to put in a water fence. I think it would have made a tremendous difference to the course. I think we would have found the horses that have phobias about jumping into water, and it might have made a big difference in the results. Unfortunately, the one area that had been used for a water jump in previous years was really unacceptable. It was in the way of the steeplechase course I had to build, and it was in the way of the access road to all the phases. I could not honestly sacrifice all the other phases just for the sake of the water jump. You cannot design a course just to put one certain fence into it; you have to include all the phases in your plans. It would have been easy to decide that, since this was the only water available, we had to use it, and to try to build the course around that water jump, but I'm glad that we didn't.

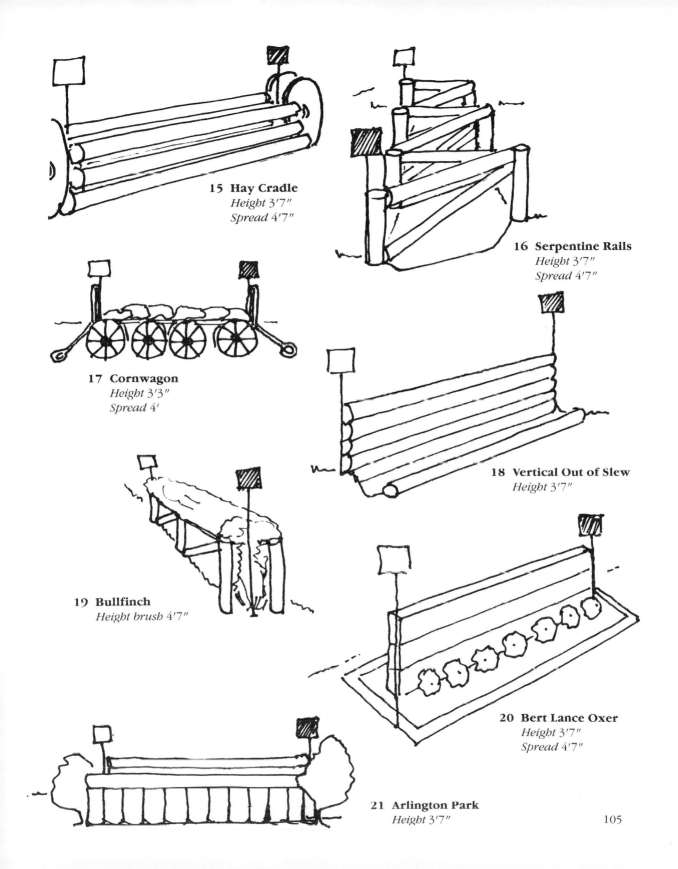

15 Hay Cradle
Height 3'7"
Spread 4'7"

16 Serpentine Rails
Height 3'7"
Spread 4'7"

17 Cornwagon
Height 3'3"
Spread 4'

18 Vertical Out of Slew
Height 3'7"

19 Bullfinch
Height brush 4'7"

20 Bert Lance Oxer
Height 3'7"
Spread 4'7"

21 Arlington Park
Height 3'7"

105

The course did its job. It jumped more easily than the riders thought it would during the course walk. I did notice that after the horses finished a great many of them were very tired and would not have been able to go another 100 yards. The heat did take its toll.

I had designed another course for this Young Riders Championships two years previously, at Flying Horse Farm in South Hamilton, Mass. I think that the course at Flying Horse was perhaps more difficult because of the nature of the terrain; it was constantly going up and down hill. But the size of the obstacles, and the massiveness of the material used to construct them, did not differ greatly between the two courses.

Bruce Davidson was coaching the Area II riders and he told me that the course had enough problems to challenge the riders without overfacing them. Jack Le Goff said that the competitors would have to do some real riding to get around, and that if he were the TD, there was not a single fence that he would alter. The comments from these two experts made me quite happy with the way the course had turned out.

Daphne Bedford, Rider

Our first impression of this course was that it was enormous, massive—all the fences were built of such gigantic materials, great beams and logs. The second impression was that we were going to have to do a great deal of twisting and turning. You could see where the original course had been built in the existing fence lines—one fence line had at least ten fences along its length. Finally, the terrain was very flat indeed.

The Area II team walked the course with our coach, Bruce Davidson, who was tremendously helpful. He knew all our horses and told us what to expect from them at each fence.

I was feeling some of the pressure of being the defending champion, a feeling that Bruce understood well. Bruce talked to all six of us before nominating four riders for the team. He asked me to be the fourth rider on the team, and I was appointed team captain. As clean-up rider I would have to ride according to whatever happened to the rest of the team.

As it turned out, we had some bad luck—one of the riders had a fall turning into one fence, and although she was not penalized for a fall she did pick up some time faults. Another team member had a stop, and one was eliminated. By the time I rode, the team had no chance to win, so Bruce told me to go on and do whatever I could.

I had two time faults on the steeplechase course, although I am not sure why. It was a flat easy course, but I finished it with two penalties. I must have miscalculated; I know that Kilts can make the time.

The first five jumps were good galloping fences. Kilts jumped well over the first and second ones—he loves those big fences. At the third fence I jumped the ditch and rails at the spot where there was a good straight line to the fourth fence, the Trakehner. Kilts put in a gigantic leap over the Trakehner. The Hayrack was another big bold fence.

The sixth fence offered us the option of jumping two separate fences or a big oxer. Kilts was jumping so big that he had no trouble at all making it over the oxer.

Then came the only hill on the course. It was more of a molehill than anything—it just sat there in the middle of the track. There was a rail fence at the bottom. I thought that we would have to attack the rails and then hook back to keep in control going over the top of the hill and down the other side. Kilts jumped up big and I was saying "Ho, ho!" and kept him together as we went over the top. This is the kind of fence that he does well because he is such a pony. Coming down the other side I took him over toward the left side where there were two fences. Bruce had instructed all the team riders to ride this side, and sent the two individuals over the oxer on the right. The problem with the oxer was that you had to be in exactly the right spot as you came down off the mound. I think either way would have jumped well.

The course demanded lots of turning and twisting. No sooner did you jump a fence than you had to pull around and twist back on the path. However, just as you were getting tired of the twisting and turning, Richard (the designer) somehow managed to give you a nice big galloping fence as a reward.

The course turned back to the same hill, or molehill, further along and there was a big upright gate on top of it this time which looked enormous. The option was most unattractive and Bruce told us all to jump the gate. None of us liked the idea. There was a little step down just before the gate and I thought Kilts would take off from the lip; as it was he stepped down into it, jumped up and hung a leg on the gate, but kept his balance. It was a big fence, and I was lucky.

I angled the rails over the drop with no trouble—Kilts is really handy over fences like this. The big oxer again gave us a chance to fly over a fence. The little horse was jumping really big that day and this was exactly the kind of fence he enjoyed.

The next fence was a strange-looking one. One of our riders had a stop here. We felt so sorry for her as she had been in the lead up to this point. I had no trouble picking a line through.

We went on to the Sunken Road, which had attracted a great number of people. Kilts handles this type of fence well because he is so handy; he can pop into and out of anything like this.

The drop fence rode well, as did the next big oxer. The zigzag fence in the depression had looked just enormous when we walked the course but Kilts gave me his best fence on the course here. He flew through the air. It was exhilarating, and we galloped on over the wagons.

At the next fence up into the woods Boyet Stevens, who was riding as an individual for our Area, had been worried about his horse so Bruce had told him to really go for the fence. When I did the same thing, Kilts took off about two strides back and gave me quite a shock. Afterwards Bruce told me that the advice was for Boyet's horse, not mine!

We then zigged and zagged back and forth, obviously to add distance to the course, and had a couple of sharp turns over the bullfinch and another oxer. The final fence was big and solid and posed no problems.

Kilts gave me some of the best fences of his life on this course; he went clear and jumped as well as ever. We finished the competition just a fraction behind the leader. If it hadn't been for the time faults I picked up on steeplechase we would have been first.

I have now been to three of these competitions and the courses have all varied. I think that this course was perhaps less demanding than the one at Flying Horse (Mass.) because the terrain was so flat, and the course in Canada had more combinations and thinking fences. But for a championship course this one did what it set out to do.

Part Two
Preparing for the Event

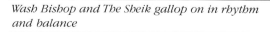

Wash Bishop and The Sheik gallop on in rhythm and balance

4 *Basic Dressage Philosophy*

Torrance Watkins Fleischmann

USCTA Rider of the Year 1980
Bronze Medalist, Fontainebleau
Alternate Olympics 1980

Torrance Watkins Fleischmann on Severo

Torrance Watkins Fleischmann has been eventing for over ten years. She first caught the attention of the USET selection committee with her chestnut horse, Severo, and her gray, Red's Door, but she captured the heart and imagination of a whole generation with her now famous partner—the small, 15-hand pinto mare, Poltroon. Riding in Poltroon's first international competition, Torrance placed second at the famous Burghley event in England in the fall of 1979. The pair won two of the team selection trials in the spring of 1980 and placed second in the other, making them a natural choice to represent the United States in the 1980 Olympic Games.

Due to the unfortunate political situation, most eventing nations chose not to compete in the Moscow Olympics, but made their way to an alternate competition held in Fontainebleau, France instead. Here Torrance and Poltroon quickly caught the imagination of the French spectators. The slim blonde in the colorful silks on the already colorful mare won the hearts of all who saw them. Well-placed after their elegant dressage test, Torrance and Poltroon went on to win the individual bronze medal. Crowds clapped and cheered for "Le Pinto," and supporters of the pair sported T-shirts proclaiming "Pinto Power."

Once a skeptic, Torrance has become an enthusiastic convert to the advantages of correct dressage schooling. Here she outlines her thoughts on the benefits of dressage for every event horse.

To me, dressage schooling is at the heart of every challenge my horses have to face in the future, from show jumping to cross-country to steeplechase, but I admit that I never used to feel that way about it. I was one of those people who had to be dragged out to practice by the hair, yelling and kicking and beating my hands against the ground, saying "I don't want to do dressage!" Dressage was such a chore because I did not understand what I was doing.

Dressage is a very involved mental and physical exercise for both the horse and the rider. Now I understand that dressage is an exciting way of building a base into the horse. You can incorporate work for all the muscles the horse must use during the cross-country phase, which in my heart is the part of the sport I like best. It is tremendous to know that every single muscle has been so well-conditioned, so disciplined and relaxed by dressage work, that the horse is perfectly ready to meet the demands of the endurance test. If someone had tried to convince me five years ago that I would say this, I would have looked them square in the eye and said "Yech—you are *way* off base."

Dressage means conditioning the horse's mind, and tuning the responses so the horse and rider become a pair, an entity. Watching dressage does not always give that impression, since often what you see looks like a fight. This to me is a shame, because not all riders truly understand what real dressage training can do for a horse.

I am very unorthodox in my dressage schooling, probably because I do not have a dressage arena *per se* to school in, and I very rarely have the advantage of working in one. When I take a young horse out to do flat work, I work in several different areas on our farm. I work the older horses in one particular place that is slightly flatter than most. I can set up an arena there but I tend not to. When I schooled Poltroon and Severo, the only time we worked in an arena (except when I worked with Jack Le Goff, Mike Plumb, or Jim Wofford) was when we entered the dressage arena under the gun in competition

Dressage schooling can take place anywhere. Here Tad Coffin warms up Bally Cor in a field

and I believe this is what kept my horses so fresh. They did not go in and look miserable; at least I never felt that they were miserable. The resulting test was exciting to me because the horses gave spontaneous responses to my mental commands. The horses did not anticipate the next step, and consequently every move was fresh and elastic. If you're not careful, the rider can make dressage dull, like a form of punishment you'd devise for prisoners in a camp somewhere.

*Mary Anne Tauskey readies
Marcus Aurelius for the dressage
ride*

With young horses I am very careful not to drill too much on dressage. Jack Le Goff is so good about saying "gymnastic your horse on the flat." I want the young horses to enjoy their work, so I will do a lot of my dressage schooling during their daily hacks.

My primary objective with a young horse is to encourage the horse to relax and trust the leg and the seat. The best way to do this is to be quiet and to ride the horse in a long frame. So many riders ride their horses into a Pre-Training dressage test with the horse cranked into a Prix St. Georges frame. The young horse will become nervous when pushed into an artificial frame. The horse must learn to relax the back and the hind end. I aim for relaxation especially in the horse's early schooling, but sometimes I too grow impatient and cram the horse into a frame. When this happens I remind myself that the training of the horse is progressive, and that a young horse is not ready to be a Third Level dressage horse.

During the first year of work I expect to be able to get the horse to accept the hand, to lengthen the frame, and to move away from the leg. I try to get the horse to move from behind so

James Wofford on Carawich display beautiful balance and harmony during the dressage test

that the horse is pushing off its hindquarters. I do not know if that is what most of the books say, but this is what I like to feel. In the long run I want these horses to be able to run and jump safely at speed, yet still be able to expand and contract their frame, even when they are galloping cross-country.

I like to use the shoulder-in exercise from the very beginning. I ask for it going down the road from one side to the other. I also use haunches-in, but without drilling the horse in a ring. I use voice commands during transitions and praise the horse when it does well. I want to teach the young horse to balance itself as it contracts and expands its frame and I try to do this where it is easy, on a slope or going up a hill. I want the horse to be happy in its work. I do a great deal of work at the rising trot to encourage the horse to move forward. I try to teach the horse to respect and respond to the seatbones, instead of pulling on its mouth. I sometimes use a breastplate as an aid and pull on that instead.

I start the young horse with a soft bit and no spurs, then I progress to using small spurs. (I am not comfortable with a dressage whip; I do not know how to use one properly.) I try to correct any stiffness in the horse as soon as I can so that the horse's neck and shoulders will be supple. I try to get the horse to ooze around my leg.

If the horse is well-balanced in the canter I will start using counter-canter quite early on. I teach the young horse to move laterally away from my leg in the true canter as a beginning. If the horse has trouble with its balance in the canter or the gallop, I work on a circle and use half-halts to try to correct the horse and balance it. I do canter departs and halts and use my voice to help obtain the halt. I find I can get a proper half-halt in the canter sooner than I can in the trot and I use the walk-canter departures early on in training.

Blue Monday gives David O'Connor a lengthening of stride at the trot

Each time out the horse will make mistakes that need immediate correction. But I never drill the dressage work and I vary the location and work routine as much as possible.

I cannot be disappointed if a young horse does not develop a true lengthening after the first year of work. If the horse is not willing to go forward I will put it beside an experienced horse; usually the young horse will try to match the older one's longer strides and learns to lengthen that way.

If the young horse can go forward from the leg, lengthen and shorten easily and be supple in its neck and shoulders, I am quite content for the first year of training. The level you will reach in a year depends on the horse. Early dressage training should not be too complicated. I take the young horses to minor dressage schooling shows during their first year, entering them in Training and First Level tests, and provided they do well and do not get sour I will take them to several Pre-Training and Training level events. All of this is to get the young horses used to going to shows away from home.

The more a horse learns, the less the rider has to move, and the less the rider moves, the better the horse's balance becomes. As the horse relaxes and responds to the rider's aids, giving with its back, you will find that there is a moment when the horse actually "fills up your leg" and you can do whatever you want to with it. I heard the feeling described once as "having your stirrups start to hum;" you feel as if the horse and your legs are in complete harmony. The magic of riding a test on Poltroon or Severo was to be able to *think* of the movement and have them perform it. It seemed almost like instant communication, mental telepathy. The horse's concentration deepens as its education progresses. Someone asked me how my own concentration level could be rated during a test, on a scale of 1-and-10 and I replied that it was absolute 10, but also remains spontaneous so that I have the flexibility to reorganize anything that gets out of line. I am certainly not programmed for a test and my horses are not programmed either.

All the time I spend working on the flat pays off for me on the cross-country course. My horses are responsive and are able to use every single muscle fluently. Dressage schooling is the guts of the cross-country riding. A typical example of what is needed for three-day event horses was one of the problems set by the course designer at Radnor in 1981. The Dog Kennel was a real test of the horse's ability to shorten its frame. It was a vertical fence set on a downhill slope, and it was a "very vertical," the fence looked nasty, yet for so many riders it rode easily. The first eight fences had asked the horses to expand, and suddenly they were faced with a downhill vertical. All of those horses had to set back onto their hocks and listen to their riders. The rider could not play around with the horse's head but had to bring his shoulders back over his hips and have the horse come right up in front so that its knees would come off the ground quickly in order to make that vertical. If horse and rider were steady for the vertical, the following oxer (the "dog house") came very easily. Without the basic flat work, those riders and horses would have been in trouble.

I enjoy my dressage work and I enjoy riding the tests, but the real test of my flat work comes out on the cross-country course. If I know my horse is well-schooled on the flat, I know it will be responsive and athletic over fences.

5 *Gymnastic Schooling Over Fences*

Edward E. Emerson

Edward E.—Denny—Emerson on Core Buff

Edward E.—Denny—Emerson originally taught high school English and sold real estate in his native Vermont. A lifelong fascination with horses led him to eventing, and with his small, tough, part Morgan, Victor Dakin, Denny was selected to represent the United States in the World Championships in 1974. He was part of the victorious U.S. team that won the gold medal from the British on their home ground. Since then Denny has been an active competitor with several other horses.

Denny is another rider who passes on his knowledge to students. He and his wife, May, run Tamarack Hill Farm in Strafford, Vt. as a combined training center. Many of Denny's students have been successful in both the junior and national open competitions. A man of great energy, Denny is in demand for clinics all over the U.S. His gymnastic jumping exercises have become gospel to many combined training enthusiasts.

In 1982 Denny took over the presidency of the U.S. Combined Training Association (USCTA) and is turning his efforts to continuing the tremendous growth in the sport experienced under the leadership of Neil Ayer.

Gymnastic jumping is a series of exercises that use rails or fences placed in such a way that they help predetermine the horse's take-off point and predetermine the length of stride through a line of jumps. There are countless variations on the ways this can be done and many of them are most useful for the three-day event horse. Gymnastics can be used to develop a horse's confidence in its own jumping ability, including jumping bigger fences than it would otherwise be ready for. Gymnastics can help correct such jumping faults as rushing, twisting, knee-hanging, jumping hollow-backed with the head in the air, chipping into fences, and jumping crooked. Gymnastics can develop a horse's boldness about jumping into a maze of rails and help teach it to go where it is directed. Gymnastics can help the typical sprawled-out Thoroughbred that runs on its forehand to shorten and regulate its strides, and to rock back and jump off its hocks. Finally, gymnastics can help the inexperienced rider feel the jumping motion without worrying about getting to the correct take-off point each time.

If I have a green horse that has never jumped before, I will first set out a single rail on the ground and walk the horse over it. The horse should learn that there is nothing to be nervous about. Next I will put the horse into rising trot and trot over the same rail. If the horse is not particularly hot it will accept this exercise easily.

Once the horse will trot over one rail, I will add several other single rails around the schooling area and just trot around, changing direction frequently, in rising trot, simply trotting over the ground rails here and there. When the horse pays little or no attention to the rails I will then place four or five rails in a row about four-and-a-half feet apart. I bring the horse back to the walk again and let it walk through the series of rails on a loose rein. If the horse puts its head down to sniff at the rails, or even if it goes through hitting every third one with its feet, I remain calm, pat the horse and walk through again. If the rider stays calm and positive, the horse will soon realize there is nothing to be excited about.

When the horse is calm in the walk, I ask it to pick up a trot and go through the line in rising trot, letting the horse discover for itself the swinging stride that will carry it over the poles. I do this until I am sure the horse has accepted the exercise.

Some trainers then add a little X jump (crossrail) after the row of cavaletti but I prefer to let the horse jump just a single little X standing by itself. I think this is less confusing to the horse. The X should have a ground line on either side of it so that it can be jumped from either direction. I just keep the horse trotting into it. There is a very definite rhythm if the exercise is done correctly, the horse comes to the fence, trot, trot, trot, rocks back over its hocks and pops over. I am looking for that rhythm; I do not want the horse to come at the fence and fall on its forehand.

Once the horse can just trot over the little X, I then return to the line of rails on the ground and add another X—about 9 feet from the last rail. Then I have several options. I can add another X 9 feet further from the first X, making a bounce, but I usually will put a second X about 18 feet away (one stride) from the first one, to start building up the grid.

My next moves will depend on the way each horse reacts. Some horses might trot over the rails, pop into the combination and crawl out over the second fence. In this case I may dispense with the trotting poles in front of the little combination and just ask the horse to jump the two Xs. The rails on the ground can put a horse onto its forehand because they tend to draw its head down to look at them. I think that a horse should be able to trot through the rails and then jump, but sometimes this seems to confuse the horse. I study each horse's reactions and act accordingly. Sometimes I need to put up more rails at the side (as wings) because the horse wobbles through the line.

At the heart of any trainer's use of gymnastics

Right: May Emerson guides a young horse through a gymnastic line. Here the horse rocks back on its hocks for take-off as May gives full freedom of rein (Photo by Mike Noble)

Below: The horse concentrates on the next element as he lands (Photo by Mike Noble)

Left: May continues through a simple one stride line (Photo by Mike Noble)

Below: May leaves the young horse alone so the mare can sort the jumping techniques out for herself (Photo by Mike Noble)

The distance between cross-country fences requires careful study. Here Jack Le Goff and USET riders watch Mary Anne Tauskey pace off strides in a combination

must be the knowledge of "true" distances. Distances will obviously vary between a 15-hand, pony-gaited horse and a lumbering giant, but the following are basic guidelines: for trotting poles in front of a small fence, the rails need to be set four-and-a-half feet apart, and there should be 9 feet from the last rail to the fence; between a small X or vertical fence, approached at a trot, use 18 feet to make the horse take one stride; if you want to add another small fence two strides away you will need 33 feet.

All riders and trainers need to develop their own stride so they can pace off the distances between fences correctly. I draw a chalk line on the ground, then another one 24 feet away. I make all my students pace it off, then ask them how many feet they have found in the distance between the two lines. Pacing a distance is a skill that should be developed, or else you'll end up

carrying a measuring tape around. Most riders do not bother to develop this skill, but they should. You can really confuse a horse by putting a combination at a 16-foot distance when you meant to use a 19-foot one.

Distances between fences basically involve multiples of 9, 10, or 11 feet. As the horse's training progresses, you can adjust your distances accordingly. For example, if you want to discipline a horse that is getting careless, you can increase the height of the fences but keep the distances short. For the green horse jumping low fences out of a trot, multiples of 9 feet should be used. If you progress to higher fences, then you should increase the distance between each fence to multiples of 10 and then 11 feet. All these distances are for schooling purposes and can be used safely in an indoor ring or enclosed ring. When you get outside to a normal course you will want to use multiples of 12 feet.

The classic distances used for courses are 12 feet for a bounce, 24 feet for one stride, 36 feet – two strides, 48 feet – three strides, 60 feet – four strides, and 72 feet – five strides. What this means is that when the horse clears the fence, it will land about 6 feet out from it, take four 12-foot strides (48 feet) to the next fence and take off 6 feet from the actual line of the fence, for a total of 60 feet. In other words, the landing and take-off take up 12 feet of the 60 feet. When you are walking a line, you can do it either by backing up against the landing side of one fence and counting all the distances to the front side of the next one, or you can start six feet out from the fence and pace off the distance up to 6 feet in front of the next fence.

You cannot expect to teach the horse to jump through complete grids all in one day. The schooling takes several months of gradually increasing the demands on the green horse and making sure it accepts each new step before adding a new exercise. Each horse should be allowed to progress at its own rate, with care taken not to overface the horse. Once the horse has learned to jump a simple X, I ask it to jump an X followed by a small vertical fence with a rail in front of it. In all these exercises you should always have a rail on the ground to give each fence a ground line. Once the horse jumps the vertical calmly and in balance, add another small vertical another 18 feet away; or make the vertical after the first X into a small oxer. As the horse progresses you can raise the first X or you can turn it into a vertical and you can play around with the formations, using verticals or oxers.

Ideally the horse should jump with style. I want the horses to rock back onto their hocks and to propel themselves into the air with their knees up and even tucked under the chin, to drop their heads, round their backs and curve around the fence. (This arc over the fence is called the *bascule*.) The highest point in the horse's flight should be over the highest point of the fence. Few horses do this well naturally, but they can be taught to do so.

Apart from natural ability, much of correct jumping is a matter of balance, especially at the take-off point. I find that the average horse can lengthen its stride much more readily than it can shorten it. If the horse jumps from a low unbalanced position without its hocks underneath it, it is much more apt to jump flat (rather than bascule) without bringing up the knees.

To encourage a horse to shorten its stride, I use three, four, and five one-stride oxers with 18- or 19-foot distances between them. I jog into the first little X or vertical very slowly, put my hands forward on the horse's neck and look down the line. I let the horse work its own way through the line.

Gymnastics may be used to correct many jumping faults but, again, it is up to the trainer to analyze the faults and know how to correct them.

If the horse stops in the line or swerves out halfway down, perhaps you forgot to add only one element at a time and built too many fences too quickly. Go back to the X to the first oxer and add one element at a time after the horse has jumped the easier task several times. It may be that you are under-riding. Try closing the leg more, clicking at the horse, using your voice, or tapping the horse with your stick. You can effectively "shut the door" or hole with a pole placed as a wing.

If the horse jumps in too big at one fence and has trouble at the subsequent elements, you should bring it into the gymnastic again to see if it has learned from the mistake. If not, lay a landing pole seven to eight feet beyond each fence. The horse will not want to land on these poles and should make the trajectory of the jump shorter and higher. You can also roll the ground

May Emerson on Forfeit, a 4-year old stallion who was getting too bold and over-jumping his fences. Here landing poles are placed 7½ feet after the fence to make him land sooner

Here Forfeit drifts to the right through a five-element gymnastic line. Drift poles were later used to correct this problem

line on the second fence back (out from the fence) a little to make the horse rock back onto its hocks sooner.

Some horses will not want to go forward and will become sticky and unenthusiastic. When this happens gallop forward actively all around the ring, when you land after the final fence, then repeat the exercise in a more active trot—this time, hopefully with more zest.

In contrast, some horses set their eyes on the maze of poles and charge into them. I find starting green horses much easier then reschooling a rusher. Horses rush for many reasons and rushing may have so many causes that I would rather not oversimplify the answer. A lot of horses rush because they do not like to jump; they see all the rails, fling up their heads, and try to run through them to get the chore over with. Others rush out of fear, or because they lack balance, or because they are being over-ridden. I have had horses that could not go through a gymnastic grid. With these horses you are better off going back to cantering single fences and teaching them that they cannot run through the rider's hand. I have spent upwards of an hour cantering a confirmed rusher and jumping until the horse was so tired its tongue was hanging out. This did not look

A horse's eye view of a gymnastic line. Even a green 4-year old, properly schooled, can learn to negotiate this "sea of rails" confidently

very pretty but I was not hanging on the horse or chasing it, I was just trying to relax it. Interestingly enough the exercise had a very strong carry-over to the next time we jumped that particular horse. There was a case where gymnastics did not work; these exercises are not infallible.

Horses that swerve towards one corner or the other of the jumps are looking for more room between fences so they do not have to shorten their stride. You can prevent this by placing a drift pole on the ground on the side the horse tends to drift towards.

Some horses jump with hollow backs, holding their heads in the air, a fault usually caused by the rider's hands. The horse may have been caught in the mouth so much that it no longer dares to use its head and neck in a bascule. In this situation I place the rider's hands on the neck with a loop in the reins to absolutely guarantee that the rider cannot grab the horse's mouth. If the rider's balance is poor I will make him or her hold the mane through the entire line. No matter what, the rider must *not* catch the horse in the mouth.

The horse that hangs its knees may be doing so because it is unbalanced. Just the use of gymnastic lines will gradually help correct this because it will teach the horse to shorten and rock back on its hocks, giving it more time to get its knees up. If the horse is lazy and careless I can roll the ground rail back under the actual fence to create a false ground line. This will make the horse hit the fence and perhaps persuade it to try harder. Be careful with this correction, however, as it can be abused and should only be used by an experienced trainer.

In addition to improving the horse's style, normal gymnastic lines (and cross-country varieties of gymnastic lines) can help the horse develop considerable boldness. For example, you can build a line, fence by fence, starting with an X with 9 feet to a vertical for a bounce and, when the horse bounces through with confidence, you can add an oxer at 18 feet for a bounce followed by a one-stride. When the horse masters that, add a second one-stride (18 feet to another little oxer) and, when the horse jumps this well, add another oxer, 33 feet or two strides away. If the horse gets flustered at any point, back off. But if your horse is full of confidence it may grow overconfident and start jumping too boldly, in which case you must add the landing poles 7 to 8 feet after each fence. Once the horse has mastered jumping down a maze of poles it will tackle even cross-country fences with confidence. Often on a cross-country course the rider will have to ask the horse to jump into a maze of rails and the horse must go where it is directed. Gymnastic lines will have helped the horse acquire the necessary confidence.

This gymnastic line offers several elements for training—trotting poles, fence, landing pole, and oxer with drift pole

A gymnastic line with a cross-country twist. A fence, a bank, 10 feet to a bounce, 20 feet (one stride) to a drop. All of the distances are easy and encourage confident jumping (Photo by Mike Noble)

In general work I keep returning to gymnastics, even with my experienced Advanced horses, York, Victor Dakin, and Core Buff. Even if I am going out to do a stadium jumping school, I will have a gymnastic line set up somewhere and I will jump through that a few times before I jump a course.

If I find that my horse is beginning to get rank, or is jumping flat, I will return to the gymnastic line. Three-day event horses, especially, have a tendency to get a little flat because of the cross-country work and they are also inclined to be quick and aggressive, which is what we ask them for cross-country. If the horse will come to a fence the way Victor or York does—if it will back itself off and set itself up—you can afford to ride it forward to the fence. I find this kind of horse far and away the easiest kind to ride. But Core Buff, who is a better jumper in the sense that he can jump a bigger fence, tends to get a little strung out. I spend more time with him in the gymnastic line. It is so easy for him to stand off before a fence that he is not always very careful at times—jumping is almost too easy for him. Victor, who did not have much scope, knew that he had to meet each fence just right; he was such a canny little devil that I would ride forward at a fence and I could feel him backing himself up under me as if he was getting his momentum through speed; then he would rock back on his haunches and launch himself up. All the pictures show him with his knees way up by his shoulders. If you hold a golf ball at arm's length and drop it, it will bounce back up to your hand, but if you slam that same golf ball onto a concrete floor it will bounce way up over your head. I believe that horses like Victor get a lot of their spring from speed. Victor always felt as if he were struggling through gymnastic lines if the fences were of any size. For Core Buff, gymnastics are the easiest thing in the world since he can use his knees and jump up but he needs gymnastics because he has the inclination to open himself up too much. York was the perfect middle man—he could do either.

You can teach the horse a great deal about jumping cross-country fences by using the gymnastic lines. Many cross-country fences on any course above the Pre-Training level require a lengthening and shortening of stride. (So do some Pre-Training fences, but only if the course is not designed properly for that level.) Unlike Victor Dakin, who can gather himself easily, most Thoroughbreds can lengthen themselves all day but have a much harder time gathering themselves. With these horses I would overemphasize the shortening exercises. I know I can always count on them to open their stride. Many three-day event coaches and trainers make a big mistake in not making sure that the horse rocks back onto its hocks and jumps up. They think you have to spend more time teaching the horse how to gallop. Galloping is a natural instinct for the Thoroughbred. I have done enough show jumping and have been around enough show jumping trainers to know that if you accentuate the horse's ability to rock himself back and jump, you are teaching him the more difficult thing. If you can teach the horse that thoroughly then, when it gets into a coffin, or in front of a water fence where you do not need to take-off from too far away, or in any kind of puzzle jump where the horse must jam its hocks under itself and jump up, it is more prepared. The lengthening will take care of itself.

On the other hand, if you have a horse with a straight shoulder and a shorter stride who finds it difficult to lengthen, then I think you need to use your gymnastic line differently. The only way I used gymnastics with Victor was to keep them long and low and gallop him forward. I needed to teach Victor to land inside a combination and keep going forward.

Gymnastics are also very good for improving a horse's form over fences. You can almost shape a horse's position in the air by the way you build a fence. You can play with it until you see results. You can put the front rail higher, or the back rail higher; you can square the rails up, you can roll the ground line back under the fence, or you can

The Rider's Position over Fences

Many event riders look to the stadium jumping phase of an event with a certain amount of trepidation. Clearly, anyone who has watched many horse shows as well as events can discern that the show riders, especially the equitation riders or "graduates" from the equitation ranks, ride stadium courses with a greater poise, precision, and style than most of their eventing counterparts.

In Medal-Maclay classes, riders are judged subjectively on their form, pace, control, and style over fences. These riders compete every weekend for months on end, jumping thousands of fences a year and constantly striving to do the job correctly. The best Medal-Maclay "graduates," such as Mike Plumb, William Steinkraus, Buddy Brown, Mike Page, Conrad Holmfeld, James Kohn, Bernie Traurig, and Mary Chapot, moved easily into the top ranks of show jumping or eventing. They have such a terrific foundation in work over fences that they can adapt to greater demands.

Event riders, on the other hand, have special demands on their time, which prevent them from working so much over fences. Dressage is very time-consuming and requires systematic, seemingly endless practice. Even more demanding physically is the fitness program, which requires hours of road work and galloping. A horse undergoing conditioning for cross-country cannot be asked to jump the hundreds of fences necessary to make his rider sharp and tuned for the stadium jumping.

This lack of time and energy for practice is not the only problem. I am pretty much convinced that event riders, in general, need to take a much more systematic and correct approach to the elements of style and control over fences.

Mary Anne Tauskey and Marcus Aurelius show excellent form during the stadium round at Ledyard (Mass.)

roll it out from the fence. You can move rails around until you see your horse change its style, until you see the shoulder and the knee beginning to come up, and the horse beginning to use its head and neck. Through the correct application of gymnastics, by shaping the fences, you can change the way the horse uses the parts of its body.

For my riders I will put up a vertical fence and an oxer and send them down over the vertical, back over the oxer, half circle over the vertical, down over the oxer again and so forth. This way each rider jumps a lot of fences and develops an eye for a single fence, but the horse can get sloppy this way, so I will usually return to gymnastics for the horse. The exercise makes the horse pay attention, as though it arrives at the fences thinking, "There is a lot in front of me and if I'm not careful I'm going to sting myself or get hurt." So many three day event horses tend to jump flat. I like to feel that the horse's withers are coming up at me in the air. If the head goes down, the knees seem to come up when the horse is over the middle of the fence and the hind end flips up. The horse curves (bascules) in the air like a porpoise or dolphin leaping out of the water.

For show jumping I find that we ask the horse to do two almost contradictory things. We want the horse to be coming positively forward with lots of impulsion, but in balance. It is fairly easy to get impulsion, by sending the horse forward energetically; and it is fairly easy to get balance, by lifting the horse up and back. But it is difficult to get both together. The tendency of the American sporthorse, or Thoroughbred, is that as you send it forward, it opens the stride and gets longer and on the forehand, losing its balance. If you want the horse to wait and lighten in front, the engine dies and you have a horse that lunges off the ground but doesn't have enough impulsion to make a long distance. The challenge is to create enough energy behind and to give the horse the freedom it needs to jump well, but not to let all the energy "out the front door." You

need to come forward to the fence with both impulsion and balance so you are trying to create two almost contradictory qualities. Using gymnastic lines is one way in which you can dictate the approach, because you ride positively at the line and the line tells the horse that it had darn well better stay in balance because the fences are too close for it to be able to flatten.

With Core Buff I would set up a 3′9″ vertical with 18 feet to a 4′ high oxer, 19 feet to another 4′ high oxer, then around a loop I would set another single 4′ oxer. The oxers were good-sized fences with a spread of some five feet. He would come in, back up over the line and then jump the single oxer much more carefully than if I had just jumped him over that by itself. If you have a horse with less jumping ability than Core Buff you would use smaller fences, but the principle is the same. You are trying to *create* the ability to jump the fence.

If you watch good show jump riders they are always riding forward. You might see them take back but only with a quick action, a brief half-halt. You have to have something in your hand in order to be able to half-halt. You see many event riders creeping toward the fences because it gives them more time to see a spot. However, if you ride positively forward and you see that you want to shorten your horse you can half-halt and the horse will accept it, if it is in balance. The horse will not accept a half-halt if it is on the forehand. Your job is to teach the horse to keep itself in balance as it moves forward. Gymnastics are a wonderful way to accomplish this goal.

Novice Jumping

The beginner must first learn to post to the trot. The thrust of the trot is the same (on a smaller scale) as the thrust over a jump. The rider must also learn to use his eyes to find a focal point to look at over the fence. "Don't look down" is a constant reminder.

The rider must learn to release the rein over the fences. The first, most basic release mechanism is to grab the horse's mane halfway up the neck. This accomplishes several things. It allows the horse to use its head and neck instead of getting hit in the mouth by an unbalanced rider. It also puts the rider's upper body in the correct position and supports the upper body.

The lower leg must be pressed against the side of the horse over the fence with the heel pressed well down. If there is enough weight in the rider's heels, this will prevent the lower leg from swinging back, which is a very common fault.

After the jump, the rider should halt on a straight line away from the fence. These are all exercises that make up the cornerstone of jumping position and technique.

Intermediate Jumping

Once the rider no longer feels that it is necessary to grab the mane, it is time to move on to the intermediate stage. The second accepted method of release is the crest release. Rather than gripping the mane, the rider rests the hands on the neck and presses down on them. Placing the hands too low on the withers or the lower neck prevents the horse from using the head and neck. But if the rider's hands are thrown too far up the neck they cannot support the rider's upper body. It is the press factor that supports the upper body. The crest release should be used two or three strides before the fence to begin with and only a moment before as the rider becomes more proficient.

Intermediate riders should begin to think in terms of the line to the fence and the turns on the course. The rider must wait for the turn and not lean in and out corners, just as the rider must wait for the horse in the flat work.

If the rider develops a habit of ducking the upper body over the fence you can practice approaching the fence in a two-point contact in forward position; this helps the rider keep up with the motion. One solution to ducking forward is to pick a focal point somewhere beyond the fence—this keeps the rider from over-anticipating.

If the rider drops back in the air over a fence, he or she should approach the fence at a closer, more forward angle than normal, even to every fence around a course.

Some riders have the tendency to jump ahead of the horse. The rider stands in the stirrups so that the crotch and waist are almost ahead of the pommel. This is a problem of overanticipation and the solution is to canter over small fences and to sit and wait until the horse leaves the ground before going forward. In all these instances the upper body should make a minimum of motion but should close quietly as the horse thrusts upward off the ground.

As the rider becomes more proficient, the position over fences includes a closed steady leg with the heels driven well down. The release should be automatic. The angle of the hips should close and open as the horse leaves the ground, jumps the fence and lands and the eyes should be up and looking ahead.

Once the rider's position has become stabilized, the rider can concentrate on acquiring an eye for distance. Relaxed riders, especially those who are relaxed in their arm and hand, often have a good eye for distances. A rigid arm denotes a rigid eye. The rider should slide into the take-off, keeping the arms supple and releasing the rein in a smooth, fluid motion that follows the horse's motion over the fence.

In approaching a fence there are three zones:

1. The balancing or setting-up zones, where the rider has to adjust the horse's balance, direction, speed and length of stride.
2. The zone perpendicular to the fence, in which the rider tries to relax with a soft supple arm, looking intently for a distance.
3. The take-off point, where the rider must look up and beyond the fence.

Event riders tend to "push for the fence;" they see the first distance they can and "go for it." This makes the horse rush and jump long.

Practice can improve the rider's eye for distance. You need to work on short and long options. Take a distance and ride it with short striding two or three times, then take the same distance and try for long striding. Perseverance makes the difference. Rodney Jenkins has jumped hundreds of thousands of fences; most event riders only jump hundreds.

The rider must learn to shorten the horse to get a short stride and to lengthen it to get a long stride. The rider can predetermine the horse's stride in the approach and make each jump different. Practice over a 30-foot in and out, for example. Ride it in two strides and then in one stride and repeat the exercise.

When riding an actual round you should make each jump as smooth as the next. Consistency, based on years of practice, is what counts when the chips are down. We have to learn what is correct form, what are the common faults, and how to correct them.

6 *Conditioning the Event Horse at the Pre-Training through Training Levels*

Edmund Coffin

Edmund—Tad—Coffin and Bally Cor

Conditioning makes the horse fit and increases his endurance performance with less wear and tear on feet and legs. The idea is to work his heart and lungs in short intervals, let him recover a bit, then work him again. The following schedule for a Training level horse provides an introduction for the horse and rider at the lower levels to the principle of interval training.

An important factor during gallops in interval training is to monitor the horse's respiration. Taking the horse's pulse is not practical since the horse is not likely to stand still after his gallops. I depend instead on the respiration rate, and notice particularly how quickly the horse recovers after the gallops. Most horses, especially if they finish going uphill, will pull up blowing. If their breathing comes back down to normal fairly soon, then the horse is starting to get fit. If he is still huffing and puffing 10 minutes later, that should tell you something.

Different horses have different respiration rates, especially half-breds. Some are high blowers while others can barely be heard. Each horse is an individual and each conditioning program must be approached with flexibility and be geared to that particular horse.

A horse that is fit should be in good general condition—not too thin, not too fat. Horses that look tight and drawn, are probably overworked. The horse may be fit, but he's also worn-out. Should this start happening to your horse, slow down—you're doing too much. I've seen a lot of Training level horses like this, and many others that have little fitness at all and finish a course blowing hard. Now this is where interval training comes in—with a schedule you know where you are all the time. Interval training works the heart and the lungs. The horse develops enough muscle and wind fitness, and what I call "base" to get around any kind of course. The gallops for the conditioning schedule will be discussed later.

The Walk

The walk is a very important part of the program. No matter what you are doing—conditioning or working on the flat—the first 15 minutes should always be spent at this gait. The hacking walk should be active (without hurrying) with the horse moving in a nice, long frame and using himself. I like to work horses on a long frame with the nose fairly low to the ground because this helps develop the free walk, which is so important in dressage tests. You do not have to walk like this all the time. It's a good practice to lengthen and shorten the reins from time to time. Take up the contact, then let the horse reach for the bit as you lengthen the reins. This encourages the horse to remain steady as you adjust the reins. Ask the horse to move forward at the walk and then come back. It's important to remember that the horse must have more than one gear at the walk. From the normal walk, the horse should be able to move forward into a more "active gear," without jigging.

Using hills at the walk helps put muscle on behind, as well as teaching the horse to balance himself. Some horses tend to wander or fall apart or jig on hills. In this case the horse should be steadied with more contact and leg and encouraged to maintain the same rhythm whether going up or down hill.

Flat Work

Depending on the individual horse, you might start a particular day with work on the flat and hack afterwards, or hack first and flat work last, or intersperse the hacks with flat work. Stiff or tense horses often benefit from a relaxing hack first, but with the average horse I would prefer to get my "dressaging" done at the start. Then, if there are any problems there is time to work them out and adjust the hack accordingly. However, if you wait until the end of an hour-and-a-half hack, and then have problems on the flat

this could mean being on the horse's back for two to two-and-a-half hours. For horses that do their flat work first, a nice hack through the countryside can be considered a reward.

A good way to accustom horses to getting down to business wherever and whenever they are asked is to find different level areas on the hacks and practice some of the dressage movements there. This will be most helpful when going to competitions.

The Trot

Conditioning trots and regular trots are basically the same. The horse should be round, in balance, and using himself. When doing three conditioning trots (trot sets), I'm likely to vary them. The first trot might be in a slightly longer frame, while the second could include some sitting trot, or perhaps some lengthening, while the third might even include a short canter. The whole idea is to get the horse moving forward at the trot in a balanced frame, yet add enough variety in this part of the schedule so that the horse continually benefits from its schooling.

The Gallops

I like to see the horse moving in a slightly longer frame for the gallop—round and in balance. The horse should not gallop with the head on the vertical and the neck shortened. If the flat work has been done properly, you should be able to lengthen the rein and ask the horse to lower his neck and stretch his nose out and down a bit. He should be on contact—not feather-light, but not pulling either—and moving in a nice balanced frame.

While galloping I suggest that the rider bridge the reins in a single bridge. (A single bridge is formed by placing one of your reins across the neck and holding on to it with both hands, which provides you with a "bridge" across the neck to use for support; a double bridge uses both reins crossed in this way.) I personally feel that the double bridge is limiting. The green horse should learn to become stabilized at the gallop at 350–400 mpm before learning to lengthen and shorten at the gallop. If the horse is going well, I will jack up my stirrups at least three holes. If the horse is not behaving then it's easier to sit back down and reorganize the horse if the stirrups are not quite as short.

Be sure to include hills in the gallops as this teaches the horse to balance himself and develops fitness. It is better to gallop downhill at, say, 300–350 mpm, and to go up hill at 400 mpm. After the horse has learned to balance himself downhill, then at an event he can be ridden more forward to make time. Keeping the downhill conditioning gallops on the slow side also saves wear and tear on the horse's legs.

Scheduling of Events

I recommend that the rider compete a Training level horse about every three weeks. This gives the horse one week to recover, and then two weeks to work out any problems that occurred during the last event. Also, this way you can go the whole season without giving the horse too much time off. Should the horse compete every two weeks, then after three or four events it is necessary to give him a very easy month. Another drawback here is that with only two weeks between events, there is little time to polish up any cross-country problems after easing up for the first week following the event. Here again the event schedule depends on the individual horse and the difficulty of the Training events— and, of course, on the area in which you live and compete.

Tad Coffin and Bally Cor descend a steep slope to the second fence cross-country in the 1976 Olympics, Montreal, Canada

Schedule for Training the Horse from Pasture to First Event

1st Week	**On Lunge**
Mon.	30–40 min. active walk, with saddle, bridle, and cavesson, and loose side-reins.
Tues.	45 min. active walk; 1 short trot approximately 3 min.
Wed.	50 min. active walk; 1 short trot approx. 3 min. each direction.
Thurs.	Same.
Fri.	1 hr. active walk; trot 4 min. each direction.
Sat.	1 hr. active walk; 3 sets of 3-min. trots.
Sun.	Day off—hand walk, graze, or turn out.

2nd Week	**Lunge and Ride**
Mon.	Lunge 1 hr. active walk; three 3-min. trots.
Tues.	Lunge 1 hr. active walk; two 3-min. trots each direction.
Wed.	Lunge ½ hr.; two 3-min. trots each way. Ride ½ hr. at walk.
Thurs.	Same.
Fri.	Lunge ½ hr.; two 3-min. trots each direction; ride ½ hr. at walk; include one 3-min. trot.
Sat.	Ride 45 min. active walk; include one 3-min. trot.
Sun.	Day off—hand walk, graze, or turn out.

3rd Week	
Mon.	Lunge ½ hr.; two 3-min. trots each direction. Ride ½ hr. at walk; include one 3-min. trot.
Tues.	Hack out 50 min.; include two 3-min. trots with a 3-min. walk in between all trots. (The 3-min. walk between trots [and later, gallops] is the interval of rest given the horse between each set or repetition, thus the term *interval training*. Vary the length of the interval from 3–4 min. at this level.)
Wed.	Hack out 50 min.; include two 4-min. trots.
Thurs.	Ride 1 hr.; include three 3-min. trots.
Fri.	Ride 1 hr.; include three 4-min. trots.
Sat.	Ride 1 hr.; include three 4-min. trots and one short canter.
Sun.	Day off—hand walk, graze, or turn out.

4th Week	**Total time on horse's back per day = 1 hr. 15 min.**
Mon.	Hack 1 hr.; include three 4-min. trots and one short canter.
Tues.	Four 3-min. trots; one 4-min. canter. Lay out cavaletti poles on ground 4'6"–5' apart and trot over poles while doing last two trots.
Wed.	1 hr. including four 4-min. trots; two 3-min. canters.
Thurs.	Same as Tuesday.
Fri.	Same as Wednesday.
Sat.	Do above trots and canters and include cavaletti with cross-rails 18 ft. apart.
Sun.	Day off—hand walk, graze, or turn out.

5th Week	**Total time on horse's back per day = 1 hr. 15 min.**
Mon.	Hack—include some gentle hills while doing three 5-min. trots.
Tues.	Gymnastics. Work over cavaletti and add cross-rails, then 18 ft. (one stride) to a small 2' oxer. Should do total of 20 min. at trot with breaks at walk.

Wed.	Flat work. Start to work on transitions and lengthening, slight increases of work at canter; hack.
Thurs.	Gymnastics. Work over cavaletti and include cross-rails, then 18 ft. to a small oxer and 29–30 ft. to another small oxer. Total of 20 min. trot plus 10 min. canter (always with interval of rest at walk).
Fri.	Flat work. 30–40 min. Practice movements in Training and Pre-Training level dressage test; hack.
Sat.	1st gallop—hack, then three 5-min. trots and one 4-min. canter. Mark, pace off, or measure 350 meters so as to learn proper timing.
Sun.	Day off—hand walk, graze, or turn out.

6th Week   Total time on horse's back = 1 hr. 15 min.

Mon.	Hack out—include some hills and include ½ hr. trotting with some canters, with intervals between.
Tues.	Gymnastics—warm up at trot work over small 3′ cavaletti oxers during three 5-min. trots for 40 min.
Wed.	Flat work. 1 hr. on flat with breaks.
Thurs.	Trot single fences—warm up at trot; jump 1½–3′ vertical and oxer at rising trot—10–15 fences. (When horse jumps from the trot in a good rhythm and good frame, he learns to use himself; also teaches the rider to learn to wait at a fence).
Fri.	Work in dressage ring—practice entrances, being on center line, movements, and transitions. Minimum ½ hr.; maximum 1 hr. Make sure horse is relaxed and has a good attitude.
Sat.	2nd gallop—hack, then three 5-min. trots (with 3-min. walk in between); two 3-min. canters at 350–400 mpm. Make sure horse is quiet, relaxed, round and is moving in longish frame in a good stride.
Sun.	Day off—hand walk, graze, or turn out.

7th Week   Total time daily = 1 hr. 30 min.

Mon.	Hack—include three or four 5-min. trots using hills. Also do some flat work on level areas (accustoms horse to working in different places away from home).
Tues.	Work on flat; trot and canter some single fences at home.
Wed.	Hack—work on flat on level places in countryside.
Thurs.	Canter single fences; trot first 3,4,5 fences; then canter 8–12 single fences.
Fri.	Dressage in ring—minimum ½ hr., maximum 1 hr. Then hack.
Sat.	3rd gallop—hack, then three 5-min. trots (always with 3-min. break at walk in between); Gallop three 3-min. at 350–400 mpm.
Sun.	Day off—hand walk, graze, or turn out.

8th Week   Total time daily = 1 hr. 30 min.

Mon.	Hack using hills; work on flat wherever you can find level areas.
Tues.	4th gallop—hack, then do three 5-min. trots; then three 3-min. gallops at 350–400 mpm.
Wed.	1 hr. hack plus ½ hr. light flat work.
Thurs.	Show jump—always warm up by trotting single fences. Then canter single fences including some combinations with two elements (10–15 fences).
Fri.	Dressage in ring; then hack.

Sat.	5th gallop plus cross-country school*—three 5-min. trots; 4 min. gallop at 350–400 mpm; then 4–5 min. at 400 mpm including some simple cross-country fences *i.e.* hunting panels, stone walls, coops, logs, etc. Important that horse stays relaxed and in control. *Have hard hat, gloves, stick, and spurs.
Sun.	Day off—hand walk, graze, or turn out.

9th Week   Total time daily = 1 hr. 30 min.

Mon.	Hack—include some light flat work on level areas.
Tues.	6th gallop—hack, then three 5-min. trots. Gallop 4 min. at 350–400 mpm; 3-min. break; 5 min. at 400 mpm (increase to 450 mpm, then back to 400 mpm, 3 or 4 times).
Wed.	Hack 1 hr. plus 20 min. minimum flat work.
Thurs.	Show jumping—do not jump entire course, but work on elements of course *i.e.* 2–3 fences at a time, and combinations.
Fri.	Work in dressage ring; practice different movements.
Sat.	7th gallop and cross-country school (similar to 6th gallop)—three 5-min. trots. Gallop 4 min. at 350–400 mpm; 3-min. break; then gallop either 4–6 min. at 400 mpm or do two 3-min. gallops at 400 mpm. Include cross-country fences—slightly more difficult ones if possible.
Sun.	Day off—hand walk, graze, or turn out.

10th Week   Total time = 1 hr. 30 min. (Schedule is slightly different 2 weeks before first event.)

Mon.	Hack; light flat work.
Tues.	Show jumping—trot and canter individual fences; then jump course of 8–10 fences.
Wed.	Hack; flat work.
Thurs.	Cross-country school—short course of 10–14 fences. Gallop 4 min. at 350–400 mpm with 3-min. break; gallop course at 450 mpm over course 1–1½ miles long, taking about 6 min.
Fri.	Hack 1 hr. 30 min. at walk.
Sat.	Dressage in ring.
Sun.	Day off—hand walk, graze, or turn out.

11th Week   Total time = 1 hr. 20 min.

Mon.	Hack; light flat work.
Tues.	Practice dressage test in ring with someone watching.
Wed.	Gallop—three 5-min. trots; gallop 4 min. at 350–400 mpm; then gallop 6 min. at 400 mpm (increase to 450–475 mpm, back to 400 mpm, four or five times. Finish at 500 mpm).
Thurs.	Hack 1 hr. 10 min. plus 20 min. minimum dressage.
Fri.	Show jump—trot and canter individual fences; then jump a course of 10–12 fences.
Sat.	Ship to event.
Sun.	First event.

(Easy week afterwards.)

Note: This conditioning schedule is intended only as a guideline. It must be adapted to the individual horse, taking into consideration what he has been doing, his general fitness, how easily he gets fit, the type of terrain you will use, etc.

Some additional tips:

Avoid clipping the horse in cold weather until he begins sweating when working—or not until 3rd or 4th week. If absolutely necessary to clip, then use a quarter-sheet when you ride.

Feed should be increased gradually as the schedule becomes more demanding.

On the lunge: 1. The side reins should be adjusted so that the horse is round, yet in as long a frame as possible. 2. Walk should be active without rushing. 3. Trot should be round from the start and in a long, low frame. Trot should be relaxed with careful attention to regularity and rhythm. Do not ask for lengthened strides. 4. Be sure horse responds well to all voice commands; maintains circles without cutting in, stays relaxed and quiet, and is generally obedient.

First canters should be done in forward seat and no faster than ordinary working canter.

In flat work work in *large* circles, figures, serpentines, changes of direction, etc.

If horse tires at any time during the schedule, back off immediately and adjust program accordingly.

Everyone needs assistance as it is impossible to train entirely from paper. Be sure to avail yourself of an instructor from time to time.

Gallops at this level are primarily to teach horse to move in this gait in a settled and relaxed attitude. Should horse get fit easily, then only gallop once a week (Saturday) and make the gallop a little longer. If horse needs more work on jumping, substitute work over fences for Tuesday gallop.

Galloping twice a week—no more than 4 min. at 400 mpm plus 5 min. at 400 mpm.

Galloping once a week—should work up to 6 min. at 400 mpm plus 6 min. at 400 mpm.

7 *Conditioning for the Upper Levels*

James Wofford

USET Three-Day Olympic
Team member 1968, 1972
Silver Medalist, Fontainebleau
Alternate Olympics 1980

James Wofford

Red-haired, blue-eyed, blessed with quick intelligence, a sharp wit, and boundless energy, Jim Wofford has spent a lifetime immersed in the study of equestrian skills. Born to an old cavalry family, he spent his youth at the famous American Calvary School at Fort Riley, Kansas and was exposed to the teachings of some of the best American riders of the thirties and forties. Jim's father, Col. John Wofford, represented the United States in the Olympic Games in 1932, he went on to coach the American Prix de Nations and three-day civilian teams of the 1952 Olympics, and served as the first president of the USET.

The excitement and challenge of the Three-Day Event, the ultimate competition for horse and rider, was a natural attraction for young Jim. With the great Irish horse, Kilkenny, Jim represented his country at the 1968 Olympics in Mexico; in the 1970 World Championships at Punchestown, Ireland where he finished third overall to win the individual bronze medal; and in the Olympic Games in Munich in 1972. He then found a replacement for Kilkenny in Carawich and placed fourth at Badminton in 1979 after being a member of the bronze medal World Championship team in Kentucky in 1978. In 1980 Jim and Carawich captured the individual silver medal at the alternate Olympics in Fontainebleau, France.

In addition to serving the various equestrian organizations that control the sport, Jim has been steadily building a reputation as one of the finest coaches of young riders. His students constantly turn up in national competition and many of them have gone on to become international riders in their own right. Jim imparts his vast store of knowledge with ease and logical application. His pragmatic approach to conditioning both horse and rider has helped many young riders to understand the demanding sport that Jim has spent a lifetime studying.

Many conditioning programs can produce a horse that is "fit" enough to cross the finish line with energy to spare. Most riders who reach the higher levels of eventing have developed their knowledge of conditioning from years of exposure to both competition and competent coaching. However, the situation changes at the Preliminary level, where riders are moving up from horse trials to their first participation in a full-scale three-day event. All too often, horses arrive at the finish line of Phase D exhausted and even in distress; worse yet, many of them fail to complete the full endurance test. Many riders at Preliminary three-day events do not know how to condition their horses and therefore devise their own hit or miss systems of conditioning, with "miss" all too frequently resulting in an inadequately prepared horse. It is for these riders that I have developed these guidelines for conditioning a hypothetical horse for its first three-day event, taking the Essex Three-Day Event in June as a goal.

There are a few general ideas that I would like to elaborate upon, which might be helpful while working with the conditioning program. Before we launch into this conditioning program I must emphasize that *it is only intended as a guide,* and not as an iron-clad rule. Each horse is an individual and must be trained accordingly. There are many variables to be taken into consideration such as age, condition, temperament, and the soundness of the horse. Since there is a need for some sort of program to help riders condition their horses with minimum stress, one must start somewhere. This *general* schedule should be used with flexibility in mind.

Before starting the interval training schedule to prepare a horse for its first Preliminary three-day event, there are several important factors which must be considered. The horse must have:

1. Competed at the Preliminary one day event (horse trial) level with satisfactory results.

2. Had no lameness or lingering illness.
3. Been wormed within the last sixty (60) days.
4. Had the teeth floated within the last sixty (60) days.
5. Had a current blood chemistry report, with the red blood cell count of better than thirty five (35), and a hemoglobin count of better than twelve (12), or be on a program to correct any deficiencies.
6. Regularly been cleaning up a balanced meal, fed at least three times a day, with amounts suitable for the horse's size and temperament.
7. Been in steady work for at least sixty (60) days previously. The horse should now be capable of 1½ hours hacking at the walk and trot over rolling terrain.

Once you start your schedule you will need to keep a diary to ensure that your work is logical and progressive. This will also help you keep track of your horse's performance. You cannot follow a training program mechanically; each horse requires an individual routine. If your horse is cold-blooded and sluggish, add more fast work in the later stages of training. If he is hot-blooded, use fewer, longer, cantering sets and try to get him to settle in his work.

Turn your horse out daily if you have the facilities. Turning out and long walks are your best defense against horses that get an edge too soon. When the schedule calls for "walk" this does not mean idling along; the horse should go on a long frame in an energetic lively walk. The horse relaxes at the walk, but still must work the muscles. I used to have my riders walk the horse on the bit but many younger riders do not have the idea of picking a horse up for a hundred steps and then letting it stretch out; they go out, pick up the reins, and the horse goes along at two miles an hour on a restricted neck for an hour. When they come back, they have barely gotten to the corner of the pasture. I have changed that now and ask them to hack along on a loose rein.

Vary your route while hacking as much as possible to keep your horse's attitude fresh, but

James Wofford and Carawich share a quiet moment before the vet inspection

stressed you can place your hand on the horse's side, just in front of the girth and feel the heartbeat. You can also invest in a stethoscope and learn to monitor the heart through it. Taking the horse's pulse requires some practice but it pays off in being able to monitor its conditioning program.

Practice dressage work little and often. Plan your work so that your horse warms up gradually and moves on to his most difficult movements and transitions, then end the period doing the movements he does best and enjoys most. Never end the work period on a bad note.

When you school over jumps, there is no need most of the time to school at heights over three feet (3′). Instead strive for style, cadence, and self-carriage by working over gymnastics and grids (see Chapter 5). If your horse quickens or stops, don't get excited. Analyze the reasons and deal with them in a logical fashion. Practice maintaining your composure so that a calm, methodical approach becomes second nature to you. If you lose your head at home, you will lose your ribbon at the event.

Once you start schooling over show jumps don't worry about timing your horse's stride. Give him the correct direction, impulsion, and speed, then make him do the rest. If you make him dependent on you, you will be in trouble on cross-country day.

Be alert to any change in your horse's attitude, his appetite, coat, droppings, appearance, muscle tone, or anything else, no matter how small. You have to train the whole horse, so that he arrives on dressage day of the event in perfect mental and physical condition. Never overlook any detail, no matter how small or large. *There is no such thing as too much trouble for an eventer.*

The steeplechase and show jumping of modern eventers is generally poor because not many of the riders go racing, or showing. Riders need to jump as many fences as they can, which is not always easy with only one horse to ride.

I ask all riders who are going to do a three-day

do your canters and gallops under the same conditions throughout the training cycle in order to cut down on the variables involved, such as temperature, footing, and terrain.

Keep your horse's individual pattern in mind when doing your pulse and respiration ratios. The individual pattern (*i.e.* how quickly your horse usually recovers) is more important than some statistical average. The horse's pulse can be found under the jawbone, between the two branches of the jaw. On some horses this can be difficult to locate easily. After the horse has been event to do something else besides riding to get themselves fit. I ask them to do a lot of their warm-up trots before the gallops in two-point position—a half seat, in very short stirrups, flat track length. This conditions and strengthens the rider. In some people the ankle joint and the achilles tendon bother them in short stirrups and they must work at strengthening them. If riders are working two horses and are fairly athletic themselves I can let them go. But if they have two horses and are not athletic, they still have to do something for fitness for half an hour a day. The activity varies from person to person—running, swimming, tennis, whatever they enjoy—but they have to do something for half an hour a day that is going to speed up their pulse and respiration. I always tell riders "it is not the first mile of a three-day event that you get ready for—it is the last mile." That's when the horse gets tired and that's when he needs help from the rider, yet that's when all these kids come undone—their backs give way, their knees give way, they start moving around in the saddle and they get pecked off because they are not strong enough. The trainer can prevent this by insisting that the riders be as fit as their horses.

I do not dictate any specific kind of exercise for the rider. Some people love swimming and hate running. Some people love to jog and are built for it. What is important is that the rider enjoys the exercise and improves his fitness. When recovering from injuries I have gotten ready for an event by walking up and down hills for two hours a day wearing a rubber sweat suit.

When you are getting a horse fit you have to take into account that it is harder to get a young horse fit for the first three-day event than for subsequent ones. It is necessary to teach the

Beth Perkins and Hot Shot Shawn gallop on during cross-country

horse to gallop and jump at speed. If you are getting ready for a spring three-day event (Essex in this case), you have to school a lot of your fences at 520 meters per minute. Aside from the combinations or any fence with a terrain difficulty, you have to make yourself school at 520 mpm, which a lot of riders will not do. Some riders go straight from cantering at 400 mpm to galloping at 600 mpm. Being both brave and stupid, they just drop the reins and give the horse a kick and away they go. Such riders will not finish a three-day event until they develop a sense of pace.

I use my own eye to develop a sense of pace. I watch them jump a fence and then say "come again a little faster, or come again a lot slower," and try to put a feel for the correct speed into their heads without having them look at a watch, so that they develop a feel for the horse's rhythm. Sometimes I work over a measured distance but not very often, because I am more concerned that they feel what is going on. If we do work on a track with the furlong poles, I will be very precise and accurate and make each rider do a half mile and take 12 seconds for each furlong pole, which is just to help them develop their feel. I will encourage them to go a couple of poles, establish their pace, and then gallop to the next pole without looking at the watch to see if they are still on time at the correct speed. If you have made a mistake in training and missed a gallop, don't just go to the event and put another nickel into the horse's withers, trying to get another mile out of him at 520. If it isn't there, then all the speed training in the world cannot help. The rider must feel what is going on. You must develop your feel and not go along as if you had a speedometer on the dashboard.

Jenny Willet on Feelin' Groovy clear the Mushroom Flat at Chesterland (Pa.)

Above: Karen Stives and Silent Partner jump one of Radnor's massive steeplechase fences in fine form

Below: Speed and balance are required over steeplechase fences, ably demonstrated here by Tom Glascock and Traesaigh

One thing the rider training for his first three-day event must consider is that at some time within the last four gallops you have to plan a steeplechase school. It takes a very experienced horse to jump through brush fences. In many parts of the country the problem is simply finding a place to school. If you live in Kansas, for example, you have to go out and cut some cottonwood branches and stick them in a brush box. Use whatever materials you have at hand.

It is best to start schooling the horse over hurdle-sized fences at about 3'3". If you go ahead and stick up a 4'6" brush box and go thundering down to it, you are probably going to give the horse a bad experience. You will confirm the horse in overjumping, whereas if you jump a brush fence that is between 3' and 3'6" the horse will start to get a bit casual. After four or five repetitions he will notice that he does not have to clear it. The concept you are trying to teach him is that he can alter his arc and jump through the top of the brush. I only school a horse at steeplechase once unless it is absolutely horrible, because there has to be a balance in the horse's skills. You want the horse to jump just through the top of the fences, but not actually steeplechase them. Keep in mind that the horse has to come back in thirty or forty minutes and jump something very solid on Phase D. I am concerned that the horse jumps out of its stride and that it gallops economically, neither throwing in extra strides, nor standing off and making enormous efforts. I want the horse to jump easily so that it will not take more out of itself than it needs to.

We are lucky in Virginia in that we have several point-to-point trainers around. I go to school my horses at steeplechase when they have a flight of hurdles set up. I let the horses come through the flight once at cross-country speed, then I let them come through again faster at 600 to 620 meters per minute. If the horses are very green, I will sometimes take them to local point-to-point courses after the races are over and let them school a mile while the fences are still set up. I let each horse go over a couple of fences at cross-country speed and then let it come right down to its fences at steeplechase speed.

Occasionally, I let one horse follow another. If I have a really sticky horse and another one that jumps easily, then I will let the green horse follow the other one.

One steeplechase school is not really enough, but will be adequate. This steeplechase school should take place within a month of the actual three-day event. I try to get the one-day events under their belt, and arrange it so that I have a two or three-week period between the last one-day event and the three-day event. During that time I school over a much more technical show jumping course than I think the horses will face, and I give them a steeplechase school.

My own background is so traditional that I have never gotten far away from the old fashioned methods of conditioning a horse. My motto is "long and slow," so all my conditioning schedules emphasize that end of it. I am always uncomfortable with speed because I know what happens when you start going fast.

As far as dressage schooling goes it will depend largely upon the individual horse. Let us suppose that your horse is a five- or six-year-old that was shown lightly as a three-year-old, did Training level events as a four-year-old, seems to be sound, and starts Preliminary as a five-year-old. Then I will train him to maintain a First level frame, to lengthen and shorten his stride in the walk, trot, and canter, and I will leave him at that level. If he is a seven- or eight-year old, I will have other things that I think he should be working on right up to the last two weeks or so of the 90 day schedule. I will work on confirming his shoulder-in, introduce him to haunches-in, two-track work, counter canter, and some vestiges of collection. This is not yet true collection, but I do start to compress the horse's frame a little. This prepares him for the Intermediate test, which is the hardest step up in dressage for an event horse.

In terms of the show jumping work it also depends on the horse. With a horse such as the one I have described above, that has been shown and perhaps also hunted for a season, you would not have to worry about the show jumping very much. However, you should continue to set up technical problems: turning, distance problems, optical problems (hanging a cooler over the oxer) . . . all the old tricks. Horses should see a lot of different things during their schooling sessions, because they have a tendency to ride very green when they go to an event, much greener than a horse that has been on the show circuit for a year.

Nowadays in Area II we have the luxury of being able to select events that fit the horses we are training for the Essex (N. J.) Three-Day Event. Any showing you are going to do should be done in December and January. In February you should start your technical work. Horses should be walked up into shape for thirty days, then dropped to thirty minutes of walking per day. Next begin to walk, trot, and canter on a long hold, and then intensify the work. Two weeks after that the grid work and the gymnastic jumping should begin, and so that 90 days before the three-day event, the horse is ready to start jumping individual fences at the canter, and to start slow cantering or galloping work, even if you are still working indoors because of the weather. Many of my conditioning schedules start when the horses are still working indoors.

You should examine the horse's legs every time you do a gallop, and during the last thirty days of the schedule, the legs should be exam-

A fit horse and rider clear a big, solid table at the Preliminary level

ined every day. The horse should be prepared for the work it does. He can get hurt at any time, but he should not succumb to injury. You can get a horse fit for a Preliminary three-day event by working up to three ten-minute canters; *i.e.* no speed at all. This can work if the horse is a Thoroughbred—if the horse is a half-bred it will not work as well.

You can get a horse adequately fit by swimming; I personally have had limited experience with this technique, and my experience has been that past a certain point swimming does not work. I have had horses in training for a CCI come to me out of the swimming pool, where they had been swimming thirty minutes twice a day. This is an enormous amount; some racehorse people think twenty minutes straight prepares a horse for a stakes race. I gave one of these horses out of the swimming pool a training gallop (with several other horses) and I used a moderate speed, accelerating to cross-country speed in the second set. The horse that had been swimming was not fit. He looked fit, his top line looked good, he was carrying less flesh and his legs did not blow up after the gallop, but he did not handle the requirements of galloping up and down hills as well as the other horses. There were five horses in the group and I watched this one particular horse closely. It took him two or three sets of gallops spread over two weeks to catch up. After that he was fine, but I felt that if we had tried to run the horse in an event right out of the pool, he would have pulled up in the middle of the cross-country course. The only real reason for swimming is to avoid concussion (hitting the ground) if the horse isn't sound, and if the horse is *that* unsound you have to ask yourself if he should be preparing for a three-day event. If there is a temporary injury or unsoundness while you are gearing up for a Preliminary three-day event, remember that there is always another three-day event. You may have to wait for four or five months, but there is another one coming. If you are training for an International three-day event, you are not going to make the

event anyway if your horse is unsound. You cannot always use "bute," and any serious injury at all will put your horse out. The veterinary examinations are, and should be, very stringent. The old days of having a second lieutenant riding a $400 remount are gone forever. I used to say that if your horse had enough heart, scope, and was marginally sound, then you could live with him. If he had a mild arthritic condition or similar condition then "bute" could help it, and if he had other more serious problems then nobody could live with it. Nowadays a horse has to be sound if it is to be an event horse.

In setting down this conditioning schedule I am going to take the 1982 Spring USCTA Omnibus Schedule and name specific horse trials and combined tests for a hypothetical horse that is being prepared for the Essex Three-Day Event. People who live in other parts of the country can take this schedule as a guideline and modify it to the competitions in their particular part of the country. Amazingly enough, I have had several people in the past seven years come up to me and say, "Thank you so much for your schedule in the *USCTA News*." I thanked them and they went on to say: "And do you know, we followed it right down to the wire and it worked just great." I asked, "Every day? You never had a shoe come off, or an overreach?" "No, we did everything you told us to." Ignorance is bliss, but this truly made my hair stand on end.

As you study the schedule you will see that if the horse does some other type of wind work, I will skip a gallop day. Usually I will put a longer interval between a one-day event and the next gallop. Probably I will not gallop until the following Saturday, depending on whether I have two or three weeks between a one-day event and the three-day event.

In conditioning Intermediate and Advanced horses I do not increase the number of gallops but rather the speed of each gallop. I rarely use three 10-minute gallops any more, although I used to use three "tens" a fair amount. I do not see that much difference between three "tens"

and three 8-minute gallops. I do see a great deal of difference between three 6-minute gallops and three 8-minute gallops; however, beyond that, I get the feeling that good horses can go on forever. Cantering below 600 meters per minute is purely aerobic work, therefore I do not think that longer canters improve the horses' fitness. To improve their fitness I use speed and/or hills. I use hills as much as possible for the walking and galloping, and for three-day horses I use hills in addition to the normal gallops.

As you develop a feel for the speed of the horse you can feel each gear as you go through it, 520 meters per minute, 550 meters per minute, 570 meters per minute, and so on. Most Thoroughbreds, if they are intelligently conditioned, can sustain a speed of 550 meters per minute over a cross-country course, but at 570 mpm, just 20 meters per minute faster, many of them can no longer hold up. Most horses can gallop at that speed, but they can no longer jump 4' fences from that pace. They cannot roll down to a maximum square oxer, or an open ditch, and just keep coming. It is not just how fast the horse can gallop, but whether it is able to gallop at speed over what is in the way.

Intelligent conditioning means you will have a horse that can handle all the requirements of the endurance competition and still come back on the third day and jump the stadium jumping course. Haphazard conditioning can result in disaster either on course, or in the horse's mental and physical well-being. Each important competition needs months of careful preparation so that the horse has the best possible chance of competing to the best of its ability.

An event horse must be able to handle all varieties of terrain. Here Rebecca Coffin and Zinker steadily descend a slide

A proposed conditioning schedule for a horse that is to compete at the Essex (N.J.) Three-Day Event, Preliminary Level, at the end of June.

The horse has had 30 days of walking work, and has had another 30 days of dressage and gymnastics as well as more hacking.

March 28	Combined test at Chaddwyn, Pa.
29	1½ hr. walking
30	Three 5-min. trots at 220 meters per minute (mpm) with 2-min. intervals in between followed by three 6-min. canters at 400 mpm with 3-min. intervals in between
31	1½ hr. walking
April 1	1 hr. walking plus dressage schooling
2	Ship to event and ride in
3	Sedgefield Horse Trials Preliminary Division
4	Sedgefield Horse Trials Preliminary Division. Ship home
5	Turn out
6	1 hr. walking
7	1½ hr. walking
8	1 hr. walking plus 30 min. of dressage in fields
9	1 hr. walking and 30 min. of dressage
10	Gallops: Start with a 5-min. trot at 220 mpm; 2 min. rest; another 5-min. trot at 220 mpm; 2 min. rest; a third trot of 5-min. at 220 mpm; 2 min. rest. Then do three 4-min. gallops at a speed of 400 mpm with 2-min. rest intervals in between.
11	1½ hr. walking
12	1 hr. walking plus dressage schooling
13	Gallops: Three 5-min. trots to start, at a speed of 220 mpm, with 2-min. rests. Three 6-min. gallops at a speed of 400 mpm with 2-min. rests.
14	1½ hr. walking
15	1 hr. walking and practice show jumping individual fences at 3'6"
16	Ship to one-day event and ride in
17	Loudoun Horse Trials
18	Loudoun Horse Trials. Ship home
19	Turn out
20	1 hr. walking
21	1½ hr. walking
22	1 hr. walking plus dressage in fields for 30 min.
23	1 hr. walking and 30 min. dressage
24	Gallops: Three 5-min. trots at 220 mpm with 2-min. rests. Three 6-min. gallops at 400 mpm with 2-min. rests.
25	1½ hr. walking
26	1 hr. walking plus 30 min. dressage
27	1 hr. walking and show jumping school over individual 3'6" fences
28	1 hr. walking plus 30 min. dressage
29	Gallops. Three 5-min. trots at 220 mpm with 2 min. rests. Three 6 min. gallops at 400 mpm with 2-min. rests.

30	1 ½ hr. walking

May 1	1 hr. walking plus 30 min. dressage in fields

2	1 hr. walking plus a show jumping course set at 3′6″ (jump whole course twice).
3	1 hr. walking plus 30 min. dressage
4	Gallops: Three 5-min. trots at 200 mpm with 2-min. rests. Three 6-min. gallops at 400 mpm with 2-min. rests.
5	1 ½ hr. walking
6	1 hr. walking and practice dressage test
7	Ship to horse trials and ride in
8	Blue Ridge Horse Trials
9	Blue Ridge Horse Trials. Ship home.
10	Turn out
11	1 hr. walking
12	1 ½ hr. walking
13	1 hr. walking plus 30 min. dressage in fields
14	1 hr. walking plus 30 min. dressage
15	Gallops: Three 5-min. trots at 220 mpm with 2-min. rests. Three 4-min. gallops at 400 mpm with 2-min. rests.
16	1 hr. walking
17	1 ½ hr. walking
18	Gallops: Three 5-min. trots at 220 mpm with 2-min. rests. Three 6-min. gallops at 400 mpm with 2-min. rests.
19	1 ½ hr. walking
20	1 hr. walking and practice 3′6″ show jumping fences
21	Ship to horse trials and ride in
22	Green Spring Valley Horse Trials
23	Green Spring Valley Horse Trials. Ship home.
24	Turn out
25	Turn out
26	1 hr. walking
27	1 ½ hr. walking
28	1 hr. walking and 30 min. of dressage in fields
29	Gallops: Three 5-min. trots at 220 mpm with 2-min. rests. Three 6-min. gallops at 400 mpm with 2-min. rests.
30	1 ½ hr. walking
31	1 hr. walking and 30 min. dressage

June 1	1 hr. walking and practice show jumping over 3′6″ individual fences

2	1 hr. walking and 45 min. dressage
3	Gallops: Three 5-min. trots at 220 mpm with 2-min. rests. One 6-min. gallop—begin at 400 mpm and do last 2 min. at 450 mpm. 2-min. rest. One 8-min. gallop—begin at 400 mpm and work up to 520 mpm for the last two minutes.
4	1 ½ hr. walking
5	1 hr. walking plus 45 min. dressage
6	1 hr. walking plus a stadium course set at 3′6″ (jump whole course twice).

7   1 hr. walking plus 45 min. dressage
8   Gallops: Three 5-min. trots at 220 mpm with 2-min. rests. One 6-min. gallop—begin at
        400 mpm and work up to 520 mpm for the last 2 min. 2-min. rest. One 8-min.
        gallop—begin at 400 mpm and work up to 600 mpm for the last 2 min.
9   1 ½ hr. walking
10 1 hr. walking plus 45 min. dressage
11 Ship to horse trials and ride in
12 MCTA Horse Trials
13 MCTA Horse Trials. Ship home.
14 Turn out
15 1 hr. walking
16 2 hr. walking
17 1 ½ hr. walking plus 45 min. dressage
18 Gallops: Three 5-min. trots with 2 min. rests. One 4-min. gallop—begin at 400 mpm
        and work up to 550 mpm for the last minute. 2-min. rest. One 5-min. gallop—begin
        at 450 mpm and work up to 650 mpm for the last minute.
19 2 hr. walk
20 1 hr. walking plus 45 min. dressage
21 Gallops: Three 5-min. trots with 2-min. rests. One 6-min. gallop—start at 400 mpm and
        work up to 550 mpm for the last minute. 2-min. rest. One 5-min. gallop—start at
        450 mpm, work up to 650 mpm then to 800 mpm at the end.
22 2 hr. walking or ship to event
23 Ride in
24 Ride in
25 Essex Three-Day Event—Dressage
26 Essex—Endurance
27 Essex—Show jumping
28 Ship home.

Note: All gallops should be done on a track or otherwise suitable footing. A steeplechase school may be substituted for either
the second or third of the last gallops

8 *Bringing the Horse Back to Work after a Rest*

Karen Stives

USCTA Rider of the Year
1981

Karen Stives

Karen Stives is yet another New Englander who has risen to the top of international competition through sheer diligence, lots of hard work, and plenty of natural ability. At one time she contemplated trying out for both the U.S. three-day and dressage teams in the same year—an idea she discarded after riding in two separate selection trials in the same weekend! With her reliable Thoroughbred, The Saint, she has represented the United States in international competition, and pins her hopes for the upcoming seasons on her Canadian-bred Silent Partner.

Karen considers each horse as an individual and offers her advice on the best ways to cope with the extended rest periods necessary for any international event horse.

After a season of hard competition an event horse needs a break, a vacation from his daily routines. After a major CCI, or international championship, many people believe that the horse deserves a full six months rest. However, after age nine the horse still needs to do some daily walking. As the horse ages, it can lose muscle tone that can never really be replaced if you let the horse stand idle. It is possible to bring a horse back to compete at the international level after a protracted rest, but it will lack some of the ability it showed before.

Whatever the age of the horse, it will need to be let down and relaxed for a considerable time after the efforts of the season. After the rest period the rider is then faced with the chore of bringing the horse back into work—you cannot take the horse out of the field and run it in a three-day event the next week.

No one can give you a precise routine for bringing a horse back into work after a rest. Each horse is an individual. You learn by trial and error, and it requires a tremendous amount of common sense, which is the key to good horsemanship. One of the most important things in establishing a successful rapport with your horse is learning how to read the signals he gives you. Volumes of knowledge are useless if you cannot apply them to your specific situation.

Bringing a horse back to work after rest depends on many factors. First of all, what kind of rest did you give him and how long was he out of work? A good example of an "active rest" is what I give my Advanced horse, The Saint. He is 14 years old and tends to stiffen up very easily. He worked hard in 1980 and after Fontainebleau, the alternate to the Olympic Games in August 1980, I gave him two weeks of turn-out, then gradually started to go for short walks in the woods, working up to about an hour a day. He continued the walks plus the turn-out until December, when I started to lunge him. This routine kept his back strong and his legs moving.

The ideal way to rest a horse is to have access to large multi-acre pastures, and providing your horse is reasonably sound and sane, you can literally turn it out and not bother it for six weeks, or two or even three months. I like this because the freedom is great for the horse's mind, and the large area gives his body room in which to move. The horse essentially returns to natural living.

However, many people are not fortunate enough to have large acreage for turn-out and must rely on stabling where the horses are turned out for two or three hours a day. I do this with my other two horses, Silent Partner and Silent Knight.

The Canadian-bred Silent Partner is only eight years old and is a quiet type of horse. I evented him at Training level in 1978, and Mike Plumb took him Preliminary in 1979. Then I rode him at the Preliminary and Intermediate levels in 1980. That year he had done everything we had asked him to do, and had won or placed in every event. He had earned the right to be left alone.

My other horse, Silent Knight, is older and has an entirely different type of temperament. He is basically not an easy horse to ride; even on a supposedly relaxing hack he will not even walk. Nevertheless I feel that his body should do something, although I prefer to leave his mind alone for a mental break. Both horses will have a busy season after their rests.

How I start my horses back into work depends upon their personality as well as their breed, soundness, age, and specific weak spots in their training.

The first thing I do is to look ahead to the upcoming season's schedule and decide when each horse's first competition will be. Since I hoped The Saint would go to Badminton in April 1981, I started him back to work in December 1980. Silent Partner and Silent Knight were not finished with their competition schedules until the end of October 1980, and were not slated to compete again until the end of April 1981, at a less demanding level, so they started back to work in January 1981.

Next I must consider how long it takes each

horse to get fit. I do not want them to get too fit too soon, for there is a long season ahead.

Silent Partner was bred to be a Canadian Mounted Police horse but he turned out to be the wrong color. Because he has some Percheron in his breeding, he takes forever to get into condition. Last year I did all the gallops (interval training) for the Advanced level, just to get him fit enough to compete at Preliminary level.

Silent Knight, on the other hand, is a Thoroughbred and I think he was born fit. Incidentally, he had been out of work for a year and a half when I bought him in August 1980. I immediately put him back into training and was able to compete him at Shepley Hill (Groton, Mass.) in September and at the Radnor (Pa.) Three-Day Event in October of that year. All this attests to the fact that this horse can get fit almost overnight. He stays half fit even when he's out of work, due to his nervous energy.

Soundness is the one area where there is no compromise. You must consider your horse's history. Has it had problems in the past? Talk to your veterinarian and your blacksmith and work closely with them. Getting the horse fit again is a team effort. The most important thing is to know your horse. Check it daily, before and after work. Be aware of any physical changes, such as heat in a leg, and swelling of the tendons, weight loss or gain, and be aware of changes in attitude. That is the way the horse communicates.

Now that the horse has been evaluated it is time to get down to business. The key is to stick to basics. Usually you start a horse back in the winter and you have plenty of time before competitions begin. Concentrate on making everything *quiet, forward,* and *straight.* These

Karen Stives and Silent Partner preparing to enter the dressage ring

principles apply to every horse in every phase of the sport. The approach or method used, however, will vary depending on the horse, the rider, the trainer, and the facilities available to you. Just because you do not have an indoor ring does not mean you cannot get the job done. Mike Plumb did not have one throughout most of his career, and his horses were always fit enough. Having a ring, or access to a ring does admittedly make the task easier. But be resourceful—make a manure track, salt your existing outdoor ring, or if you can afford it, arrange to spend January and February at a facility with an indoor ring.

I like to begin my horses on the lunge line. I start The Saint with just a cavesson since he is disciplined enough to perform obedient transitions. Lungeing him allows him to begin to trot and canter without any weight on his back, thereby lessening the strain on his aging body.

When I talk about lungeing I do not mean having the horse go around and around in circles *ad infinitum* until he is totally bored. I ask the horse for continuous transitions and changes of direction, and sometimes I use the whole ring, moving along with the horse. Frequent transitions also prevent the horse from losing its balance, falling on the forehand, or getting too rapid.

Lunge work can be alternated with hacking. I might lunge one day and hack the next. I work my horses according to the way they "feel" and adjust my program accordingly.

However, working Silent Knight on the lunge is something else altogether. He delights in trotting faster and faster, ignoring me entirely. He also delights in dropping his back and when I pull on the lunge line in an unsophisticated effort to re-establish some semblance of control and rhythm, he bends his neck and swings his haunches to the outside. This definitely will not do, so I use a chambon, adjusted loosely to get his head out of the rafters and to work on lifting his back. I also use side reins of equal length to help keep him straight and to prevent him from fall

Well-known eventing sisters Bea Perkins di Grazia and Beth Perkins hack their horses quietly at Ledyard (Mass.)

ing on his nose. I will also work The Saint in this tack, after he has been in work for a week or so in just the cavesson, to help supple him. For those riders who have never used these particular devices I would not recommend doing so unless you can use them under knowledgeable supervision.

I like to start the horses on the lunge because I can watch them at work, observe the way they move, and spot any problems. I lunge for short periods at first, about 15 to 20 minutes, and gradually lengthen the time. I keep some horses on the lunge for approximately two weeks before starting to ride; I alternate others between lunging and riding.

Throughout the first month that the horse is back in work, I concentrate on the principles of dressage—quiet, forward, and straight. There is no real need to adhere to a strict schedule at this point. I like to vary my dressage as much as possible—what I do and where I work. Dressage need not be confined to a ring. I ride around jumps, or I go out on the trails.

Trails are a good place to practice shoulder-in, turn on the haunches, lengthening and shortening of stride. Fields along the way are excellent areas to practice different dressage movements. Variety is the keynote. I also use different terrain to improve the horse's balance. Horses, particularly green ones, are less tense when they go away to shows in new surroundings if they are worked in different areas.

In February, or whatever the second month is, I introduce cavaletti and gymnastic jumping. I prefer the fixed cavaletti instead of poles on the ground. Poles can be awkward if they are not constantly readjusted, or if a horse hits one of them. Height is of very little importance at this time. I work on form, attitude, and confidence. The standard gymnastic is a cross-rail, 18 feet to a vertical or oxer, then 21 feet to the next jump, 30 feet for two strides, and 42 feet for three strides. It is necessary to adjust the type of fence, distance between jumps, and the frequency of the sessions according to the level and experience of horse and rider. My horses jump once a week at the most, but a green horse or rider might require up to three sessions a week in order to secure the basics before the season begins.

Toward the end of February and throughout March, I try to find a few indoor hunter shows, dressage shows and/or two-phase events. These allow me to school over small courses away from home without the pressure of being at an event. It is great for the mental relaxation of both horse and rider.

Once your horse has been in work for two months, you want to start to consider a more concrete program. The overall plan should look something like this:

Monday: Hack outside and dressage
Tuesday: Gallop (hack to and from)
Wednesday: Dressage (also hack)
Thursday: School over jumps (hack out and do a little dressage)
Friday: Dressage
Saturday: Gallop

This is my *basic* schedule that I use all through the season. Again, be flexible and vary the work according to your horse. For instance I will hack to and from my gallops, hack before or after dressage and perhaps do some hill work. On jumping days I might also hack out and do some dressage on the way to the jumping area.

The weekly schedule prevents you from getting trapped into doing the same thing day after day. I almost always try to get my horses out twice a day, especially The Saint, because I don't like to drill him for long periods of time. Often my "other" work is a one to two hour walk or perhaps a lunge. Sometimes I "pony" one of the horses, which keeps the weight off his legs and is also a good (efficient) use of time. For horses with potential soundness problems you can swim them or use a treadmill. Bear in mind also that turn-out is an important extra if you can arrange it. Horses need some time to be alone, too.

Remember, "the schedule" is merely a guide. My theme throughout is to be flexible—read your own horse. There are lots of ways to vary your schedule to suit his physical and psychological needs. If you need help constructing a program for your horse, first analyze your situation and analyze your horse. Then seek the advice of and assistance from some knowledgeable person for such a program.

No matter what specific program you use, the horse will need to be brought back into work slowly and methodically, over a period of some 60 days. After this initial work the horse can begin a 90 day schedule leading up to a major three-day event (see Chapter 7).

Bruce Davidson and Might Tango galloping on at the Lexington (Ky.) World Championships, 1978

Once your horse has been back in work again for several weeks, your conditioning program will probably include at least one weekly gallop. At this point, I would like to mention something about galloping itself. Before I started working with Mike Plumb in the fall of 1978, I didn't even know that you were supposed to gallop your horse to prepare for an event. He taught me the mechanics, *i.e.* how often, how long, and how fast. I was so totally preoccupied with this new concept that he was unable to get through my thick and stubborn skull *how to* gallop. This is an art unto itself.

I arrived at the USET training session with Jack Le Goff (Spring 1980) just dreading the first gallop. Prior to this, I had almost mastered the art of maintaining a given speed (providing it wasn't too fast) on an absolutely flat track. I knew that I didn't have a prayer of keeping the pace on the hills at Blue Ridge, let alone being able to lengthen and shorten my horse's stride. In order to control my big horses I had put a lot of hardware in their mouths. And I knew that Jack would insist on a plain snaffle! Surely total humiliation was just around the corner. Jack would be appalled at my uneducated ways and send me home. But I was in for a big surprise because just the opposite occurred. Jack decided that he would take me on as his big challenge, for I had been allowing my horse to become so unbalanced going down hills that I would get run off with going up hills. The longer the gallops the worse I got. Not surprisingly, the key concept in working out this problem was the same as it was on the flat: balance. A horse can't be balanced without being engaged behind. Back to basics again. Take off the fancy bits, put on a snaffle, and get to work on those hindquarters. Easy to say, but to do?

Jack's first step was to work on my position. A rider must be in balance with the horse. If the rider needs the reins for support, then chances are the horse will too. For a while I did all my trot work in "half seat" position, which strengthened my legs and improved my balance. Try this exercise without touching the horse's mouth and work on maintaining your balance. Work at this up and down hills and even grab the mane for balance if you have to.

The next thing I learned was how to keep my hands "on the line" to the horse's mouth, not above or below, by using a single or double bridge and to shorten my stirrups for balance, adjusting the length according to the speed the horse gallops. Then I was in a position to work on balancing my horse over varying terrain. Jack has a marvelous expression, "Put your horse on bail." I had been keeping mine locked up in jail with my hands. I would get tired and then let him loose or drop him, resulting in a most unbalanced horse. I needed to find a happy medium by being in balance on my horse, with an elastic contact with his mouth.

The next step was to work on my horse. In the initial gallops the purpose is to build up the muscles and train the horse. The speed work to develop the wind comes later.

When my horse became unbalanced, or out of control, it never occurred to me that perhaps I could interrupt the gallop. I thought a four-to six-minute gallop was just that—do or die. Jack suggested that when trouble occurred I should stop and reorganize. This could mean doing a halt, a reinback, a circle, trotting a short way, doing shoulder-in or just leg-yielding for a few steps. Then I could proceed in a mannerly fashion. This is a marvelous exercise and should be repeated whenever necessary, particularly with the young horse who is still learning.

Most conditioning gallops are done at 375–400 mpm. Once you have mastered keeping your horse in balance consistently at this speed, the next step is to try to lengthen and shorten the stride, or to go forward a few strides and come back. Do this for just a short distance at first so that the horse does not get carried away with the idea of lengthening. If the horse gets heavy or is just running, then he has fallen on his forehand. Remember, then—reorganize, rebalance.

Essentially what we are talking about is "dressage" at the gallop—balance, engagement, lengthening and shortening of stride. Keen horses can be galloped on the slower side. (Incidentally, if I interrupt my gallops to reorganize and this takes a bit of time, I might add a minute to that gallop).

This should sufficiently prepare the Training level horse for competition as well as provide an excellent base for those wishing to compete at higher levels. (Later, when you are in the final stages of getting ready for a three-day event, you can introduce lengthening at the end of the gallops.) Jack suggests that we work the aggressive horses over long slow distances and the quiet ones for shorter distances at faster speeds. I like all my horses to work up and down hills. The hills require more effort so you can work at slower speeds and reduce the stress factor considerably.

9 *Equipment for the Event*

Sally O'Connor

Sally O'Connor (Photo by Susan Sexton)

By the time an event rider reaches the Advanced level, the accumulation of equipment that goes along to each event has reached staggering proportions. At the lower levels, however, not nearly so much is required, and riders starting an eventing career should keep the amount of equipment they acquire to the bare essentials. At the Pre-Training level a saddle, bridle, adequate halter with a lead shank, grooming utensils (including a wash bucket and sponge), and shipping boots or bandages will see most riders through any horse trial. At the lower levels it is not necessary to outfit the horse with a complete set of galloping boots; if the legs are left unclipped the horse's natural hair will provide enough protection.

Most Pre-Training courses are a mile or so in length and the speeds are not fast, so it is not really necessary to put the horse up in a poultice after the event.

At the Training level, competition begins to be somewhat more serious, but it is still not necessary to make any great outlay for equipment. In addition to the requirements for the Pre-Training level it might be a good idea to acquire a pair of bell boots to prevent the danger of an overreach, and if you are contemplating progressing to the Preliminary level, now is the time to start building a supply of screw-in studs, the tap to thread the holes for the studs, and a T-shaped cleaning device to clean the threads. Studs take a little time to put in but with practice you will soon become proficient. It is a good idea to get them well in advance so you can make an arrangement with your farrier, who makes the holes in the shoes for the studs and puts in the threads. Most riders stuff the holes with cotton in between events to keep the holes as clean as possible.

You may also want to consider front galloping boots at this time. If you feel your horse needs a running martingale for better control, now is the time to try one. After a Training level horse trial i might be wise to put the horse into a poultice to ship home and to leave the poultice on overnight to prevent the legs from filling.

Do not blindly follow the latest fad. Just because one of the USET team horses was wearing a particular piece of equipment, do not rush out and buy the same for your own horse. Most equipment is designed for a specific purpose; before you buy it, be sure you know that purpose and whether it applies to your own horse. If your horse does not need a drop noseband do not buy one, but if you feel that the horse will go better in one, be sure that whatever type you buy is properly and comfortably fitted and does not restrict the horse's breathing.

There are three types of breastplates available and if your saddle is inclined to slip when you go up or down hill you might consider investing in one of these. If, on the other hand, you have a horse with good conformation and a saddle that fits well you will probably not need one. The hunting type of breastplate seems to keep the saddle well forward and it conforms to the horse and is comfortable. The polo and webbing racing breastplates are lighter and work better with a lightweight saddle. The important fact to watch is that this type of breastplate does not restrict the freedom of the horse's shoulders.

A fishnet cotton cooler helps your horse cool off in hot weather and if you event in a cold climate you should think about getting a wool cooler to prevent chills. Blankets come in every size, shape and color, and can be quite expensive, so you should shop around for the best possible bargain. (Many people wait for the annual sales to buy blankets for the following season.) If your horse is to be worked and clipped in winter, a turnout rug (New Zealand type) of canvas with straps around the hindlegs to keep it in place is a must. Again, be practical and consider your own particular needs rather than buying unnecessary rugs because so and so has them.

By the time you get to the Preliminary level you will have accumulated quite a box full of equipment. It pays you to keep it all clean and in good repair. If you are planning to ride in a Pre-

liminary three-day event you will have to consider the weight factor. (Remember, weight is not considered in the Young Rider division.) If you weigh under 165 lbs. with your saddle you will be required to carry weight to make up the difference. If you are faced with the prospect of carrying weight, check the weight of your saddle. Saddles vary greatly in weight and by riding in a heavier saddle you can save up to as much as 8 lbs. of lead. Conversely, if you are too heavy you might consider switching to a lighter saddle to reduce the load on your horse.

Weight pads come in many designs; for those who do not have to carry a tremendous amount of extra weight, the racing pad, or steeplechase pad with pockets along the side is quite adequate. It is best to stuff the lead into the pockets in front of the rider's knee and behind the leg. Avoid the pockets under the flaps of the saddle, as these can press into the horse uncomfortably. One type of weight pad concentrates all the weight over the withers, which relieves the horse's back but can definitely affect the horse's balance and make it unsteady; it does not allow for proper weight distribution and is not recommended.

Ideally, two-thirds of the extra weight should go in front of the saddle and one-third behind. Some weight pads have pockets only in front of and behind the saddle and that works out well.

The usual practice is to put a saddle cloth under the weight pad when tacking the horse up to prevent any rubbing. If you do have to invest in weights you need to practice galloping with the pad in place a couple of times before the actual competition to make sure that both you and the horse are comfortable with this new piece of tack. However, it is not advisable to do all your preparatory work carrying any amount of extra weight because this increases the strain on the horse unnecessarily.

One of the most disastrous things that can happen is to have the weight pad slip out during the competition, which of course would mean elimination. Be sure to have straps sewn into

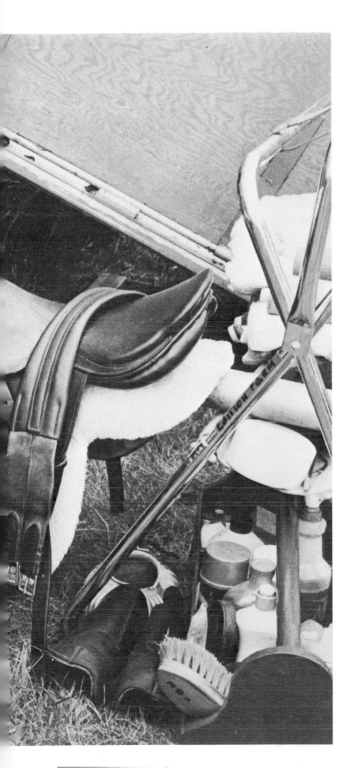

the weight pad so it can be firmly secured to the saddle.

At the Preliminary level, riders might want to add back boots to the array of tack the horse will wear. Protective boots can save the horse from injury if they are properly fitted and put on. Bandaging the horse against injury is acceptable, but must be done by a knowledgeable person.

When considering any piece of equipment you must evaluate your own situation and your horse's needs. Burdening yourself with extra tack is not necessary. You must make careful lists of just what you will need for your own well-being and that of your horse. Do not be a slave to fashion; be practical.

Intermediate Course Ship's Quarters, Md. (1981)

Patrick Lynch

Patrick Lynch has a full-time job as farm manager for the USET headquarters at South Hamilton, Mass., but he takes time off each year to design the courses for the Ship's Quarters Horse Trials, which are usually held in April at the Maryland home of Mrs. Sallie Robertson.

Patrick came to course building naturally. His father ran the riding program at McDonogh School in Maryland and Patrick has been helping with the outside course there as long as he can remember. When Patrick's sis-ter designed the first courses ever built at Ship's Quarters, Patrick got in on the act, and became fascinated with the philosophy of course design at the different levels.

His job with the USET has led to several trips abroad, where he has had the chance to study courses in other parts of the world. He keeps adding to his file of designs and picks the brains of other course designers whenever he gets a chance.

Totally involved in the careers of the team horses, Patrick has helped many of them get their start at the upper levels by designing challenging but eminently jumpable courses for them.

Patrick Lynch, Designer

Whenever I go anywhere I try to take pictures of the fences. I have a file cabinet full of pictures. If the General (Gen. Jack Burton) is going off to be an official at Boekelo in Holland, for example, I give him my little Instamatic camera and ask him to take pictures of the course. Richard Newton and I try to design courses that are fun for both the rider and the horse. We try not to build any traps.

The Intermediate course at Ship's Quarters has evolved slowly and is unique in that it is often used as a spring selection trial for the USET riders. Before I go on vacation in the fall, Jack Le Goff and I sit down and he will say that we need more combinations, or more of this, or more of that, and I work out in my head what I would like to do. We discuss the whole course. Some years he makes changes; other years he makes none at all. When I design something like the combination on the hill, we get together and work out the distances to be used. Some fences he asks me to raise and others he asks me to lower. I also find the course interesting because Richard Newton supervises the construction. There is nobody who builds fences as well as Richard does, and he will also look at the design and come up with some ideas that never even crossed my mind. In that respect the course is the product of three people's ideas.

When course designers try to outsmart the rider, too often it is the horses that suffer. That has always been my biggest source of dread, and it is the reason that I do not get much sleep on the night before the cross-country. I worry that I have made a big mistake in the design. Sooner or later if you design enough courses some horse is going to get hurt, and I just hope that it will not be because of something I have done. I try to design a reasonable course that will be safe for the horses and riders.

The Site

The course at Ship's Quarters runs down two sides of the valley, and there are two or three fairly steep hills. When you design a course, you have your basic terrain and you have to make the best use of it. There is no way to build a flat course at Ship's Quarters—it would be impossible. We use both sides of the valley, which also makes the course ideal for spectators because they can see so many fences from the top of the hills. I personally think it is easier to design good fences where the terrain varies. In places where the land is as flat as a pancake every part of the obstacle has to be manmade, even the ditches. At Boekelo in Holland, where the Dutch must have ditches for drainage, the first seven fences had ditches in them and when we got to the eighth fence they had built a ditch!

At the Intermediate level you are designing fences for fairly sophisticated riders with horses that are well along in their education. You can dictate that some fences have to be taken fast, and some more slowly. It is no longer just a matter of the rider getting out on course and kicking on. At the Preliminary level you see riders who have no idea of how fast they are galloping, and sometimes this catches up with them if someone does not tell them they have to pay attention. Even at the more advanced levels you will occasionally get people who have not figured out how fast they are going, and when they keep going like that sooner or later they will,

unfortunately, end up upside down. I believe that the main idea of a course designer is to try to protect the horse and to ask fair questions of the rider. The penalty for not answering the question correctly should be a run-out or a stop, not a fall. Enough falls are caused by the rider's mistakes without having more from design mistakes.

The Intermediate course at Ship's Quarters is designed for early in the season. I try to design a course that will help get the horses going each year. I think that it is greatly a matter of instinctive "feeling" as to what is fair, and that feeling is developed over the years. Many of the horses at Ship's Quarters may be competing in the Intermediate division for the first time. In addition, I have come up with a course for the Open Intermediate division, which is used as a USET selection trial for those riders who are trying out for whatever big competition lies in front of them that year.

The Course

The purpose of the first fence, no matter what the level, is to get the horse going. You need something that will get the horse jumping and galloping on.

At the Intermediate level the second fence should be along the same lines, but a little more difficult. You are still trying to get the horse galloping in a rhythm. At Ship's,Quarters the second fence is in the fence line with a downhill approach. It is almost a parallel rails. The front rail is slightly lower than the back one,

but there is some drop-off into the next field on landing.

I then put a snake fence over a ditch that runs across the field. This is a fence that needs to be ridden boldly but as there is a sharp left hand turn immediately after it the rider has to remain in control. If the horse is running off, the rider will have to make a much larger turn than necessary and lose some time. The snake fence is not particularly wide but with the ditch underneath it the horse needs to be bold. The left-hand turn takes the horses down beside the third fence on the Open Intermediate course, a combination which is considerably more difficult. After they gallop through the stream, there is a right-hand turn into what is essentially a coffin a sloping vertical and an 18 foot distance to a revetted ditch. I simply framed the stream with telephone poles. For an Open Intermediate fence or an Advanced level fence, I would add a fence coming up out of the ditch. With a 6' ditch most of the horses can handle the spread, so there is no threat of falling in it. It is not even very deep, so for the Intermediate horses and riders it is not difficult. If there is a fence added afterwards the horses have to adjust; they cannot approach so slowly that they cannot get out on the far side, and they cannot come so fast that they bury themselves on the other side.

I used an 18-foot distance here between the rails and the ditch because I had been to a course-building clinic given by Frank Weldon of Great Britain, and he said that 18 feet was a

1 Ascending Rails
Height 3'7"

2 Rails and Drop
Height 3'8"
Spread 4'

3 Lexington Snake
Height 3'8"
Spread 5'

4a,b Ascending Rails and Ditch
Height 3'8"
Spread at ditch 6'

5 Bank to Road
Height on bank 3'9"
Spread at ditch 4'6"

Illustrations by Linnea Wachtler

good distance to use in this situation. This is not a big, bold fence but it requires the horse to be a bit clever.

We have two banks up onto the road, and both of them have been used for the Intermediate level. The smaller one has been there for some time, and the larger one has had dirt piled on top of it and a ditch added at the base. It is a fair-sized fence for an inexperienced horse but no problem for the horse who has jumped similar obstacles before.

The course then goes on over a large galloping stretch of land that is usually used for crops. I had to design a fence for this field that was moveable and came up with a big brush steeplechase fence. If the land is farmed, you have to construct a few fences that can be picked up and moved out of the farmer's way. I try to build as wide a facing on this fence as possible because it does sit out there in the middle of nowhere, and it is important to offer a fair fence.

I realized that by this time on the course I had not given the horses and riders a big spread fence yet so I added the big oxer down by the dressage ring. They approach this downhill, after flying over the steeplechase fence. It is a test of control—if they are out of control they could end up in the middle of it. It is still a galloping fence, but the rider has to retain control.

The next fence is another snake fence set over uneven ground. It is very vertical and never seems to jump very well—I think because of the ground line

more than any other reason. It puts the horses in a bad spot. One real problem is that it is always jumped in the same spot. The year it rained during the event there were a couple of falls at this fence. I am not really happy with it, but the horse is fairly well along in the course here and perhaps needs a more difficult question.

The water fence comes next. I am very happy with this water jump. I like the idea of having a water jump that can be drained after it is used. The stream does not run through it and fill it up with silt, so the footing stays consistent. We are lucky in having a spring there that keeps running through the worst drought, and we use that to fill the obstacle and let the water out of the dam after the event. We have built up the dam and revetted it so that I have many options for fences both in and out of the water. We always grass over any place where we enlarge something or do any great earth-moving operations and let it settle. The bottom of the water jump is clay and we put a great deal of gravel on top of it, to prevent the horses from breaking through. If you are going to invest a lot of money in a water jump like this it needs to be as versatile as possible. I have a fair amount of leeway with this one.

In 1981 I sent the Open Intermediate riders across a bounce into the water. I do not remember having seen anything like that in this country before. It rode so easily that I shall use it for the regular Intermediate division from now on. The Intermediate riders had just a single rail

before the water and their problem was to hold the line going through the water and out the other side. If they jumped too far to the right and didn't make the turn, they slid right by the flag.

The Intermediate riders galloped on through a stream and came upon a vertical fence set diagonally on a natural rise from the old streambed. The rider had to pick a line carefully here in order to take off at a good spot. If the horse went too far to the left the fence would be too big, and if it went too far to the right and jumped up the rise, it might wind up in a difficult position. I do not remember anyone having any particular problem here.

The next fence is just in the fence line but it contributes to the series of problems at the bank combination that follows because the fences are definitely related. The bank has vertical rails down into a pit, a jump up onto the bank and a single rail off the bank for the regular Intermediate riders, and an oxer off the bank for the Open Division. Here I believe it would be unfair for the regular Intermediate riders to have a high and wide fence off a bank. This is a fence that requires the rider to come into it very much under control but then to be very aggressive through it.

From here they go around the hill to the Helsinki. The ground is not level here—it goes up a rise and the fence is set on a slight rise where a fence line ran through at one time or another. You have to pick a spot for the take-off and the ground drops away on the landing side. It is not a fence that could be used on a Preliminary course; a Helsinki is enough of a problem for that level without having undulations in the ground line. I am not 100% satisfied with this fence—it rarely jumps nicely or smoothly, and I am not sure whether that is because of the footing in front or because of the drop behind.

The next fence offers two options; it can be taken as a bounce or as a vertical with a wide sweeping turn to another vertical. I think this has worked out well. The rider can go along the hill and turn into the bounce, or go straight, jump the vertical, and turn back and jump the second vertical. The fence is essentially two L's close together. The bounce is set at 16 feet and the rails are 3'8" high. It is set up downhill; I do not think that you would build a downhill bounce for Preliminary level horses. The fence works well—quite a few people choose the slower option. The longer the fence is there, the more people take the bounce. Every time you build a new type of fence the riders scratch their heads at first and then they find out that it works and no one ever complains again. On the other hand, even at courses like Badminton (England) there can be a fence like the pheasant feeder. It can be there for years and not cause any problems, and one year it jumps up and grabs two or three people.

After this fence the rider turns right and gallops back toward the top of the hill. I built a diamond fence on the hill with a curved wing behind it, which is really a combination, but sometimes we cheat a little in the way we number the fences. Here there is the option of jumping a right-handed or left-handed corner, and for the Open Intermediate riders we leave a gap in the middle, so they can jump a vertical rail, then go through the hole in the back and jump the wing. You could probably use the same type of fence for a Preliminary course but I do not think that you would put it on the side of a hill; it might be easier to jump one of the corners on the flat. I like to include corners on a course to give the riders a chance to practice them—these corners are not difficult. The first year I built it, the diamond just sat there by itself and I think that just about everyone jumped one of the corners, even though they could have jumped through the middle. This year we put in two trees, just to make the gap look smaller than it really was. I think a lot of people took the middle route because it was a good school for the horses.

When I designed this fence I went out to study the site with the basic idea of it in my mind, and then I went home and drew it out on graph paper to try to figure out the right distances. Then I went back to the ground and laid out the rails and hoped that it would look right. If it didn't, I had to rethink it. As it was, this turned out to be a very educational fence for the horses and riders. There is a certain amount of luck involved in coming up with a design like this—it either works or it doesn't. Fortunately this works very well indeed, especially when we are doing the USET selection trials.

I think you should try to include as many educational fences as possible at the lower levels. Once the horses get to Badminton, if they are not well educated, you might as well forget it. I believe that course designers should make a point of being educational when they are designing for the lower levels. We are trying to create problems that will help horses and riders when they advance to the Olympic Games. For instance, we do not know what the Germans will build at Luhmuhlen for the World Championships, but we look at the kinds of courses they have produced before and we try to come up with the same type of fences. I can truthfully say that I got the general idea for several of the fences I have built for the USET Selection Trials in 1982 from fences at Luhmuhlen. My second fence is almost exactly the same as the third to last fence at the European Championships in 1979—a vertical to two steps down, but without the V they built in Germany. They also had a vertical on top of a hill. I copied that with a vertical on top of a rise. It is the kind of fence that you cannot stand too far away from at take-off because you are going downhill. You have to get as close to the base as possible, yet still have enough room so that you do not get buried under it.

The combination on top of the hill that came next has been there for several years. It consists of three angled rails. For the first year I included it on the Open Intermediate course, and had just the three rails. The following year

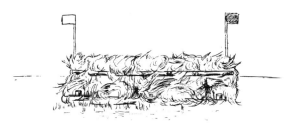

6 Bullfinch
Height brush 4'7"
Height rail 3'3"

7 Spread Rails
Height 3'9"
Spread 5'3"

8 Sneaky Snake
Height 3'7"

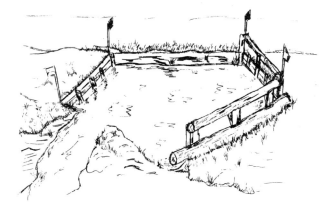

9a,b Splash and Out of Water
Height rails 2'3"
Height on bank 3'
Depth water 10"

10 Rails on a Slope
Height 3'9"

11 Gate
Height 3'9"

12a,b,c The Lynch Challenge
Height 3'3"
Drop of 5'
Height on bank 3'6"
Height rails on bank 3'

13 Helsinki
Average height 3'8"

14,15 Side by Side L's
Height 3'8" for both

16,17 The Paddock
Height 3'6" for both

18 Post and Rails
Height 3'9"

I decided to run the regular Intermediate division over it and put in some extra panels so that, if riders were not confident in themselves or their horses, they could weave in and out through it. Obviously this option would be for a lesser horse and the rider would not have the same time advantage as anyone who went straight through it. The fence has now been there long enough that almost everyone goes straight through it—the riders know how to jump it. Many riders take different lines through, although more and more they take the line down the middle. In the first year they did not do this.

After that, the course goes back down the hill, makes a left-hand turn and goes over a big vertical fence that has been there for years. Here it is a matter of control—of getting the horse back together after the steep slope downhill so the rider can make the turn.

The final fence is a big stone wall and oxer with a straightforward gallop to the finish.

Karen Stives, Rider

My overall impression of this course was that it was a good Intermediate course, especially for the beginning of the season; it was a course to get a horse in gear for the year. I really liked it—the course rode well.

The first fence was a simple inviting rail fence which posed no problem at all for Silent Partner. My account of riding this course will be quite uneventful because my horse has so much scope. Unless he has to deal with a really scary looking obstacle, everything is easy for him. He can handle any distance and height, although he could be braver about ditches and banks. I rode off towards the first fence with no worry in my mind, whereas if I had been on a horse that tended to run down onto the forehand or jump flat, I would want to be careful here. With Silent Partner I could just canter down and jump the fence.

The second fence had a slight drop after it, but again with Silent Partner this type of fence poses no problem because he is so quick. On another horse I would need to "set up" for this type of jump.

The third fence was a snake rail with a wide ditch underneath. Here I really needed to ride to the approach, as this is the type of fence he will really look at. I did not have to worry about where he met the fence, but I had to ride forward and make sure that he got over it.

Then we came around a corner to the ascending rails and ditch. This resembled a coffin fence and the distance between the two elements was very short. Silent Partner is a big horse and I had to ride very forward to this fence because I knew he would look at the ditch on the far side. I thought that he would suck back in the air over the rails so I did not worry unduly about the short distance, but I did have to worry about getting over the rails.

The same thing applied to the next fence, a big bank and ditch up onto the road—I really rode forward to it. Silent Partner needs some added incentive approaching ditches and there was a big ditch in front of the bank.

Silent Partner just galloped up to and went right over the top of Fence 6, the Bullfinch—it was no problem for him to clear the whole thing!

If I had been riding The Saint at the big oxer that followed at the bottom of the hill, I would have had to really set him back and make sure that he was balanced, because if he met it wrong he would be in trouble. But the oxer was a piece of cake for Silent Partner; he just ran down and flew over the fence. If he had met it wrong it probably would not have mattered much—he could jump it from anywhere.

The Sneaky Snake can be a problem for a horse that does not have much scope. If the horse does not approach it boldly you can get down under

19a,b,c Zig-Zag
Height 3'5"—3'9"

20,21 The L
Height 3'8" for both

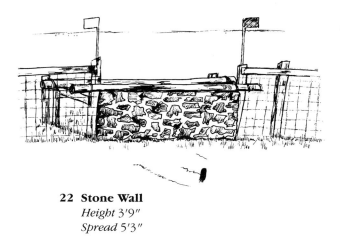

22 Stone Wall
Height 3'9"
Spread 5'3"

the rails and have a fall. But Silent Partner took right off at the lip of the fence. He has such scope that if he gets a bit braver about some of the optical problems, he is going to be a horse that I will be able to take all the big options with. He has that much jump.

The water came next. Here again is a fence that I had to ride quite hard; the distance was slightly awkward in the water and he hung a leg coming out of it. It was a low fence in, very straightforward and not the cause of too many problems. It was a good water fence for the beginning of the season, and there was a good jump into enough water so that the horse could feel it. I liked it.

The next fence sat on top of a small rise, and it did not matter if my horse left from the bottom. Although Silent Partner is a big horse he is tremendously adjustable and like a cat with his front end. It is really nice to have a horse like Silent Partner to ride cross-country.

The gate was another vertical fence and I had no trouble. Silent Partner can come down and jump a gate either out of stride or not. The bank that followed made these two fences into a combination and I rode well forward—he went up and off without hesitation.

The Helsinki was a tricky fence. I did not like it when we walked it, and I thought it would not ride well. I have seen a lot of people ride it with difficulty. The ground is uneven. The upper panel is the most attractive because the ground is flatter, but there is a big dip right about where you would want a horse to take off, so most of the riders opt to take the middle panel. It is just not a great fence to ride.

On the next fence you have the option of jumping two sets of rails with a semi-circular turn, or you can do what I did—turn the corner and jump a downhill bounce. The tight turn sets you up perfectly for the bounce, and the corner really helps you prepare. I hate to come to a bounce in the middle of a field, but if you come off a turn you have already gotten your horse back. The downhill slope helps the horse carry over the second rail, and the distance was not too short.

Fences 16 and 17 were a most interesting combination. Some people ran through the middle of the pen, went through the gap and on over the rails beyond. I jumped the uphill corner to the vertical, and Silent Partner bounced it—his choice not mine! You had to keep your line to jump the corner and still make

the next fence because of the distance problem, so it was definitely a rider problem. If you have a talented horse then the horse can make the decision to bounce out. This fence has caused problems before; I have seen riders come in at too much of an angle and have run outs. It is a challenging fence for the rider.

The vertical on top of the hill is the type of fence that can catch you off-guard, as it was low and uninteresting. The horse wants to run up the hill and get on the front end; the fence does not make the horse want to gather itself for the jump.

The ZigZag is another rider fence, but you need a little help from your horse, too. You have to maintain your line. I came around and took a bounce and then jumped the one stride. The one stride was very short but the horse tends to look down the hill on landing, and that backs him off. It rode fine, and as long as riders keep the line it has ridden well every year.

We then galloped down the hill to another vertical, and here is a fence where you want to be

sure to keep the horse together coming off the hill. I started balancing the horse as soon as we landed over the ZigZag. I set myself against him so that his hind-end would stay under him downhill. I took the fence as a one stride in-and-out, turning in the air over the first element.

The last fence was a big oxer, and I just let him gallop down to it because I knew that he would not look at this type of fence—he is just going to jump the fence from wherever we approach it. It's a wonderful feeling!

This was an ideal Intermediate course at the start of the year. The course offered water, a bank, a type of coffin, some gymnastic fences, some galloping fences, and fences where you had to work on the line. It presented a lot of questions but with no real trappy fences. It was not just a course you could gallop around—the course made you and your horse think.

Part Three
The Event

Cindy Irwin and Orient Express clear Breedence Bounce at Chesterland (Pa.)

10 *The Dressage Test*

Torrance Watkins Fleischmann

Torrance Watkins Fleischmann on Red's Door

When riding a dressage test at any level, you should not worry about silly little things upsetting the horse. You cannot be riding into the dressage arena and think "Oh my God! The flowers!" Granted, we do not school around pots of flowers every day but you can get your horse accustomed to them, and you must not allow them to distract you. Do not ride into the arena thinking, "My horse doesn't like flowers," because that will affect your test. The test that follows here is the F.E.I. Three-Day Event Dressage Test (1975) at the Advanced level.

When I first approach the dressage arena I try to make my approach in the gait that I find my horse is most at ease in. I will also, if I feel confident in my horse, try to do something quite dramatic, a lengthening, or maybe a shoulder-in, if that is the horse's specialty. Usually you do not have a great deal of room to do anything fancy. If I am trying to keep the horse's blood down I might just walk in. The walk to canter transition is a very easy move for me; I like it, and I can get it better than I can the trot to canter transition. It is a tidy move and the judges think, "Ahh! Well in hand."

The judges cannot help but see you; they might be writing comments on the previous horse but they will look up to see you as you go by, because it is human nature and they want to know about you. I smile and say, "Good morning," (or "Good afternoon") as I ride by the judge's box, and I also thank the judges at the end of the test. It is my moment to shine but they have to sit there and watch me. The judges I like the best are the ones that write the most comments; I want to hear their opinions, and I want them to know that I am most appreciative.

You are allowed 60 full seconds after the whistle is blown before you have to make your actual entry into the ring. What most people don't seem to realize is how long 60 seconds is. The whistle can blow when you are not organized to go in yet, so take your time. I always have to remind myself that there is a lot of time in one minute. I can remember once in 1978 at the selection trials at Chesterland when Severo flipped out. I entered the collecting area and his nerves were just absolutely addled, so I did two extended canters after the whistle blew, still made it into the ring on time, and the horse came right down to his halt and stood. Years before I would never have done that. I would have

---

Bea Perkins di Grazia prepares for the dressage test on The Sheik

---

picked up the reins at the whistle, the horse would have been addled anyway and I would never have gotten a halt—he would have done a pirouette instead and it would have wrecked the test. As it was he placed in the top six. It would have been a disaster had I not learned to keep my head. I am not sure where all that composure came from suddenly, for I certainly did not have it in the beginning. I think it came from getting to know my horses better, from being able to put my leg on a nervous horse, as you would put your hand on a nervous child's head to say, "I'm here," to relax the child. A horse will relax the same way if he has confidence in you.

The salute to the judge comes while you are at

the halt. I am beginning to enjoy the salute, I am getting to be ham enough to want it. The salute is saying to the judge, "O.K., Mr. Judge, here I am." If you present a hurried, rushed salute, the judge will think that the whole test is going to be hurried and rushed. However, if you are worried that your horse is going to bust out of its skin if it doesn't move forward, you can fake the halt. Don't rush the salute, but on the other hand don't wait around. There is a way of halting and doing your salute as the horse puts his last foot on the ground whether he is in trot or canter. The quicker you move your hand on the horse however, the more your back is going to move—since your hand is attached to your arm, which is attached to your shoulders, which is attached to the backbone! The horse will feel you move. You must know if your horse tends to be nervous yet still try to do your salute in slow motion. There is a choice of words I use when working with nervous horses and nervous students; I tell them to work slowly in their minds.

Bruce Davidson canters Golden Griffin around the dressage ring before the test

If you can slow their minds down you can obviously slow their bodies down.

If you have a horse that will come to the halt and stand there, make much of the salute. Make a big to-do about it. I think there is nothing more dramatic than to have a horse come in, halt square, and to see the rider take his time about the salute. I always have a feeling that I would like to be able to take my hat off. It is so dramatic when a gentleman takes his hat off. I think it is also important to dress properly; you are going to ride better if you know you look good.

Using the arena to the greatest extent possible aids your performance. You must move off from the halt absolutely straight with the horse underneath you; if you allow your shoulders to precede your horse and get nervous about going forward your horse will never be straight, he will

"Make much of the halt and salute." Torrance Watkins Fleischmann on Severo

Karen Stives and Silent Partner demonstrate a balanced turn off the center line

he will fall to the outside with the shoulders. You see this happen all the time. Instead of allowing the horse to proceed, the rider anticipates the turn, and as a result the horse falls on its forehand with its head bent too much to the inside, and very often it will move with an uneven stride. The exercise of decreasing the circle by sitting taller and taller so that the horse can move right under the apex of the rider will help you to prepare for riding this turn. Use that exercise coming out of the turn and you will sit tall. Wait and allow your horse to move under you through the turn so you can allow the horse to move out into the medium trot.

I used to believe that the horse had to be bent on the medium trot circle and every time I tried to bend my horse with the inside rein, the horse would break stride. The rider must support the horse with the outside rein and the outside leg so the horse will bend on its own. The horse should be "wrapped around your inside leg" at this level of training and should respond to the pressure of the inside leg. The horse needs the rider's support, especially in the medium trot, because it has to stay in balance and has to get lower to the ground to extend the frame. If you get ahead of the horse and bend the head to the inside, you will break stride. Ninety percent of the time the rider causes this error, not the horse. The medium trot is one of the most dramatic moments in the test, and may determine the judge's attitude towards you right at the start. If you can do this move well, you would probably be able to break at the canter later in the test and the judge would forgive you.

You have to prepare the horse for the medium trot. So many people drive the horse instead of allowing the horse to stretch out and say, "Look at me." When I am teaching students there are many ways I have found to give them this feeling. One is to ride a circle and have the riders allow their hands to go forward, keeping their shoulders back and following with the hips; suddenly they feel the roundness and think, "Hey, this is fun!" You must also keep the horse almost

fishtail all the way down the center line. In the 1975 FEI Three-Day Event Test you have to track to the right and almost instantaneously go into a medium trot. The fact that the medium trot is very early in the test leads me to do some medium or extended trot in my warm-up before I hit the arena, just to get the horse tuned to my leg, to get it moving forward. I try also to carry forward the feeling I had in the canter during the entrance. I find that a horse trots spectacularly after a canter so I allow it to carry through. I allow the horse to move forward under me. Many people do not allow the horse to move; they try to move *for* their horse and the horse becomes unbalanced.

Many riders overbend the horse's neck to the inside. If you use too much inside rein on the first turn you will lose the horse completely, and

Bruce Davidson and Might Tango circle at the medium trot

straight on the circle. If you have been working on the lateral work correctly the horse will give you the necessary bend. I used to be one of the biggest culprits; I used to bend and bend and bend my horses in the nose, ears, eyebrows, and in the fifth vertebrae, but there was no bend in the back! As a result the haunches could not keep up and the horse would break to canter.

The medium trot seems just beautiful to me. Both Severo and Poltroon have taught me a lot about medium trot—they both get low to the ground behind and just explode because they enjoyed doing it. Remember to sit back to the point where you think you are behind the vertical, although in reality you are not. The hind end of the horse gets lower, and your hips must remain very supple so that the horse feels free to move behind. Medium trot is a spectacular feeling, perhaps the most dramatic feeling I have ever had since I began to enjoy dressage.

So many dressage problems result from rider errors. In the transition down from the medium trot you must keep the horse very straight so that you will keep the points you get on the circle. The entire movement does not end until you've completed the transition down and you can ruin your whole mark with a poor transition. You must be able to soften your back and shorten the movement of your hips and allow the horse to come down without a whole lot of work up front.

Sheer elegance—Bea Perkins di Grazia and The Sheik during the dressage test

We all override with our hands. I think that the quieter you are in the dressage test, the better, even if the horse performs badly. If you are quiet you may often be forgiven by the judges. I realize that it is the horse that is being judged but I also think that the cumulative marks below the line count for so much, since they are doubled by coefficients. So many horses are beautiful movers but their riders are distracting to watch, with their hands up above their chests as they move about on top of the horse. Why not let the horse do the job?

In the downward transition you may well have a judge sitting at the end of the arena at M and he should not see the inside of the horse's head until you hit the corner, so the transition from medium trot to working trot must be very straight. If you have a beautiful transition in dressage, just think of what you can do cross-country. This is what amazes me about dressage.

The next move is the turn at A followed by a half-pass left. Use the corner well, since none of the judges at this point can see how much the horse is on the forehand. If you have lost the horse somewhere in the medium trot, you can be clever and use that turn to get him back. You can almost turn the horse on the haunches to get him back and the judges will not see you. They will see the flexibility of your back, and if you can soften your back and use the turn to elevate the horse in front, you could very well get away with it. As you come to the center line to do your 10-meter turn, your horse should be right underneath you. In the 10-meter half circle or turn onto the center line, allow the horse to move out in front of you. Often riders shorten the front end, so the horse picks its way around with the hind end usually outside the front end, thereby destroying another mark. Give the horse time to do the half circle and try not to lean in; then when you hit the center line do your half-pass. Wait for the haunches to straighten, position the horse, half-halt, organize, and go. Organize is another word for a half halt to me, but it is more of a mental action than an actual half-halt.

Remember that, in the half-pass, the biggest mistake you can make is to let the horse lead with the hindquarters. The second most serious mistake is to let the front end reach the track first and then shoot forward without waiting for the haunches to catch up. The old exercise of going down the center line, or the quarter line, or even your stone walls, or your paddock fence at home, and doing a couple of steps of half-pass then forward again teaches you to feel where the hindquarters are.

I found with Poltroon that it took a while to develop the half-pass. The one thing she really enjoyed was lengthening, so I would do two steps of half-pass, maybe even only one, just until I could feel her back get round, then I would let her go forward and do something she liked. So she began to think that half-pass was not all that bad and began to give me more steps just as long as I let her do her thing afterwards. I believe that if you introduce a move that the horse does not particularly like, or that it does not understand, then you should let it do something it likes and appreciates. Then it does not mind doing the difficult movements in a test.

I find a horse like Southern Comfort (Monty) very difficult because he is programmed to anticipate everything. He has one set of orders, one routine, and has never been given a selection. We often fought over this. He would do exercises like shoulder-in, a lengthening forward, and halt. Then he would canter but I could not get him to do another lengthening at trot. All he knew next was to change the canter lead. If I brought him down to trot he would pick up the other lead, a very difficult move to get out of a horse. So I now find that most of my time with Monty is spent going through the fields, not even working in a dressage arena, because he knows the arena too well. During the first test I rode him in at Shepley Hill (Ma.), I could feel his anticipation in every single move and yet I had never practiced the test with him. Obviously his whole warm-up routine and education had centered around the test.

Torrance Watkins Fleischmann and Red's Door in final preparation for the dressage test at the 1978 World Championships, Lexington (Ky.)

done when the *rider's* body is even with the letter—not the horse's head, the horse's nose, nor the horse's chest, but the *rider's* body. So you have to know just how many strides it takes to prepare for a halt. Make a big deal out of the halt. Drop your hands and sit there. This is your moment to shine. You are saying "Look at me, boys." What fun to be able to do that well. Then rein back, remembering that a horse backs up with diagonal legs. Close your leg and allow the horse to back under you without shortening the frame in front, and remember that the horse must step forward on the last step back. It should go back, one, two, three, four, five and forward. You'll present a very pretty picture.

About this time in the test, provided everything is going well, your mind should be completely clear. If things have gone wrong you still should present a picture of satisfaction in hopes of gaining a point or two.

How well I remember that cold, rainy Ledyard event in 1977. I was fortunate enough to ride my dressage test on the second day but it was one of the very few times that one would have wished to ride on the first day. It was one of my first Advanced events, something special. I was riding Red's Door. The wind was blowing and the rain was falling so hard that I kept dipping my top hat so the water would fall off the brim. The tails of my coat either hit the horse hard or they were streaming straight down. Cameras were rolling because film crews were shooting the movie, "International Velvet," and the tarpaulins on the cameras were blowing around. The rings were in the middle of the polo field. My ring had a canal all the way around it where everyone had ridden before me. There was no way to avoid this canal, and the horses were up to their hocks in mud. Going by the ring for the first time I realized what it must look like and I started to laugh. I howled. I don't know what made me laugh, except that it was so darn funny. I dipped my hat and the water poured off and the Swiss judge looked at me as I laughed. I was thinking, "Oh well, he doesn't know me

After the half-pass you have to let your horse move out because the half-pass is contracting and the minute it ends you must let the horse go forward. Use the next turn to soften his back so that he comes to the halt without being contracted. A horse that comes into the halt in too tight a frame will more often than not back up.

I firmly believe that this halt is also part of the showmanship. You can create such a good impression and, of course, you can also lose so much. First of all you are right in front of the judges; they cannot miss you. The halt should be

Eventing continues rain or shine. Here Tad Coffin and Bally Cor await their dressage test in the pouring rain at Ledyard (Mass.)

from a hole in the wall. Who the heck is Torrance Watkins?" So I laughed and said, "Good afternoon." It was not a great test, and Red's Door was out of control most of the time as he tended to be. He was not a great mover and he had to use his head and neck to regain his balance all the time. But he got a much better score than he deserved because I had laughed so. The judge got to the point where he just sighed and said, "Ahh! Isn't she charming!" I figure if showmanship worked there, it will work anywhere.

At this point in the test, when you are right in front of the judges, you have to be able to smile and sit tall. Now is the time to remind yourself to elasticize your back.

Moving from the rein-back immediately into the trot the rider must not precede the horse. This is a difficult move because some horses are not quick off the ground. You go on around the next corner and move straight into the second medium trot on the circle. Chances are that this circle will be better than the first one, so allow it to be. Again, don't anticipate; wait for the horse to move out under you. The movement is not over until you have made the transition back to the working trot. Then you set your horse up again in the corner and move into the second 10-meter half circle and the half-pass.

At this point it is a good idea to think about the general tone of the test. By this time I am lost in the test. I have not allowed confusion to enter my mind for a long time; I am having fun and I really expect to enjoy myself in the ring. By the time I have gotten as far as riding the FEI Three-Day test with a horse then the homework has been done. I should have faith in that homework and that is exactly how I feel when I ride my horses in the ring. At this point in the test on horses like Poltroon, Severo, and Monty, I feel as if I own the world. What an incredible feeling! The horses have their own sense of pride. But if the rider constantly nags at the horse, the animal will not be proud and will not look proud.

You are now coming up to the second halt, which comes just before the extension of stride. Your horse must be comfortable at the halt but powerful enough so that you know you are only ten strides away from an extension where the horse has to put out everything it possesses to knock the socks off the judges. The rider must be very elastic and the horse has to respond very spontaneously to the leg. This is where it all comes down to having the horse like you and understand you. All the work you have done before comes into play. Again the halt comes right in front of the judges, so here is another time to think, "Look at me!" And this is another time to score, because you can elevate yourself and if your horse has halted completely square, just think of the points you can earn, even if your horse is not the world's greatest mover. This is one of the times you can make up for the fact that perhaps your horse does not extend well, for example. This is one place in the test you can make up for the fact that your horse cannot move very well. Bally Cor was a prime example of this. The mare was not a good mover, but she and Tad had a tremendous presence and pride and that earned high dressage marks. The extravagant horse might lose out here because the rider fails to take advantage of the moment; while the adequate horse, who is generous in his mind and wants to do his best, can win out. The horse must have a sense of well-being, precision, and pride. You should be thinking, "This horse is going to jump better than anyone else, and right now he is going to do the very best job he knows how and I'm very proud of him." Think of the judges' impression; that feeling must come across to them. Don't go into the ring defeated by the fact that your horse has a poor gait. Tad did such a fabulous job with Bally Cor because they entered the ring and seemed to say, "Look at us." And the judges did just that.

After the halt, the way you come out of the turn is very important. If you anticipate the extension in the turn, the first three steps of the extension, if not more, will probably be bungled. You must wait but be ready and alert on the horse, and let the horse know what you want. Use the turn to elevate the horse's front end so that it is already off the ground, but don't crank up the engines going around the turn because you will lose the haunches for sure. Get yourself organized, get straight on the diagonal, then light the match. When you reach X in an extension, whether it is in trot or canter, ask again. Don't give up; don't anticipate the downward transition or the next corner.

When you get to the corner elevate yourself and the horse. A great many horses topple onto their forehand at the end of the extension so that rebalancing them becomes difficult. Young horses who have just moved up into this division find this a difficult transition. The judges can see every step you take at the end; they are just sitting there waiting for you, and if you have any trouble they will either subtract from their mark for the extension, or from the next one. I think that it is important to get the horse back during the turn. Use the corner; it is a good place to half-halt, half-halt, half-halt. *Use the ring.*

In the FEI test the first extension is ridden in rising trot, which makes the extension easier to achieve. The rider must take care not to precede the horse's center of gravity when rising, which can happen all too easily; many horses will break to canter if this happens. I have a new word I use to explain extension—*volume*. I think the feeling you get when you close your leg is akin to

*Torrance Watkins Fleischmann
and Severo at the
extended trot*

turning up a stereo. With horses that are eager to offer extensions you have to be subtle with your demands to get them back and make it appear easy. It is all a matter of grace, and at the end of the diagonal you must be tactful in getting the horse back to working trot. You must know your particular horse and know what it takes to bring him back. Use the arena; use the corner again to bring the horse back underneath you. Often the eager horses will carry their extensions around the corner, so you must try to keep them balanced by using a great deal of outside rein.

To me the extension ridden in sitting trot is more satisfactory to the rider, while the rising extension is more satisfactory to the horse, as it frees the horse's back. Around the short end of the arena you must have the horse bent correctly, and you must keep your eyes on the next marker across the diagonal. Your weight will follow your eyes, and the horse will follow your weight and seat.

Extensions should be explosive, full of volume. If I have to push my horse I do not feel that I have done a satisfactory job of training. I do not want to look as if I am having to flap my legs in the breeze. As the horse becomes more educated the rider should move less and less. At the lower levels you expect to have to do more pushing, but by the time you reach the FEI level your horse should be locked in to the rider both mentally and physically. The horse knows that a second extension is coming up and it is up to the rider to polish that extension and make it appear brand-new and effortless.

Poltroon's test at Fontainebleau was one of the most exciting tests I have ridden. In spite of the cramp she had just before she went into the ring, she concentrated more than at any other time. Her extensions were magnificent. She felt

Torrance Watkins Fleischmann and Severo perform
a controlled serpentine at the canter

as if her front feet were knocking her teeth out, but in slow motion, which is the way I like an extension to feel. The horse should take time in the suspension and remain balanced on all four legs.

As you come down to working trot from the extension you need to maintain roundness as you enter the corner. The walk follows at C, immediately after you get around the corner, so the horse must be round. The transition to walk has to be effortless but immediate, as you are once again right in front of the judge. You must work out how to perform this move in your daily routine, not wait until you are in the test. Monty has trouble with this; his transitions down are precise but he does not offer me his hindquarters. He gets nervous, and this is obvious to the judge. With Poltroon and Severo I would just soften my lower back and they would come right down to the working walk. The rider has to use the aids to tranquilize the horse and to encourage it to overtrack at the walk as much as possible. Mentally I try to think about letting the horse go in a free walk, but I keep the contact. In training my horses I use the free walk a great deal, then bring the head back little by little.

The walk is very important and the rider must take time to let it happen. Be willing to take time; do not rush. I cannot impress this upon riders enough. Do not rush. The judge must see how easy the walk is for the rider and the horse. There must be a definite distinction between the working walk and the extended walk. I believe that the working walk as ridden in the three-day test is more of a collected walk. The rider must be a showman here. Your hands should allow the horse's head to move. Allow your elbows to move with the hands to accentuate the horse's head movement, and relax your lower back. If you try to get a nice extension of the stride on the first half of the diagonal, from S to X, you can use the rest of the movement to get the horse back together again and ready for the next move.

You must try not to let the horse anticipate the canter departure which follows at A. If you have a nervous horse you really do not have to pick up the rein until the actual canter depart. Jack Le Goff advises his riders to wait until the depart if you have a horse who anticipates.

The 10-meter canter circle at A gives you time to put yourself together. I strike off perfectly straight but I am already thinking of the bend needed for the circle. If you allow your eye to move around the circle, the horse will feel your weight shift and follow. I think you can get away with making the circle deeper than normal as long as you do not go over the quarter line. It is better to use a bit more room rather than less room; it makes the movement easier for the horse. After the 10-meter circle and the return to A you should look to the point where you want the horse to hit the center line during the serpentine.

Be very accurate in your serpentine, which should consist of three perfectly round half circles. Retain the horse's roundness during the change of direction and the counter-canter. The horse's head must be bent to the outside during the counter-canter, not to the inside. The rider's weight should stay over the inside leg of the canter lead, no matter what direction the half circle takes. The horse should be allowed to take the rein and not be restricted. Once again the rider must take time and not rush the counter-canter. It is the rider's task to keep a round working canter at the end of the serpentine by being sympathetic to the horse. A lot of riders try to organize the horse with their shoulders which can throw the horse off balance and make it very unhappy. I want my horses to be happy during the counter-canter.

The horse must remain in balance at the end of the serpentine and should not be allowed to anticipate the lengthening. The rider should ride through the turn after C and soften the horse by using a half-halt. If you allow the horse to anticipate, it will be off-balance and crooked. I very rarely practice this move at home because the horses do learn to anticipate. The canter extension should start when the horse is perfectly straight on the diagonal, not before. With Poltroon, who cantered very high in front, I would try to get her to lengthen her frame, but with Severo, who had a great canter, I could really show it off. In any extension, when you get to X you should hit the button again so that the horse does not stop. Be confident, and show the judges that you are confident. Keep the horse straight in the transition down to working trot as there is a chance that it might switch leads behind at the last moment.

Use the corner to help you put your horse together after the canter extension. If you can give the horse an effective half-halt it will not anticipate the next canter depart. The second canter departure is often missed because the horse is strung out. Stay calm before the strike-off and do not anticipate the canter; the horse will strike off without a problem. Do not be abrupt. After the strike-off use the full ten meters of the circle to prepare the horse for the next move. Bring the horse back to you, let it know who you are and what is going on, and get back into the rhythm of the working canter. Make sure that you are straight and precise on the center line for the canter departure—the judges will be watching for that. Make the half circles on the serpentine nice and round, and almost come to a collected canter. This becomes the moment of control—it is more of a mental collection.

When you reach the end of the serpentine, keep the horse well under you and make the corner in balance before the second extension. When you let the horse extend at the canter, try not to drop it onto its nose. It is entirely up to the rider to keep the horse from changing leads behind. I start to shorten my back at X and prepare for the transition down so that the horse will not change. The horses will try to switch if they can, so be prepared.

Getting the horse back after the last extension is very important because that center line will come up very fast. This is where I will linger in the corner to prepare for the turn, again using the half-halt. I like the double bridle here because I can feel the horse under me and the quieter I can keep my hands around the corner, the straighter the strike-off on the center line will be. If the rider's hands are moving around, the judge will see and the horse will not be quiet. Be soft and supple with your lower back. This brief canter on the center line is a very hard move for event horses because they are full of energy, ready to run cross-country the next day, and they have just finished a canter extension. You have to be confident in your ability to keep the horse straight, and you should look the judge right in the eye. This may be the moment when you are getting run away with, but you have to smile and think, "This is wonderful!" Then the judge will think it *is* wonderful. You cannot afford to have a fight with the horse because you are heading right for the judges—you have to relax and use your seat.

Make sure your final halt is square. Prepare, and know exactly how many strides it takes for you to get the halt. There is nothing better than a snappy last halt, but the halt is not over until you have walked away from it. Do not hurry away and be efficient in leaving the arena. Show that you are happy and you may get an extra point. I try to say thank you to each judge as I leave; I just like to acknowledge each one. I finish the test by circling just before I go out and then I salute the ring steward. After that I can relax.

*The perfect ending—J. Michael Plumb demonstrates
a perfect halt and snappy salute on Laser*

11 *Steeplechase and Cross-Country*

Bruce Davidson

Individual World Champion, 1974 and 1978

Bruce Davidson and his son, Buck

Bruce Davidson is the only event rider in history to win two consecutive world championships, first with Irish Cap in 1974 and later with Might Tango in 1978. His reputation as one of the world's finest riders is well deserved. In 1972 Bruce rode Plain Sailing at the Munich Olympics and helped win a silver team medal for the Americans. On Irish Cap, he won the individual title at the World Championships held at Burghley, England in 1974; and won the individual Silver medal in the Pan American Games in 1975 on Golden Griffin. He also helped the U.S. team win yet another gold team medal in the 1976 Montreal Olympics. In 1978 he rode the young and untried Might Tango to a startling repeat victory at the World Championships in Lexington, Ky.

In April 1982 Bruce placed second on J.J. Babu to Richard Meade of Great Britain in the prestigious three-day event held at Badminton, England. One week later he went on to Italy with Beacon Charm and won another international three-day event, the Rome CCI.

Bruce's deep understanding of each individual horse stands him in good stead on cross-country and steeplechase courses, and his analysis of different types of fences helps the novice rider understand that there is more to this game than just running and jumping.

Some horses—like Plain Sailing and Irish Cap—need hardly any schooling for steeplechase. They are both strong, aggressive and bold, so the competitions themselves at the Preliminary and Intermediate levels serve as their school. However, most horses, particularly those that need to become more "gallopminded," would do well to have some sort of schooling in this phase. And most riders need experience over steeplechase fences. One does not need an out and out course to school over. Two steeplechase fences that the rider can build himself and school over from time to time are really all that is required.

One problem is that the horse that jumps well over steeplechase fences jumps flat, and this is not ideal for the rest of the event. Nevertheless, the horse must learn to jump this way in addition to being able to bascule over certain cross-country fences and those in a show jumping course. All of which makes one realize to an even greater extent what an extremely versatile animal the event horse is. The idea is not to emphasize teaching the horse to stand back and jump flat through his fences, but simply to educate horse and rider adequately in this phase so that both leave the starting box on Phase B feeling confident of success on the steeplechase phase.

Never build or school over too small a fence with the thought in mind that a small fence is a good introduction to steeplechase. This can be dangerous. A horse is just not impressed with a 3′ or 3′ 3″ fence. There is nothing to a fence that small and the horse is apt to run to the bottom of it and jump badly. It teaches a horse to chip and thus lose his confidence, which is the exact opposite of what you are striving for.

A confident landing by Tom Glascock and Truesaigh over steeplechase at Radnor (Pa.)

It is best to school over fences that have some size, say at least 3′8″ or better, and some width. The fences should also lean slightly away, and have a take-off board. To teach the horse that you mean business from the start on steeple-chase, use a speed of about 600 mpm. A less experienced rider might go at about 500 to 550 mpm, just to get the feel of it as well as to gain confidence, but then should work up to 600 mpm. The idea is to get the horse to take the initiative, take your hand, and continue his speed into the next fence rather than backing off. It's surprising how fast horses learn to run and jump through their fences rather than trying to jump over them.

If the horse is reluctant to land galloping, or if he approaches the fence reluctantly "sucking back," I'd use the bat before the fence. Another time I might go to the bat would be right over the fence. The reason for this is to help the horse learn to "take the ground" as he jumps. The horse will pick up the idea of shooting through the fence and landing at a gallop quite quickly. The bat, I'd like to point out, is not something to be abused, but rather should be used as an encouragement.

In a competition, I might even use the stick on my good horse if he puts in a bad fence. Again, I'm using it not as a punishment, but as an encouragement and saying "Come on, let's take my hand. This is a job that has to be done. We're not schooling today and you're here to be in the spirit of the competition and not to take a second look." If a horse jumps steeplechase well but has one or two sticky fences and the rider has gotten after him and given him that message—to get the job done the best he can—then that attitude will carry over onto the cross-country course. A horse that has jumped well, with his blood going and in good rhythm, will be a confident horse starting Phase D.

When riding steeplechase, one must keep the horse in balance and maintain that balance and gallop in a rhythm. As the horse approaches the fence and starts to compress himself off the

rider's leg, the contact of the hand does not change much. Keep the hands and body low and steady, and *let the horse* determine his take-off point. This is very important. Avoid trying to adjust or place the horse. Jumping at speed, a horse can stand back further from a chase fence than most riders would think possible.

Sometimes you see riders pumping and jerking with their hands on the approach, as you see occasionally in the show ring. This kind of over-riding is definitely wrong for steeplechase, and will inevitably result in a bad jump and interfere with the horse's galloping and breathing rhythm.

When riding steeplechase, the rider wants to discourage the short, engaged strides that might be used prior to a drop or combination on cross-country or in stadium jumping. The horse must gallop much faster than on cross-country, and is in more of a race horse frame. The rider should encourage the horse to lower his neck and get his nose farther out in front of him. The horse will be lower to the ground.

As the horse approaches the fence, he will no longer stay low. His head will come up slightly as he sees the top line of the fence ahead. And in doing so, he will come slightly back off the rider's hand. In terms of pounds, let's say the rider has 12 pounds of contact in hand while galloping. As the horse approaches his fence, the rider would ease up and have about 9–10 pounds of contact. As the front end of the horse comes up, the rider should then increase the leg to try to keep the same length of stride over the fence as in the gallop, so that the horse lands on a galloping stride. This is the kind of landing you want, not a landing on all four legs, which happens when the rider messes with the horse on the approach. Watch this on film sometime when you have a chance to see a movie of an event, and you will see how hard it is on the horse. First of all it breaks his breathing rhythm; the rider plops down on the horse's back, the horse's head shoots up in the air and his back hollows out. The rhythm and stride are lost. Horse and rider almost have to start over to get it

Denis Glaccum and Cougar jump fast and flat over a steeplechase fence

together again. And precious time is lost. Riding a proper steeplechase fence is all-important.

When riding in a three-day competition toward the end of Phase A, I stand up in my stirrups and let my horse gallop under me at about 400–450 mpm, rolling along in a nice relaxed rhythm, so that the horse can take a deep breath, stretch his legs, come on the bit a little, and start taking my hand in preparation for what lies ahead. I finish Phase A this way, making sure to come in a minute to a minute-and-a-half before the start of the steeplechase phase. This gives me time to shorten my stirrups, check my girth and set my watch for Phase C.

An elapsed-time stopwatch has a dial on the outside that tells you how much time you have left, and the inside numbers tell you how much time has gone by. As soon as I get to the start of Phase B—just before going on steeplechase—I set my watch on the outside dial for Phase C, say for 45 minutes. My watch is now punched to zero. For steeplechase I know the time is, say, 4 minutes and I read that on the inside of the watch. At the start of Phase B I punch my watch.

Because speed is a definite consideration on steeplechase and there is a .8 point penalty per second over the allowed time, you must impress on the horse that he is going to have to go from a halt to a gallop as quickly as possible. The idea is to get the horse on your hand, ready to gallop, to come out of the starting box as quickly and quietly as possible, and to approach the first fence in the same attitude you want the horse to have for the rest of the course.

Remember, the hardest thing to do is make up time. On the first circuit, if the horse is galloping easily and confidently, I let him go ahead. It's better to have an easy gallop, and take back and let the horse catch his wind some place on the second circuit for ten or twelve strides than to find out you are slow. This way you are still within your time. However, you must be careful not to "cut your throat," as Jack Le Goff would say, by pressing the horse too much.

Now if you are too slow on the first circuit and find you are in the bad situation of trying to make up time, you are liable to back the horse off as he won't be able to catch his wind. It is very important to know your speed with a "clock in your head" and to maintain a good steady pace on both circuits.

As soon as I finish Phase B, I punch my watch, quickly look at it, and punch it again for Phase C, which, as you know, starts as soon as Phase B is finished. Then I ease my horse to a walk, jump off, and loosen the noseband and girth. I do this while walking alongside him. Taking the weight of 165 pounds or more off the horse's back when he is blowing or gasping for air gives him a chance to recover more quickly. It also gives me a chance to check for missing shoes, glance at his boots, and run an eye over the horse to determine if he is in distress, or whether he is just blowing hard and catching his wind. I walk or jog alongside him for about two minutes, or more if the horse appears to need it, then do up the girth while still moving and remount, leaving the noseband loose for Phase C.

Roads and Tracks

Many people lose their head when they finish steeplechase and don't give their horses a chance to recover. They think they have to press right on. They get nervous about their time. But believe me, the two or three minutes spent allowing the horse to walk will pay off. Once the horse has regained his wind, you will find that he is willing to take the initiative again. Some horses that are pushed right onto Phase C develop a

Denny Emerson punches his watch before leaving the starting box to begin cross-country aboard Core Buff

Bea Perkins di Grazia carefully checks her horse's girth before starting cross-country

negative attitude, understandably, from not being allowed to recover and they lose their mental as well as physical initiative.

If you consider that Phase C takes anywhere from 25 to 40 minutes or more, depending upon the level of competition, then you can see it is not very difficult to make up two minutes. If your speed on Roads and Tracks is 220 mpm, then you figure about four minutes per 1000 meters. The first 1000 meters will then take about six minutes, or a little more. That means that you will have to do some other 1000 meters in less than four minutes to make up those lost two to three minutes. For every minute you have walked, you will have to canter a minute. Actually, a nice, relaxed canter is almost easier on the horse than a brisk trot. This way you make up time without putting any stress on the horse.

One important note—on the Official Walk of Phase C, make a note of places with good footing that are level or on a gradual decline. These are the places to make up the time at a canter.

By two-thirds of the way on Phase C you should be on time. I like to finish about a minute or a minute-and-a-half early. Should there be a marker down on Roads and Tracks or should you take a wrong turn, you still have a minute to catch up and not, again, put undue strain on the horse. It is very important not to ever be late on Phases A or C as the time penalties are very stiff—1 point for each second in excess of the time allowed.

Cross Country

When contemplating the ideal way to ride cross-country fences, first consider a few factors—the horse's level of experience, the rider's experience, the desire to be successful, and the realization that every horse requires a different plan.

Each rider absolutely needs to have a "plan." The clever and intelligent cross-country rider must have a basic plan yet must always be ready to adjust the situation as he goes along. He must know the course so well that he knows all the alternatives. The rider should walk the cross-country course so that he knows exactly what approach he is going to take into each fence. The rider should also figure out alternative approaches, in case the horse is pulling and tired. At an option fence, for example, it might be wiser to take the somewhat longer route with the easier fence than the shorter route with the bigger effort.

Before going on course the rider should find out how certain problem fences are being ridden, and then make the necessary adjustments in the plan. One good example of this occurred one year at Ledyard. There were a lot of problems at the "Coffin." Many horses were stopping at the "in." But a lot of competitors didn't realize initially that the "in" didn't have to be jumped at all. They watched other competitors stop and get eliminated without being aware that the problem could have been avoided altogether by taking a different option and going down the

Jack Le Goff and the American riders at Lexington discuss the complex World Championship cross-country course (1978)

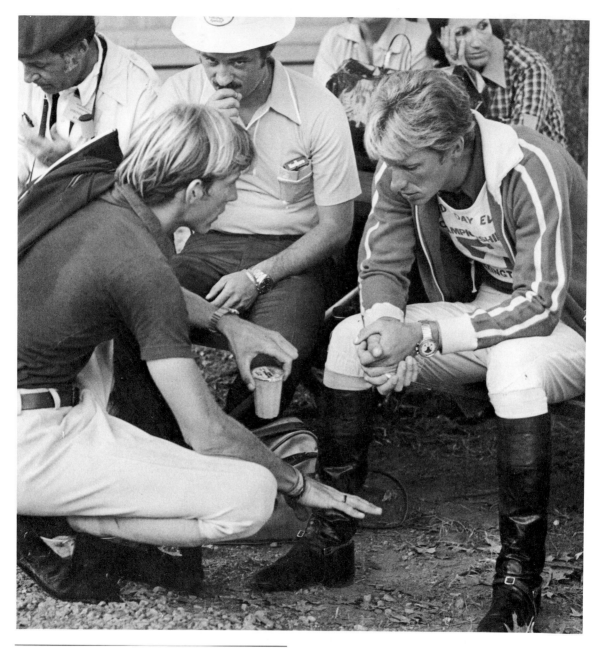

*Tad Coffin and Bruce Davidson discuss problems of
the Lexington cross-country course, 1978*

Cross-country fences need to be studied and restudied—Here Tad Coffin and Mary Anne Tauskey inspect the Head of the Lake at Lexington 1978

to see what might happen. When the horse has already said "no go", it is too late. There is no time to correct the problem, no matter how forcefully the horse is ridden.

If I'm on a big course and my horse has been a bit sticky, I'll take an aggressive attitude in preparing for a fence. No matter how much I like the horse, I'm going to like him a lot more if he lands smoothly on the other side of the fence.

Ditches

When jumping ditches, horses fear the depth. A training-level ditch is really quite narrow, only three or four feet wide. But a ditch is a psychological hazard which stops many a horse. The object in riding ditches is not to be concerned with the depth or the width of the ditch. The rider's only concern is the point of take-off.

When approaching a ditch, stay forward in the saddle, in balance, not sitting down, with the hands low to encourage the horse to lengthen his neck and to stick his nose out in front of him so that he will be looking only at the take off. The only time the rider might come back in the saddle is when the horse is trying to stop; then the rider needs everything behind the withers to get the horse out in front of him. The closer the horse comes to the take-off rail, the easier negotiating the ditch is going to be for him. If he stands off, then a three-foot ditch becomes a six-foot ditch, and you will be asking something very difficult for the young horse.

It is a good idea to let the young horse find his way a bit, providing the ditch is approached with some speed. It does no good to jog up to it, let the horse pick for the edge, and then pop over it. If the ditch isn't very deep, the horse is likely to think, "Am I supposed to jump into it and out, or what is the situation?" Approach the ditch at a gallop and it will be quite clear to the horse what he should do. But don't adjust on the approach! Think about lengthening. If the horse lengthens and is moving forward well, and then

chute, then jumping the ditch. So watch and listen to how problem fences are riding, and then adjust your plan accordingly to your particular horse and his way of going that day.

The successful cross-country rider must know all of his horse's attributes and shortcomings. This way the rider can anticipate a situation and compensate for it before it becomes a problem. If, for instance, a horse has proven to be sticky at a particular type of fence, the rider knows to start encouraging the horse before it is needed. This gets the horse's blood up and the fight ready in him beforehand instead of waiting

wants to put in one or two short strides—that's OK, even ideal. The only time I adjust stride going into a ditch is to lengthen the stride to the edge. If I get there wrong, then I have enough speed and impulsion to help carry us over should the horse need to stand back. Never arrive at a ditch with a long stride on a horse that is backing off your leg, because there will be that moment of hesitation. If the horse jumps, there is the possibility of catching his hind legs on the back edge of the ditch. Horses get hurt this way. The loss of momentum also breaks the horse's breathing and stride—all very discouraging.

With a young horse, it helps to start increasing your pace about 10 strides out or more, staying forward in the galloping position. Sometimes I almost override a green horse a few times. Soon the horse realizes that a ditch isn't scary, and that negotiating the obstacle really requires very little effort. You can increase a horse's boldness at a

Above: Torrance Watkins Fleischmann and Poltroon poised for the ditch at the base of Radnor Banks. Above right: Poltroon is well out over the ditch and concentrating on the next fence. Below right: The gallant little mare Poltroon shows her scope up over the second ditch and bank

ditch simply by giving him the option of running over it.

To help a horse lengthen on the approach, it is a good idea to use the stick well in advance. Be sure the horse has a fair chance by giving him the cleanest, most clear-cut route so that he can see exactly what is happening, thus helping to eliminate the surprise factor. The big problem with the Coffin at Ledyard is that the horse can't see what is expected of him until the very point of take-off, which startles him. That is why successfully negotiating such obstacles depends entirely on the horse's boldness.

Simple Banks

Core Buff and Denny Emerson display an extravagant leap off the Radnor Banks

When first schooling onto a straightforward bank, horses will often get a bit aggressive as they jump onto it. They find it requires very little effort to jump up. But when the horse lands on the bank, it is a different story. The horse soon realizes that it's not so easy to lower the landing gear. He will often scramble, not getting his legs completely underneath his body, and will suck back. The horse soon learns that not only does he have to jump the height like a straightforward

fence, but he must also get his legs down because the ground is underneath them.

Once the horse has taken off, the rider mustn't rely on the horse to carry him through. It's important to keep the leg on the horse in order to help him follow through with his hind legs, so that they are up underneath him where they are needed.

Caroline Treviranus and Comic Relief mid-way through the Advanced Normandy Bank at Chesterland (Pa.)

Normandy Banks

A Normandy Bank is a ditch and bank followed by an obstacle at the far side of the bank. Again the rider's main point of concern when jumping this obstacle should be the take-off point. Don't worry about the height of the bank. The speed at which you approach it is determined by the distance across the top of the bank. In other words, if the distance is a bounce, or a very tight bounce, avoid barreling down into the bank. The same applies for a tight one-stride that is still definitely a one-stride. In this case, too much speed could result in a bounce, even though the distance is too long for a bounce, which could result in a disaster. The ideal speed is a good galloping stride.

When jumping onto a bank where there is a short distance, some horses will simply change their feet instead of bouncing or putting in a short stride. It's nice when they do this and it gives the rider a feeling of confidence. But this usually happens only with experienced horses.

If the horse comes into the bank with a willing attitude, all the rider has to do is to keep riding forward. The ditch is the take-off point. Look at the take-off just as you would an open ditch. Let the horse decide for himself if he should stand back or throw in a short stride. Again, *never, never adjust the take-off to a bank.*

As with the simple bank, it is essential to keep the leg on the horse as he jumps up onto a Normandy bank. Here the horse sees the ditch and looks for the second fence while jumping, then drops his hind legs before he can get them clean on top of the bank. This either stops him, makes him fall back down off the front of the bank, or gives his legs a good whack. For this reason, the rider *must* help the horse by keeping the leg on him. Should the horse hesitate on top of the bank, the rider should be ready to use the bat for encouragement.

Irish Banks

An Irish bank is a natural-looking obstacle covered with grass, and is not revetted back with logs or railroad ties. There is ordinarily a ditch on the take-off or landing side and, on occasion, a vertical fence just beyond.

I've never known a horse that would look at a bank and try to run through it the way he might a post and rail. This is the type of fence that a horse will take himself back on. With an Irish bank a horse will either jump up onto the top, which is quite a leap—or else he will jump into the side of the bank and scramble up to the top. If the horse leaps on top, he will probably arrive there with all the brakes on in order to take a look at what's on the other side. A horse will seldom fly an Irish bank, but if he does it once, he won't try it a second time.

Sometimes a horse that lands on top of the bank and sees no obstacle just beyond might be inclined to go ahead and fly off the far side. This is acceptable. However, if there is a fence follow-ing the bank, then the horse must put his hocks up under him and slide down the bank. Few horses would leap off such a bank with complete disregard to the fence just beyond.

Riding an Irish bank basically requires the same tactics as riding a clean-cut bank. Present the horse at the obstacle at the correct speed and with enough impulsion to handle the job and he will adjust his take-off accordingly. The rider shouldn't let the reins get too long coming up onto the bank in case the horse is really strong and attacks the bank. The rider needs to be of some help in supporting the horse. Also, if there is a fence just at the bottom, as there was at Ledyard, then it is necessary to bring the horse up off his forehand and to get his knees up.

Water

Water, or splash jumps, have a definite psychological effect on both the horse and rider. The horse is instinctively terrified of being swal-

Desiree Smith and Foxie display a confident and balanced descent over the Irish Bank and Rails at Ledyard (Mass.)

lowed up by the water, and generally has not had adequate schooling to overcome this fear. The rider lacks confidence in his horse for just these reasons. It is surprising how many riders use competitions to "school" their horses in water, when this should have been part of their homework. As a result, water becomes the big bugaboo to both horse and rider. All this can be avoided with a proper and consistent schooling program.

There is little doubt that water would have to be considered one of the more difficult obstacles on any cross-country course, no matter what the level of competition. One should therefore prepare for it properly from the start. In competition, water will be presented in a variety of forms, but there are certain basic formats. The most simple one, used for young horses, asks that the horse simply jump into water, with or without a log or rail, and then proceed out. From there, obstacles can be added on the entry side directly in front of the splash, or a number of strides before, as well as on the "out" side of the water. For added difficulty, the horse can be asked to jump from water into water by placing an obstacle in the middle of the splash, or by having a drop into the splash. Depending on the level of the competition, a rider can expect to find any one of these types of water obstacles, plus a combination of one or more of these situations.

The depth of the water and the footing underneath can add another degree of difficulty to splash jumps. The present FEI rule states that the depth of the water cannot exceed 20 inches on landing, but this cannot always be controlled due to weather conditions. Before this rule was passed, the water in some competitions, like Munich, was almost 3 feet deep.

Bruce Davidson and Might Tango gallop steadily through the Swimming Pool at Ledyard (Mass.)

Organizers have fortunately given a great deal more thought to the footing beneath the water and have found a gravel base to be the safest and longest-lasting kind. Mud and soft bottoms may not only cause the horse's shoes to be sucked off, but can also cause numerous falls. On landing, the horse cannot free his front feet from the mud before his hind feet land, so the horse goes down.

Left: Karen Stives and Silent Partner jump into water. The rider keeps her weight back in order to steady the horse's landing

Right: Karen Lende and Erin's Shamrock jump carefully into the water with good control and balance

Starting the Young Horse The manner in which a horse is introduced to water will have a lasting effect on his outlook thereafter. Going into water should be a happy and fun experience from the start. This will in turn build confidence and boldness.

Water is an unnatural obstacle for a horse, so the first initiation is most important. Find a shallow stream with good footing and go back and forth through it as part of your daily routine. If you can find water that is two feet deep or so, let your horse stand in it until he is thoroughly relaxed and almost bored. Whenever and wherever you can find water, use it to advantage and take your horse through it, until he makes nothing of it.

Later take a set of show jumps down to the edge of the stream, make a little X with two rails, and trot on down over them. Continue to splash in and out in both directions. Subsequently add an X on the far side. Make the whole thing a game, and make a big fuss over your horse. Later put a little fence in the middle of the stream and ask your horse to jump from water into water.

Seek Out Water If you don't have water on your own place or wherever you stable your horse, go out and look for a stream somewhere else and try to make it as much a part of your regular routine as possible. Join clinics or find a cross-country course in your area. Pay whatever fee is required to school there and expose your horse to a real water obstacle, and to various other fences that will bolster his training. The advantage here is that you can take your time, show your horse the water, let him walk through it if necessary, and then go and jump it several times.

A competition is not the place to introduce a horse to water. This could scare the wits out of him and almost guarantee developing his fear factor, probably assuring a stop or run-out. If that happens, a problem has been created that could have been avoided.

Build Your Own Water Obstacle Building your own little splash is a nifty idea, saves a lot of time traveling about, and is not all that difficult. You can do it by hand, or with the aid of a tractor and backhoe.

Dig a hole about 18 feet wide, about 20 feet long, and about two feet deep. Line it with plastic, then put about one foot of dirt, sand, or gravel on top of it—right out to the edge, covering all the plastic. Run a garden hose into it, and there, you've got it. Go through the same procedure you used with the stream—let your horse walk around it and get him thoroughly accustomed to the water. Then· build different options.

Physical Problems Inherent in Water Obstacles Water is an unknown factor to the horse. He never knows how deep it is, yet there is quite

an impact produced on landing. Try jumping (yourself) off a small wall, or walking down the stairs in the dark, not knowing how far down or where the last step is. The impact upon landing is quite startling and severe. The knee joints seem to fuse together and your back teeth almost rattle. A horse that doesn't know whether the water is one foot or three feet deep will also land a bit stiff-legged, not knowing whether he will get stuck in soft footing that will impede his next stride, or whether he will land into gravel, which is safer but results in a stiffer landing.

The resistance factor is another problem that must be taken into consideration when the horse moves through water. No doubt you have experienced this yourself when running through a foot of surf on the edge of the beach; you tire mighty quickly.

Since splash jumps are usually placed in the last third of the course when the horse is already tired, the resistance of the water is going to further tire the horse. Care should be taken here not to plunge on through too fast, as the water's resistance has brought many a horse down. If the horse cannot get his front end up before the hind end comes down, or loses his balance on the first or second stride after landing, that's it!

Some riders have the mistaken idea that water isn't so tiring for a horse, because it really is refreshing. Not so, any more than it would be to get hit in the face with a bucket of water, or flung into a pond and hauled out, during a tennis match; especially if you are immediately expected to continue as though you've been refreshed. Instead of revitalizing the horse, a splash cross-country has only a startling, soaking, water-logged, and slippery effect on him.

The Approach The approach depends on the type of splash we are concerned with. Let us first consider a simple water jump—into water and out—with good footing and water that is not too deep. The approach should then be made at a bouncy canter. This means that the rider should have the horse "between the leg and the hand,"

A different approach into the water by J. Michael Plumb and Laurenson—the horse attempts to clear the water in a single bold leap. Mike's steady position helps Laurenson regain balance upon landing

in balance and creating a lot of impulsion, but not much speed. It's rather like a nervous accelerator that is bouncing up and down. The horse's strides are short, energetic, and up and down. This way he can hardly get in wrong at the fence. He also has a chance to see and size up the situation at hand, as he approaches the obstacle.

Actually this bouncy canter is an excellent approach for most water obstacles, with the exception of those in more advanced competition, where the ground might drop off before a large vertical into water (as at Burghley) or where it is necessary to jump over a wide obstacle before a large drop into water (as at Montreal).

If you enter water at steeplechase speed, you are definitely asking for trouble. You might well get a stop, or even a fall. Going through water at speed also creates spray that can temporarily blind the horse, and should he have to negotiate another obstacle *in* the water, the results could be disastrous. If you have a confident and bold horse and are jumping from water into water, approaching the water at the trot would be recommended. This would give the horse an opportunity to evaluate the effort required on his part, and would avoid his being blinded by the spray.

The Rider's Position I was taught to ride forward as fluidly as possible, to avoid breaking the horse's stride, or breaking his breathing, and all the while encouraging him to make an honest bold effort on the approach and take-off. Sitting way back and "hailing a taxi," as they say, can cause a horse to drop down behind and drag his legs over the fence or land on his hind feet, which in turn can bring all the rider's weight down on his back. This is a punishment to the horse for having made the effort to do what you asked of him.

Generally speaking, the rider should be in balance over his horse. The angle between the horse as he descends and the rider's upper body will widen as the drop becomes more severe.

When descending into water the rider should sit very close to his horse. Should the horse start to peck, the rider can help rebalance him by sitting up quickly, taking hold of the horse's head and picking him up. The rider's legs should act as springs to help absorb the impact on landing. At all times throughout the approach, over the fence, dropping down into water, and on landing, the rider's body should be in a good stable position so that his arms and legs can support the horse at all times.

A word of caution. If the rider is perched too far forward and the horse bobbles on landing, the rider may get thrown forward out of the saddle.

I find that the "double bridge" is most useful on drops, because it keeps my hands on either side of the withers. This helps to keep my upper body in the proper position, and at the same time keeps me from hitting the horse in the mouth.

The Effect of Water on the Rider The amount of water that gets thrown up on the rider as he goes through a splash is unimportant. The reins are already covered with sweat so rubber reins and gloves with rubber palms can take care of that.

If you fall, however, it's a different story. The horse is drenched, the rider is soaked, water is sloshing around in his boots, and the saddle is slimy from saddle soap. It's truly a unique experience. After you remount you feel like you are sitting on a greased pig, slipping and sliding around.

There you are, trying to help your horse recover from an unnerving experience, and you can scarcely stay in the middle of the saddle for the rest of the course. Even a bit of sand or mud (that some riders rub into their saddles and on the inside of their boots so they will have a little extra glue in case of problems) will have washed off in the fall. After a fall into water the rider is no longer able to perform at the peak of his ability, and is therefore less of a help to his horse for the remainder of the course.

Left: Bruce Davidson unsaddles his steaming horse after cross-country

Below: Torrance Watkins Fleischmann gives Red's Door full use of his head and neck while jumping safely out of the water at Chesterland (Pa.)

Above: Nanci Lindroth and Auchinbreck display a confident jump over a big drop fence, the Birch Rails at Ledyard (Mass.).

Right: The Quarry at Chesterland (Pa.)

If you spend some time wisely schooling a young horse, or an older horse who has had a problem with water in the past, and ride water jumps judiciously and with proper form in competitions, the psychological effect on the horse will be positive and long-lasting. Splash jumps will then become "just another" obstacle on the cross-country course.

Simple Drop

Some competitors are inclined to sit way back in the saddle when negotiating drops. Our riders are taught to sit right in the middle of the saddle, in balance. Sometimes it is necessary to lean back, but not in the exaggerated way that one often sees.

There is more to jumping drops than just getting the horse's front end over. Obviously the hind end has to follow. When the rider's weight is back on the hindquarters, or the rider has hit the horse in the mouth, and the reins have slid, the result is that the horse's hind end is strung out. The horse is prevented from basculing, which makes him hit the top part of the bank (or rail, if there is one) with the stifle or other parts of his hind legs on the way down. That moment of impact can injure the horse, and even stop the forward movement, throwing the rider off the front or over the shoulder.

The American style of keeping contact and staying in the forward position allows the horse to jump over the top of the fence with his hind end and use his back, and then to come back for the landing. This way the horse jumps clean. I think if you watch our horses, you will notice that they jump drops willingly time after time. The horses that get sat-back-on reach the point where they approach drops looking as if they don't want to jump them. They realize they are going to get hooked in the mouth, and that they are going to have to twist their hindquarters in order to avoid hitting their stifles.

Obviously a rider is going to have to lean back to a certain degree on a big drop, but not in a really exaggerated position. However, *don't lean back*—no matter what—*until the horse has his hind legs over the edge of the bank* or over any rails that may precede the drop. The rider must do what he feels is necessary the moment the horse leaves the ground or is in the air. If the horse is in trouble or has lost his balance in the air, or is going to land awkwardly, it is better for the rider to be back in a position to hold him up and take the contact before landing. Better to do this than waiting until landing to decide what to do—by then, it is too late! Even on a small drop a horse might jump way out. The rider must help rebalance the horse the same way in order to keep him from buckling or rolling.

The approach to a drop does not require much speed—a good, choppy canter or a strong trot is ideal. One of the ways you can make time cross-country is by making these adjustments as close to the fence as possible and not dozens of strides out. Adjust two or three strides out, come to the trot, drop off, and go on. The main thing is to make sure that the horse does not halt or step back on the approach. The rider must be sure to send the horse forward with his legs to initiate the jump, then stay in balance and be of as much help as possible to the horse on landing in case of trouble. The rider must be sure to pick his horse up on landing for the next stride if the horse should buckle. Momentum dictates that the horse must take that next stride, and if his front end is not up and in front of him, he will roll right over.

The use of a double bridge on the neck when riding drops prevents the rider from hitting the horse in the mouth, and it helps hold up the rider's weight rather than allowing it to flop over to one side of the horse's mouth. Even though the horse has to extend his head and neck on landing, there is less risk of catching him in the mouth with the bridged reins if the rider's weight should fall back against the reins.

J. Michael Plumb and Good Mixture come off a big drop following a combination

A Drop Preceded by a Vertical

This is the hardest kind of drop to ride. It is even more difficult when the ground drops away in front of the fence, as it does at the Waterloo Rails or the Dairy Farm drop at Burghley.

Here the rider must be concerned not only with the fact that the horse sees a clean-cut drop, but that the take-off point is right on the line. If you miss this, or if the horse hesitates, then he will be too close to the vertical. Then the fence becomes a real knee hooker, sometimes to the point that it is impossible for the horse to take off at all.

Like a simple drop, this kind doesn't involve speed, but requires lots of impulsion and "rpms." The rider can create a good deal of impulsion in the horse by keeping him between the hand and the leg. Letting the horse run through the rider's hand can result in that moment of hesitation which makes the horse lose the snap to

his knees and miss his take-off, in turn causing him to slide down and under the rail or fence.

Trakehners

The rider must treat a trakehner just like a ditch. Do not worry about the height, the width or the depth—just the ditch. The jumping problem is quite similar to jumping a triple bar. The width or height is not the main concern; the point of interest is the front rail—and how close to that you can get. Once you take off, the rest of the fence will follow because it tends to lead away from the horse.

The idea is to ride a trakehner with the same attitude you would have for an open ditch, thinking only of helping the horse get to the proper take-off, and coming as close to the edge as possible. This way the horse is concerned only with the top rail. Seldom will a nice big log back a horse off. If the jump is well-designed, the rider isn't asking the horse to stand back and clear a big, open gap under a big rail, just to jump a big log.

Should the horse start to look down or hesitate when galloping into a trakehner, give him a good, strong lift up in order to raise his head, and then go to the bat. The bat should not be considered a punishment; it's an encouragement to go forward and jump. As we have seen time and time again, once a horse stops at this type of fence, before you know it he's stopped three times.

Mike Huber and Sir Oddity fly over the Oxer Massif at Blue Ridge (Va.)

Oxers

When riding an oxer-type fence, the object is simply to be sure that the horse is in balance and is not standing too far back on take-off. The farther back the horse stands, the wider the fence becomes. Keep the horse in balance as you would in the show ring, but don't ask him to show-jump an oxer. Keep galloping, but well in balance so that the horse can pick himself up for the first part of the oxer and clear the width. If the rider asks or allows the horse to stand too far back, then the horse will really have to reach for the fence or might even put a leg down in between the rails.

In other words, try to pick a comfortable take-off point so the horse can clear the height of the fence easily, without making the width any greater than necessary.

Jumping Corners

I start schooling horses to jump corners by first using a single vertical fence and jumping over it at different angles. This way the horse gets the idea that as you canter off the angle, he should not run out down the line of the fence. The trick to it is to *teach the horse to hold whatever line you give him in his approach.*

Even if you take a 45 degree angle to an upright fence, be sure your horse understands that he still must jump the fence. Then add another rail and more standards and gradually increase the angle. Keep the fence low and not too wide, especially for a young horse. The wings or standards will help hold the horse in.

Jumping at angles is basically a balance problem. The horse has to get both his knees up equally, the same way he does when he comes in straight and perpendicular to a fence. Be sure to give the horse enough time to get accustomed to jumping off the angle before adding any width to the schooling fence.

When jumping corners in a competition, put the horse in balance about five strides out; slow him down; turn for the fence; and then allow the horse to maintain whatever speed is necessary to jump the fence well, without having to adjust fifteen strides out.

Bounces

With a bounce, the way you jump *in* is the important consideration. If the horse enters the combination well, he automatically jumps out well. The horse should jump in with plenty of rpms and on a short stride. If he jumps in too big, he will hit the second rail with his chest. If the horse comes in to the bounce flat and long and stands back from the first element when he takes off, it will be hard for him to get his hocks underneath him and his knees up. He will be on his forehand and his front legs will fold behind him; the "out" will be most awkward.

The object is to get the horse to round himself (bascule) over the first rails, and again to use his back so that he doesn't hit the rail behind and stop his forward motion.

Be sure *not* to ride a bounce as if you were riding a cross-country fence. Ride the "in" like a show jump, and be sure to maintain the contact all the way through, keeping plenty of leg on the horse to help him over the "out."

Refusals

Besides having a devastating effect on the rider and taking an enormous amount out of the horse, refusals also account for a considerable loss of time. You have to figure that *each refusal is equal to the loss of 20 seconds*. Twenty seconds doesn't sound like that much, until you try to make it up galloping. Twenty seconds and 20 penalty points can put you out of the competition.

After having a refusal, try to make up some of the time wisely. If it is a team competition, you must gain every point. When making up time be sure not to press the horse too much and take a chance of a second refusal or a fall. Once the refusal occurs, the rider should keep his head and say to himself, "I've had it now, but I must get over this fence without wasting any more time, and be on my way."

Making Time Cross-Country

The whole idea is to keep the forward motion. The rider should be out of the saddle in a good galloping position and balanced directly above his feet. He should be low enough in the saddle to encourage more direct air flow. Occasionally you see some riders galloping cross-country standing up in their irons in a rather erect position, and some sitting right down in the saddle. This is in effect giving the horse a half-halt and saying "come back to me."

It is always better, whether riding dressage or cross-country, to go with the horse instead of against him. This takes less effort for both horse and rider. While staying in balance, keep your upper body forward slightly and initiate the next stride, rather than pushing it out of the horse. Encourage the horse to lengthen his neck and to carry his head correctly, which in turn will increase the length of his strides. Again you get more direct air flow. If the horse is ridden in too tight and compressed a fashion, his knees will "climb" a bit, which will make his strides shorter.

When preparing your plan for riding the course, think about each fence carefully and decide at which fences you can "go on" and at

Juliet Graham Bishop chooses the "in and out" element of an option combination

which fences you must say to yourself, "I'd better lose a bit of time here because this fence presents a certain problem where speed might catch me out."

Consider the options that are offered with respect to the various obstacles. For instance, one obstacle might offer a corner, or a big oxer, and a bounce or an "in and out." The oxer or corner might be a hair more difficult, but if the horse is experienced and obedient, it is only one jumping effort as opposed to two.

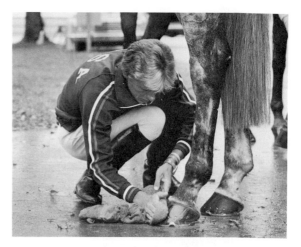

Right: Even a world champion must pay attention to his horse's appearance. Here Bruce Davidson gives Might Tango a final bit of polish before the vet check

Below: Bruce Davidson and Might Tango clear an inviting fence at Ledyard (Mass.)

Independence and Brian Maloney clear one of Ledyard's more intricate fences

When you consider that the energy required by each horse to jump a single fence is comparable to the energy that horse burns up galloping 1/16th to 1/8th of a mile, it becomes clear how important it is to consider the number of jumping efforts your horse will have to make. It's not just a time factor that's involved, but also the number of efforts over a certain distance. The less effort required of the horse, the more you can ask of him overall, and the more time you can save. For the young horse where speed is not a consideration, it is often better to take the easier option with the longer route in order to build his confidence.

Figure out where the halfway point is on the course and know what your time should be at that point. When riding the course check your watch when you get there. If you are slow, don't panic and say "Wow, I'd better get going," and blast off. Check the horse to see if he is capable of moving on. You can do this by moving him

Torrance Watkins Fleischmann and Poltroon breeze over one of Chesterland's imposing oxers

out a bit for a few strides to "listen to his motor," as Jack Le Goff would say. If the horse is tired already and you move on, you will end up exhausting him, and will risk his making some mistake at fences. The ultimate is to make the time with a horse that is not exhausted and that is still jumping well at the finish. On the other hand, it is unsatisfactory to finish with a horse that is still pulling but with a time two minutes over the time allowed.

Study the cross-country course well when you walk it so that it will be clear in your mind just where you can move on; on flat stretches, for instance. You can also make time by taking advantage of the terrain in general. Benefit from the hills and encourage the horse to lengthen his stride downhill, which is easier for him and saves time. Uphill, take back to conserve him. This is the exact opposite of training at home. There you gallop uphill in order to develop the horse's wind. Don't gallop downhill. This puts too much weight on the horse's legs.

Another consideration in trying to make time is keeping the horse in a relaxed frame, and "frame of mind," as you gallop cross-country. It is easier to adjust this type of horse's stride quickly in the last few strides before a difficult obstacle. It is *not* easy to have to make stronger adjustments many strides out with a tense or rank horse. It is difficult to make time with this type of animal.

Know your horse and the course and its terrain so well that you can best benefit from this knowledge. One or two seconds here, and one or two seconds saved there, adds up substantially and can put you in the money, or out of it.

Above: Karen Sachey Reuter and The Mast safely clear a large but straightforward first fence on course

Right: Kim Walnes and The Gray Goose at Ship's Quarters (Md.)

12 *Stadium Jumping*

J. Michael Plumb

Veteran Member USET Three-Day Event Team

J. Michael Plumb

J. Michael Plumb is a true veteran in combined training at the international level. He began his Olympic career in the 1960 Rome Olympic Games and has been a member of the USET's three-day squad ever since. A cool, confident rider, he excels in riding any horse to the best of its ability cross-country. He has perhaps jumped more horses over more fences than other event riders will ever see. In 1974 Mike rode Good Mixture to an individual silver medal in the World Championships at Burghley, England, and later rode Better and Better—a green horse untested in international competition—to a silver medal win in the 1976 Montreal Olympics. Mike has won the leading rider of the year award on nine separate occasions, and I do not believe that there is any major event in the United States that he has not won at one time or another.

Always courteous, Mike encourages young riders and offers them help from his vast store of knowledge. He has coached several successful riders, including international rider Karen Stives, and is always available with sound advice to anyone who needs help.

Although the individual gold medals in the Olympics and World Championships seem to elude Mike by mere fractions of a point, he has earned the respect and admiration of the event community in America and abroad. Here, Mike outlines the recipe for his success in the stadium jumping phase of any event.

Stadium jumping seems to be the one phase where three-day riders have the most trouble. When I give clinics everyone wants to practice the cross-country even though their basic jumping over gymnastics is terrible. Gymnastics may be less exciting than cross-country, but I believe that we need to pay more attention to the basics. Our riding has to change with the times and more people are now beginning to understand that the basics are so important. I think the stadium needs the most improvement, more than the cross-country and the dressage. Of course, it depends upon what area of the country you come from and your exposure to good instruction.

Most event riders have not had the necessary experience over stadium fences. We are lured to the sport because the people are nice and we all like to go out and ride cross-country. Then we have to worry about the jumps we cannot just gallop at and we have to pay more attention to the skill these fences require. It is one thing to jump in a straight line, but putting a whole course of jumps together is quite another. Similarly, many dressage horses can do passage and flying changes every stride, but few of them can put all this together in the Grand Prix test. We have to practice riding courses, even if it means going to hunter shows and jumping small courses.

Very rarely will you find big stadium courses at an international three-day event. Some of the biggest courses I have seen have been at the team selection trials at Ship's Quarters and Blue Ridge. But I think we will come to the point where course designers for international events

Derek di Grazia and Thriller II show excellent form over a stadium fence

will have to put up courses that are a little bigger on the third day and, when that happens, I think that a lot of riders will be in trouble. If the designers put up 10 to 12 fences at 3′11″ with maximum spreads, we will have to get on with our homework.

Tips for the Rider

To improve position I like to make riders ride a horse without stirrups while being lunged. I do not think we do that enough, especially over jumps, and this is the ideal way to start to teach the basic position. George Morris's books and Jean Froissard's book are excellent reading and seem to have the correct basic exercises; they reinforce everything that the USET coach Jack Le Goff says, and they outline the same basic education that Jack himself received in France at the Cavalry School at Saumur. Obviously one needs a nice quiet horse to work on without stirrups so the rider can concentrate on the fundamentals. Event riders do not take the time to practice all these things.

At the Training, Preliminary, and possibly at the Intermediate level you can get away with riding forward to the jumps; at the Advanced level you cannot. This is where precision riding pays off, and good riders know where they are at every jump. You cannot get them off balance or have them lose their perspective on the jump. The rider wants to find the spot on a forward stride, but sometimes you have to break up that stride, or you have to put the horse together for a jump. This technique is similar to riding cross-country but involves more precision and structure. A triple bar on the cross-country and in the stadium are ridden in completely different ways. In a show jumping round you need to find the spot for the take-off without fiddling with the horse's head because of the nature of the jumps.

Timing is very important. If a rider tells me that timing is a problem, then I know that the rider needs to work on improving his balance. It all has to do with the approach. As an exercise I will put a rail on the ground between two standards and tell the rider to make believe that is a jump, and I will ask the rider to come into the "fence" on a long stride, and then on a short stride, and back and forth. This is also good for the horse because it regulates the length of its frame. I ask for a long stride, repeat, and then ask for a short stride. Sometimes I will even set up a course consisting entirely of standards alone, and I will ask the rider to make believe the jumps are there, just to get the concentration that is needed to be able to ride a course.

Event riders are short of practice time. All the practice for the stadium jumping phase has to be done in the winter months. By the time March rolls around we have to start working on conditioning. We no longer have much time to practice for stadium because the training for all the phases demands so much of the little time available.

Over the winter months I start schooling the event horses over just a single rail lying on the ground in the indoor ring. It always seems as if event horses want to rush at their fences the first time they see them. This is good for cross-country, but the horse must also be able to see and analyze a stadium fence too. If the horse just runs at a stadium fence, he will get into trouble. I like to start by trotting over a single rail, and then over several rails on the ground and some cavalettis, thinking mainly about the attitude of the horse and making sure that it is carrying itself. Then I progress to grid work.

Above right: Nancy Bliss and Cobblestone going well-forward over a stadium fence at Radnor (Pa.)

Below right: Debbie Hoyt looks to her next fence aboard Chippendale at Radnor (Pa.)

Right: J. Michael Plumb confers with Jack Le Goff and William Steinkraus before stadium

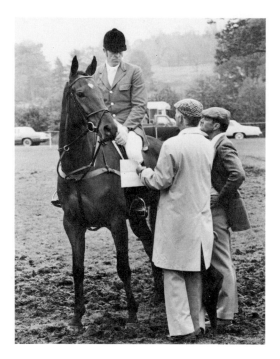

I usually keep the horse jumping small vertical fences until I am sure that his attitude toward the fence is calm and correct. If you introduce spreads too early, you add another dimension to the jump and can confuse the horse's mind. I make sure the horse can approach a maze of poles calmly and rationally until it becomes very easy for him. Then, and not until then, if I am thoroughly satisfied, I will add an oxer. I think it is hard for a horse to deal with an oxer right away as we have been doing in clinics. Verticals are much simpler and should lead to oxers. This helps the horse concentrate on the jump when he's in the grid, and it has made a difference especially for horses who like to take charge. I admit that this is a new approach to stadium for me and that it has made my life simpler.

After successfully trotting over the verticals in the grid, I will then ask the horse to canter over the same line of jumps. I will put a rail before and after a cross-rail, at about 9–10 feet from the X. For most horses who are unbalanced you need those rails. Jump them back and forth until the horse knows what you want and soon begins to do it by himself.

I then put up a course, with four fences on a 20-meter circle, with rails before and after each fence so that the horse becomes programmed. I want the horse's attitude to be quiet, even on a loose rein. If the horse starts to rush, sometimes I will add a turn on the forehand or on the haunches after a halt between fences.

The rider enters into the picture as we go along in this program. When I put up a small course I use rails that have been cut down to 6′ instead of 12′. I do this for several reasons. First, I can put more fences in the ring, and second, it puts much more emphasis on getting the correct

line. Most event riders have difficulty finding lines because they have not had the correct training, or lack control over their horses. A narrow fence makes the rider very aware of the proper line into each fence. I then add different fences to the course: combinations, roll-tops, gates, and brush boxes.

As I add different fences to the course, the rider works on getting the correct lead after each jump. Most event riders do not pay enough attention to the landing. All this work can take place in winter or early spring.

Once the weather breaks I move everything outside so the riders do not get to rely too much on the sides of the indoor arena but must control the speed of the approach and the landing.

Event riders also need to work on being able to change gears between fences. The rider must be able to send the horse forward and then bring him back. To bring a horse back, the rider must practice dropping his seat into three-point position instead of remaining up in two-point, and must be able to switch back and forth easily between the two positions. You have to be accurate in moving from two- to three-point position when approaching a jump at 400 meters per minute. I think that Bruce Davidson is the master of using a two-point position at 450 meters per minute. I don't know how he does it, but he manages to stay in two-point at this speed, and he always seems to canter a bit faster than normal in the stadium. I work too much in three-point position, but I believe that we should try to get a balance between the two. I think this is where the show people are ahead of the event riders.

The horse show riders can set a good example for the event riders but the event riders need to work more on their balance than on their form. The show people do not have to change speeds and the eventers do. There is no question that we have a lot to learn from the show riders, but they do not have to worry about fitness or about being able to gallop at 690 meters per minute. An

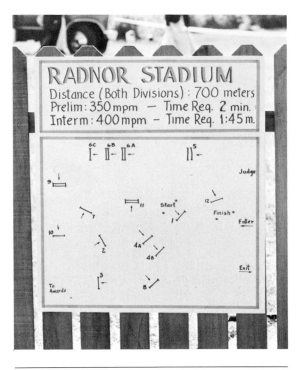

Plan of Radnor (Pa.) stadium jumping course

Riding the Stadium Course at a Horse Trial

At a horse trial the horse is still fairly fresh when it is time for the stadium jumping phase. You will perhaps need to warm up more than at a three-day event. The horse has gone two to three miles cross-country, which for a fit horse is not too much to ask.

I like to use a small cross-rail for a practice fence at an event to find out how the horse feels. I do not want to enter the ring without knowing my horse's mental and physical attitude. Most horses lose their calm attitude during the cross-country and you have to manipulate them back after the cross-country so they can go into stadium. You have to *create* a calm attitude in the horse. Once again you can use a rail before and behind the practice jump. I try to get the horses calm and concentrating, then I jump a total of perhaps ten times, changing the height of the jump and the speed of my approach. I try not to jump too many jumps because you can get so involved with the approach that you can overdo the warm-up.

Warming up properly is a difficult job at a horse trial. Often there are inadequate warm-up fences and everyone else is milling around trying to warm up at the same time. You have to be flexible enough to be able to do a good job with your horse and still cooperate with the other riders. If you have done your homework the horse should know what is expected.

When you walk the stadium course you need to look at the jumps themselves and the track of the course. Look carefully at the places where the ground is not level, and work out the striding between any fences that are at all related to each other—whether it be three, four, five, or six strides. You need to consider whether the problem involves jumping a vertical to an oxer, or vice versa, and what jumps are to be jumped on a downhill or uphill slope. A horse will carry its arc (bascule) over both an oxer and a vertical, and the arc will vary with the speed of the ap-

event rider has to be able to count on having a consistent ride over a stadium course.

Event riders seldom jump enough courses in practice sessions; they spend a lot of time practicing the flat work. I do think it is necessary to jump courses so the rider can learn what to do when riding a course, even if it is only a 3' course. I also think event riders should practice riding over fences that are a little bit bigger than the ones that will be in the competition. Riders sometimes get so involved in technique that they don't spend enough time learning how to apply it to larger fences. We have all seen how things can go wrong when eventers jump larger fences. The rider must practice over larger courses as well as small ones. I think the horse and rider should get as much mileage as possible in horse shows, jumper classes, and combined tests.

James Wofford lets Carawich relax between phases

proach. You cannot ask for a long stride if you have an oxer followed by a vertical downhill. You do not want to rush into any type of fence. At Radnor in 1980 the stadium was more of a speed class. None of us fully realized how much the time mattered or how tight the course was.

Pick your line during the course walk. If your horse happens to be very strong, you can jump some fences at an angle to save time during the course. I think you need to have practiced over a water jump and perhaps a bank as they crop up on stadium courses more and more. I often detect a tendency to have a cross-country course atmosphere in the stadium courses. I think this is difficult as we do not all have the facilities to practice over these fences.

Sometimes the riders can get too technical in measuring the striding, taking away or ignoring

J. Michael Plumb paces distances between stadium fences

their instincts. I try to instill in my riders some of their own feeling and knowledge of their particular horse rather than to say they must "take six strides here and seven here." I do not ignore the striding between related fences but the rider wants the horse to jump clean and must know that particular horse.

I pay great attention to the turns because the rider tends to lose the horse there, especially on turns that arc about eight or so strides out from the next fence. To prepare for this I like to raise my stirrups up and work in half seat when schooling on the flat at home. Some riders do not have the same control when they raise their stirrups as they do in dressage and are lost. It is nice to feel you are controlling the "engine" in the dressage, but you need to be able to do this in the stadium as well because the course constantly changes direction. I think this is where Bruce is so excellent because he can stay in control even while changing his balance.

As I approach a fence I always try to find the place that my horse is going to leave the ground, and I look at the top rail, not the bottom of the fence. I have one eye on the whole fence and one on the top rail. I watch the top rail of a vertical or an oxer, but at a coop or a triple bar I think about the bottom of the jump also. I try to find my place on each jump and that is where timing is so important. If you need to interfere with the speed in the approach to a stadium fence you can, unlike cross-country where you try not to interfere with the horse.

From the moment you enter the ring and salute the judge you must try to ride forward in balance with sufficient impulsion to carry you smoothly over each fence, and you need to know the exact line your horse should take.

Warming Up for the Three-Day Event

Warming up for a three-day event stadium course is a much more difficult proposition. You may have a tired horse so you do not want to jump too many jumps. I get my horses out walking in the morning and see how they are before the vet check, and I get them out walking again before it is time for the stadium. The warm-up should be organized so that the horse peaks when it enters the ring. I go back to basics in the warm-up, and make sure the horse is listening and can adjust its speed, but I am careful not to jump too many fences. The courses are not that complicated and as long as the horse is sharp enough I am content. I take great care to make each approach exact so that the horse will be at the right speed and in the proper balance to negotiate the fence. If my homework has been done correctly the horse should be able to get around the stadium course clean.

Princess Anne of Great Britain lines up Goodwill for a careful turn on the stadium course at the 1976 Olympics, Montreal, Canada

13 *Cross-Country Course Design*

Neil Ayer

USCTA President, 1971–1981

Neil R. Ayer

Neil Ayer served as president of the U.S. Combined Training Association (USCTA) from 1971–1981. Those ten years have been a decade of unparalleled growth in the sport of combined training, that saw the U.S. teams win the gold medals in two World Championships and an Olympic Games. By providing dynamic leadership Neil fostered the growth of the sport. Nothing was too trivial for his attention: He organized his own international level three-day event (CCI) at Ledyard Farm, acted as Technical Delegate for small, local first-time events, supported the top-level riders, and helped purchase horses for the U.S. team. But above all, Neil served the entire eventing community with great good humor and unbounded energy. It is largely due to his efforts that eventing has continued to enjoy the spurt of growth evidenced in both the number of competitors riding in events, and in the number of events offered all over the country.

Neil offers his views on the joys of eventing, and in the latter part of this book explains the principles that go into creating and building suitable courses for all levels of competition—safe, challenging courses that enable riders and horses to learn their craft as they move up through the levels of competition.

Tew cross-country courses are being built each year and, since new course designers are emerging to design them, some of the principles which have proven to be sound are worth reviewing.

Objective

The objective of a cross-country course should be two-fold: first, to test the horse's speed, endurance, and jumping ability; and second, to test the rider's skill in using the horse's talents to the maximum, so as to be able to complete the course both safely and quickly. The cross-country course must ask for all of these—not just speed, or endurance, or the ability to jump an obstacle of maximum dimensions at any particular level.

Mary Anne Tauskey and Marcus Aurelius clear the Oxer Massif at Blue Ridge (Va.)

Factors to Consider Before Designing

Before setting out to design a cross-country course, first determine that you have enough acreage for the level of competition in question. The nature of the terrain available (not counting the percentage in unusable woods or swampland, the percentage developed with farm buildings, the area "cut up" by roads and streams, the amount of acreage under cultivation, and so forth) must be taken into consideration before the following rules of thumb can be applied.

Minimum Acreage for Cross-Country Courses

	MILES	ACRES
Training Level	(1–1½)	80–100
Preliminary Level	(2–3)	100–150
Intermediate Level	(2–3)	150–200
Advanced Level	(3–4½)	200–300

Bruce Davidson and Irish Cap clear a large drop fence. The rider's stable position supports the horse upon landing

In establishing the level of difficulty for a cross-country course, take the following factors into consideration:

1. The proficiency and experience of both the horses and riders who are expected to compete in the event.
2. The time of year. (Is the competition at the beginning of the spring season or at the end of the fall season? Is the event being staged primarily for training purposes, or is it being run either as a selection trial or a championship? The fitter and better trained a horse is, the more technically difficult a course he can be expected to handle.) The distances used (minimum or maximum) will be determined both by the purpose of the competition and by whether it is scheduled at the beginning or the end of either the spring or fall cycles.

In laying out a cross-country course the designer should keep the following principles in mind:

1. Set aside the flattest and quietest area for dressage and, unless cross-country is scheduled at a different time, do not route the cross-country course either through or near this area. Pick a relatively flat area for stadium jumping with the same consideration in mind.
2. Choose an area for parking that will be large enough to accommodate all the vans, trailers, and automobiles that will be coming to the event, and make sure that its surface will hold up no matter what the weather conditions may be. Make sure that the road into and out of it will also hold up, and that none of the traffic will in any way interfere with the track of the cross-country course.
3. Ideally, locate both the starting box and finish flags of the cross-country course in close proximity to each other. They should also be reasonably close to both the secretary's tent and scoring headquarters, in an area that can be reached by vehicle so that vets, farriers, grooms, and competitors can easily get both themselves and their equipment into and out of the paddock area.
4. If possible, avoid crossing traveled roads, avoid terrain which is likely to become excessively deep after a heavy rain, or a track which calls for the course to cross itself anywhere except in a very open area.

Study the Terrain and All Available Natural Features

Before picking a track for the course, you should first walk and re-walk the available acreage in an irregular pattern, searching for suitable locations for different types of obstacles. (If available, an aerial photograph of sufficiently large scale can be most helpful.) Look for streambeds that can be converted into water jumps, ditches with good take-off and landing characteristics, natural sites for road crossing and coffin-type obstacles, banks and slopes with good footing, open areas for galloping fences, groves of trees, and natural wall and hedge lines. All of these should be plotted on a map, for planning purposes.

No course can include every possible type of obstacle, but generally speaking, in order to meet the testing and educational requirements expected of it, a course should include the following variations:

vertical obstacles
vertical obstacles with a spread
ditches
banks
drops
water
brush (bullfinch)

brush (bullfinch)   ⎫
option obstacles   ⎬ Preliminary Level and up
combination obstacles   ⎭

A solid but inviting Preliminary-level oxer at Radnor (Pa.)

J. Michael Plumb keeps his weight back to steady
Better and Better over this drop and ditch fence

Choosing Sites for Obstacles

After analyzing the available terrain, select the best sites for each kind of obstacle and place them in an order which will produce a well-balanced course. The first two or three obstacles should be fences that encourage the horse to "gallop on"—so that he will have a chance to warm up and settle into a rhythm of sorts before he has to face any "problem" fences. Therefore, do not place any difficult fences before the third or fourth obstacle on course. Put the major obstacles (combinations, multiples, and anything other than straightforward galloping fences) in the middle two-thirds or three-quarters of the course—then tail off to the finish over two or three obstacles that will require an honest jumping effort but that will not pose either technical problems or demand extraordinary athletic efforts. Water jumps always pose problems and therefore should be placed from one-half to three-quarters of the way through the course. It's a good idea to try to prepare a horse for a major effort which lies ahead by setting up a small bank before a large Normandy bank, or a moderate drop before a maximum drop, for example. Guard against too many banks, too many drops, too many sharp turns, and too many distance problems. Include sufficient problems to satisfy the testing and educational requirements, but keep the course a galloping course.

The Training Levels

Keep in mind that the Pre-Training and Training levels (and to some degree the Preliminary level) are educational and that over 60% of the horses should go clean (in the Open sections, as many as 80% should go clean.) Some horses should have problems but they should be rider problems and most of them should be run-outs. Roughly 10% of the competitors should be eliminated, either because the rider misses the

obstacle or because the horse is not prepared. There should be very few falls, and these should be of the kind where the rider is unseated. The course should encourage the horse to go on without damaging his courage. If a horse jumps boldly, lands on uneven terrain, and then falls, this reflects poor course design. A horse should never be penalized for jumping boldly. The objective is to create a sufficiently pleasant and rewarding experience for both horse and rider to encourage them to go on to higher levels.

The Intermediate and Advanced Levels

At the Intermediate and Advanced Levels (and to some degree at the Preliminary Level) the objective shifts from educating to testing. At these levels a rule of thumb would say that 25–30% of the riders should go clear, 25–30% should either be eliminated or have enough faults to put them out of the running, and the rest should experience some disobedience and technical faults. The best cross-country horse should end up on top.

Obstacles at these higher levels create testing situations by introducing problems involving unnatural distances between elements; a change of direction between elements; a change of elevation before, at, or following an obstacle; jumping into or out of water; and "controlling boldness." An example of a distance problem would be an "in and out," or a lane crossing, set at other than a natural striding distance so that negotiating it would require that it be jumped as a bounce, taken at an angle, or jumped off a shortened (or lengthened) stride. Changes of direction between elements of an obstacle usually involve both turning and either shortening or lengthening of stride, or both. At the lower levels the change of direction should be gradual, and the horse should be led through it. At the higher levels a change of direction can be an option left up to the rider (as in a Munich Pen-type

obstacle). If executed properly, a change of direction should not be a punishing experience for the horse. Even so, too many turning situations on a course can become discouraging to horse and rider and should be avoided.

A simple bank (or series of steps) up or down are all that should be introduced at the lower levels, but at the higher levels changes of elevation can be designed in conjunction with one or more jumping elements. Water jumps at the higher levels may call for an obstacle to be placed in front of, in, or following the water. This requires the horse to maintain his balance either when he lands in or takes off out of the water.

"Controlled boldness" can best be illustrated by the classic coffin-type obstacle, where the horse is asked to jump over a vertical element, proceed down a steep slope, jump out over a

Both Perkins and Irish Trick jump into the Coffin complex at Ledyard (Mass.)—Irish Trick jumps boldly—and lands looking for the final element

ditch, continue up a steep slope, and jump out over a second vertical element. This kind of combination asks a horse to be bold but at the same time to be in complete control. "Corporal Stripes" present a similar problem in a simpler way—as do both a "Crooked.S" and a "Stolen S." Brush can be employed to test the boldness of a horse. Examples would be a brush fence (of maximum dimensions) set before a drop, either onto dry land or into water or any bullfinch filled in with a thick enough pile of brush so that the horse cannot clearly see what is on the landing side.

Cross-country Courses at the Various Competitive Levels

Training Levels At Training (or Pre-Training) level, obstacles should be straightforward and inviting. All distances between elements should be set up to allow natural striding and the course should include verticals, spreads, a ditch, a simple water obstacle, a drop, a bank, a brush fence, and one or two simple combinations. No severe turns should be required between elements of an obstacle (or between obstacles) and the water in the water jump should be visible from five to ten strides away. Entry into the water should be over a "step-in" drop or a telephone pole or a small log lying on the ground.

Preliminary Level At the Preliminary level, rider problems such as option-type obstacles and alternate lines through a combination may be introduced—because at this stage of training the horse should be more responsive to the rider. A long-legged "L" with a corner option is appropriate, as is a "V" where the rider has to choose his line. Horses should be encouraged to jump boldly, but complicated fences and obstacles involving several elements should be avoided. Water jumps at this level may include a low vertical element either before or after the water.

Intermediate Level At the Intermediate level, the designer should incorporate obstacles which, in a straightforward and uncomplicated way, will require the horse to adjust (shorten or extend) his stride, slow down and speed up, turn between elements of an obstacle on the flat, jump simple obstacles requiring "controlled boldness," and negotiate obstacles at the exact point designated by the rider.

Advanced Level At the Advanced level, multiple obstacles can pose highly technical problems; they can require a change of direction, either on the flat or on a slope, shortening and lengthening of stride, acceleration and/or deceleration, and boldness—to the point of jumping "blind"—as in the case of a spread or bullfinch into water, a

vertical before a steep slope, a bullfinch onto a bank or into a road crossing, and so forth. Multiple obstacles at this level can be very difficult, but if they are properly designed and properly constructed, they should be perfectly safe.

Some Types of Obstacles that are Appropriate at Various Levels

TRAINING LEVEL AND ABOVE

Brush, Trakehner, Steps (up or down), Pen, Ditch before Rails, Rails before Ditch, In and Out, Water Jump (provided the water is not concealed from approaching horse)

PRELIMINARY LEVEL AND ABOVE

Helsinki, Tidworth, Cirencester Rails, "L" Fence, Bank out of Water, Elephant Trap, Slide, Single Obstacle on Slope

INTERMEDIATE LEVEL AND ABOVE

Corner Jump, Coffin, Bounce, In and Out (with unnatural striding), Combination Requiring a Severe Change of Direction between Elements, Combination Requiring Either Compression or Extension of Stride between Elements, Combination Involving Elements at Different Elevations, Single Telephone Pole with No Ground Line, Obstacle in Water Jump (a "Duckblind"), Echelon Rails, Chevrons (or "Corporal Stripes"), an Obstacle at Top of Slide (or Slope), a Choice-Type Obstacle (such as a "Star" or "Arrowhead"), Road Crossing (which has to be taken at an angle), Multiple Obstacles on a Slope.

Right: The first fence on cross-country should look inviting to horse and rider, as this one does—here ably cleared by James Wofford and Carawich

Right: Technical Delegate Lord Hugh Russell directs course construction at Ledyard. The T.D. inspects all fences before an event to make sure every obstacle meets AHSA specifications (Photo by Barry Kaplan)

Do's and Don'ts of Cross-Country Course Design

1. Avoid a great variety in the level of difficulty of obstacles on a given course. It is unfair to the horse to take him over a number of "give-away" obstacles and then ask him to negotiate a real monster. Both balance and a uniform standard of difficulty should be maintained.

2. Keep the position of the sun in mind. Don't head horses and riders into either the rising or setting sun.

3. Avoid mandatory flags at sites other than at obstacles. It is hard enough for a competitor to remember all the obstacles on a course without expecting him to remember a mandatory flag which the designer has placed either to add length to the course or to take the track around a newly cultivated field. It is far better to add an extra flagged obstacle to accomplish this purpose.

4. Build all obstacles with a good wide frontage (minimum of 20 feet) as this not only gives the fence a better appearance but also gives the riders a wider choice of takeoff should the footing deteriorate for any reason during the competition.

5. Make use of existing hedgelines, stone walls, ditches, and the like when selecting locations for obstacles.

6. Follow the same principles in designing for the Pre-Training Level that you would follow in designing for the Advanced Level (particularly in the use of massive material and in determining the width of the obstacle).

7. If the course must cross itself, have it do so in an open area with good visibility and at a considerable distance from the nearest obstacle.

8. When jumping from light into shade choose a light-colored building material; from shade into light use a dark-colored building material. In either case both the design and the material should provide sufficient contrast to the background so that the obstacle can be easily identified and sized up by the horse.

Some Observations about Specific Types of Obstacles

Bullfinches should be packed solidly with brush up to the maximum height allowed under the rules for the solid part of a cross-country obstacle. Then they should be filled less solidly to the maximum height allowed for a brush fence, and even more lightly to the maximum height allowed for bullfinches so that both horse and rider can see through the top. Bullfinches must be maintained and repaired throughout a competition to ensure that their appearance is the same for the last rider as it is for the first.

Brush jumps, whether single or double, should never be built with a back rail that is higher than the front top rail. The top rail in back should be lower, if possible.

Cordwood jumps (log piles) should be located near trees from which the wood could have been cut. They are not appropriate in the middle of a field. The logs should be fastened securely to that they cannot be dislodged, and the leading edge should be either chamfered or protected with a round or half-round rail.

Painted fences should be avoided, except where they look natural. Brightly painted elements are entirely acceptable in the stadium jumping course but are inappropriate on a cross-country course. Exceptions would include painted gates in a fence line; formal "garden type" obstacles (such as the "Swimming Pool" at Ledyard), obstacles carrying commercial sponsorship, and the like.

Island fences in the open are difficult to design so that they look natural. Among the possibilities would be a mushroom flat (Chesterland), a giant's table and chairs (Lexington), a harvest stand (Ledyard), or a hay rack (Burghley). The point to remember is that an island fence must be designed as a complete entity that will look more or less natural where it is located—usually at some distance from the nearest feature of the terrain.

Left: Denny Emerson and Victor Dakin clear the large brush oxer at Ledyard (Mass.)

Below: A Preliminary-level cordwood pile at Radnor (Pa.)

The last fence—At this point on the course the horses are tired and headed for the finish line. If the fence is too easy, it invites the rider to start speeding for the finish flags before negotiating the last fence—and is likely to cause the horse to make a bad mistake. An ideal last fence should require both horse and rider to think but not demand a maximum jumping effort.

Diamond fences are difficult to balance properly between height and spread and are very difficult to construct because of all the different angles that have to be cut. If one is built, it should be constructed of large rails (8″–10″ in diameter).

Water jumps: Make sure that the bottom is sufficiently solid to withstand repeated impact. In any case, design the fence with a broad frontage in case the bottom (or the take-off) does deteriorate.

Horse and rider display confidence over a wide rails and ditch at Ledyard (Mass.)

Option fences: Set up options that are well-balanced. It is a waste of time and effort to spend hours and hours building one or more options into an obstacle if all of the riders are going to choose to take it just one way.

Ditches: The bottom of each ditch should be solid, just as in a water jump. A take-off rail is advisable. At the lower levels, if a ditch is over two-thirds of the maximum width allowed at that level, the landing edge should be sloped to avoid injury to a horse that lands in it.

Inappropriate (unnatural) fences would include picnic tables (if set with a table cloth, plates, cups, napkins, etc.), tires (unless sponsored by a tire company—in which case the monetary reward may offset the pain as well as the appearance, which resembles the entrance to a dump), and pens with stuffed animals (unless exceptionally well-executed). In general, any obstacle that does not fit in with the surrounding landscape and terrain should be avoided unless it has a meaningful motif or promotional reason for being where it is.

Left: Mary Anne Tauskey studies the massive Serpent, one of the toughest fences on the World Championship course at Lexington (Ky.), 1978

Below: Susan Palmer and St. Finnbarr jump boldly off a complex bank

Banks of all sorts must be built, filled, and compacted several months in advance of the competition so that horses will not punch through the surface while negotiating them (this principle applies to all earth-moving operations). Banks should be high enough at any particular level to require the horse to jump up onto and down off them, as opposed to running over them.

Tables, benches, mushroom flats, etc. should be built substantially so that a horse can safely bank them (jump on and off).

Slides generally should be avoided, as they tend to deteriorate during a competition. If they are used, adequate maintenance must be provided. Downhill fences provide a fairer and better test of the horse's ability than do slides.

Drops must be designed so that the horse is not subjected to extensive physical strain if he jumps boldly. Make sure that the landing is smooth and gently sloping, with good footing.

Multiple obstacles require a great deal of anal-ysis and thought on the part of the designer, to ensure that they are appropriate for the level in question. Keep in mind that only at the Intermediate and Advanced levels should a multiple obstacle completely test a horse's ability to slow down, accelerate, compress and lengthen his frame, and turn, especially on a slope or in water.

Narrow fences should be used only when they look natural as part of a particular fence line or woods line or when they are designed to be jumped at just one point. They are particularly troublesome in wet weather because all the wear and tear of take-off is focused at that point.

Obstacles in fence lines should generally not be built higher than the fence on either side.

Paved roads must be covered with tanbark, gravel and dirt, or sod, or shavings and manure, or some other material that will provide a good firm footing, no matter what the weather, to a width of at least the frontage of the obstacle plus twenty feet for take-off and landing.

Denny Emerson and Core Buff take a powerful leap off an Irish Bank and ditch

Rebecca Coffin and Zinker attack an uphill combination

Derek di Grazia and Thriller II sail over the big oxer at the end of the Eyelash at Ledyard (Mass.)

The Cross-Country Course at Ledyard (1977)

Neil R. Ayer, facing camera, directs course building at Ledyard (Mass.)

Neil Ayer, Designer

I doubt that the design of any cross-country course is ever the result of just one man's thinking. Certainly in the case of Ledyard '77, I relied on the advice and counsel of Roger Haller, Jack Burton, Jack Le Goff, Paul Weaver, and others. I also borrowed, as others surely do, a number of ideas from other courses I had seen—and when the obstacles were completely built, I had to make a few minor alterations to comply with the requests of the Technical Delegate, Lord Hugh Russell from England.

The goals, as I saw them, in designing the course were: (1) to present a challenge to some of the top international horses and riders from Canada, Great Britain, Germany, Holland, Ireland,

and the U.S. and at the same time produce a course that less experienced horses could get around; (2) to build a series of obstacles that were both progressive and consistent in their degree of difficulty; (3) to lay out a route that would both make the best use of the many available features of the terrain, and at the same time place the more interesting obstacles where they could be seen by the greatest possible number of spectators; and (4) to use a great variety of building materials that were available locally.

The degree to which the first of these goals was met can be measured by the results. The first three places were captured by top horse/rider combinations: Mike Plumb on Laurenson, Mike Plumb on Better and Better, and Lucinda Prior-Palmer on Killaire. Of the 38 competitors who started Phase D, 18 (47%) went clean, 3 (8%) were eliminated, 2 (5%) retired, and 15 (40%) incurred penalties. Horses from ev-

ery competing country crossed the finish line, and newcomers to the international scene, like Rebecca Coffin's Zinker and Tony Provencher's Grullo Cowboy, turned in clean rounds. Both competitor and spectator comment during and following the trials persuaded me that goals (2) and (3) were achieved, and the wide range of construction materials used included silver beech, oak, choke cherry, poplar, birch, telephone poles, spruce, red pine, hickory, railroad ties, cedar, brush, fieldstone, and milled planks.

The principal challenge in designing the course was laying out a 4½-mile-long track on less than 140 acres that would neither interfere with nor cross itself.

My concept involved starting the course over a series of reasonably straightforward obstacles. The first jump (the Silver Beech Logs) could be seen from the starting box. It had a long flat galloping approach, was sloping in design, and was built of four huge silver beech logs. The second one (the Oak and Fieldstone Cradle) followed, after the track went up a hill and through a wooded area. It was an oak log cradle (with two vertical elements) filled with fieldstone and it involved both height and spread. The next fence (the Choke Cherry Echelon Rails #3,) was a long line of echelon rails constructed from choke cherry logs. It, too, was an obstacle with both height and spread, but like venetian blinds, it could look either very airy or more solid, depending on your angle of approach. The fourth obstacle (the Poplar and Fieldstone Ditch and Wall) was basically a dry ditch in front of a fieldstone wall, with a large poplar log on top of it and some smaller vertical poplar logs at the base, which in effect revetted the take-off side of the wall. It was of both maximum height and maximum spread at the base and looked simply enormous, because the distance between the top of the poplar log and the bottom of the ditch was almost six feet.

Fence numbers 5 and 6A & B (the Birch Rails and the Irish Bank and Ditch) were the first combination on the course. This was basically an Irish Bank with a vertical birch rail on both the take-off and landing sides and a revetted ditch on the landing side. Since the birch rails were parallel to each other but were both at an angle to the long axis of the bank, the problem posed here was how to pick a line that would best suit both the stride and the maneuverability of the horse. Any one of a number of striding and change-of-direction alternatives were available, and most of them were used. Horses with sufficient athletic ability to compress and extend their stride and to change their course between elements had little difficulty here.

The seventh obstacle was an Open Ditch filled with water, and #8 (the Pine Log Oxer) was a vertical fence built of heavy pine logs. The latter was originally set up as an oxer but was modified just before speed and endurance day by the Technical Delegate (TD), who asked that the back rail be removed for two reasons: (1) Because of the heavy going

caused by the incessant rains, he wanted to reduce the severity of the course a bit, and (2) the back rail was difficult to see in the approach.

Obstacle #9A, B, C & D (the Creation On The Hill) was the second combination which got its name during the course construction, when my wife Helen asked, "What, pray tell, is that Creation on the Hill?" It was built of peeled red pine rails and offered a number of alternate routes through it. Even though the distances between elements were natural (with no need for the horse to either lengthen or shorten his stride), it was the type of combination fence that evoked an enormous amount of study.

The tenth obstacle was an Elephant Trap of maximum dimensions, set up with an open galloping approach and designed in hopes of producing a big jumping effort. Fence 11 (Hobo's Hideaway) was at the edge of a flat field. It was set at the top of a fairly steep slope down to a blacktop road, which was covered with gravel and loam so the horses wouldn't slip on it. As Mike Plumb points out in his commentary, it was conceived to test both the horses' boldness in jumping "into space" and their athletic prowess in negotiating the obstacle itself, the steep bank, and the road.

The Golfers Bench (#12 and #13) served as a turning point approximately halfway through Phase D. It was put in to see how well the horse and rider could jump an obstacle with both height and spread, make a sharp U-turn, and then come back over the same obstacle (at a different

flagged panel)—all without going outside the Penalty Zone.

Next in line was a Bullfinch (#14) built of cedar. This fence, stretched between five hickory trees and set behind a hickory rail fence, was designed to pose the classic question, "Does the horse have sufficient confidence in his rider to jump an obstacle through brush without really being able to see what's beyond?" At this level of competition, virtually all horses just sailed right on through.

Fences 15 and 16 made up the elements of the Swimming Pool (or Water Jump), a fairly formal structure of white painted posts, logs, and pickets, which surrounded a rectangular, brook-fed pool with an adjustable spillway (to regulate the depth of the water). Water always causes its share of problems on a course and is included for this very reason; and this case was no exception. Though it was numbered as two obstacles, this was, for all practical purposes, a combination. Weldon's Wall (fence 17, named after Col. Frank Weldon, the Director of Badminton, who was TD for the first international event at Ledyard in 1972) was put in to ask the horse to jump over a water-filled ditch with a medium-height wall built of beams beyond it. This obstacle looked all the more forbidding because of the distance (5½ feet) between the top of the water and the top of the wall.

The approach to the Woodcutter's Lot (fences 18 and 19) was the longest galloping stretch on the course—a good opportunity to speed up the pace and slice off

1 Silver Beech Logs
Height 3'11"
Spread 5'7"

2 Oak and Field Stone Cradle
Height 3'10"
Spread 4'3"

3 Choke Cherry Echelon Rails
Height 3'9"
Spread 5'9"

4 Poplar & Field Stone Ditch & Wall
Height 3'9"
Spread at bottom 7'9"
Spread at top 5'7"

5 Birch Rails & Irish Bank
Height (rails) 3'9"

6a,b Ditch and Birch Rails
6a: Spread 4'   6b: Height 3'10"

7 Open Ditch
Spread 10'5"

Illustrations by Joseph Martin

8 Pine Log Oxer
Height 3'11"
Spread 5'9"

9a,b,c,d Creation on the Hill
    9a: Height 3'8"   *9c: Height 3'10"*
    9b: Height 3'10"   *9d: Height 3'7"*

10 Elephant Trap
Height 3'9"

11 Hobo's Hideaway
Height 3'3"
Spread 5'2"

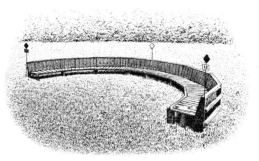

12,13 Golfer's Bench
Height 3'10"
Spread 5'

14 Hickory Bullfinch
Rails: Height 3'11"
Brush: Height 8'
Spread 2'6"

15,16 Swimming Pool
In: Height 3'9"
Out: Height 3'7"

a few seconds from one's time. The Woodcutter's Lot was basically a pen-type jump, which required a 90 degree turn between the two elements. The first element was a maximum dimension cordwood pile, and the second part was a saw table (also of maximum dimensions), which was made more difficult by the absence of a continuous ground line.

The next four obstacles were the Tidworth (fence 20, made of silver beech logs), the Rails and Grave (fences 21A, B, & C, made of peeled red pine logs), the Orchard Rails (fence 22, made of hickory logs) and the In Flight (fence 23, made again of peeled pine and named because it resembled a flock of waterfowl flying in V-formation). All of these presented less severe questions but were still designed to pose some problems. The Tidworth had to be negotiated at the lowest point, where the top logs appeared to cross, or else had to be jumped at a height considerably higher than 3'11" (in other words, it was a steering problem). The Rails and Grave, a three-element combination on an uphill slope, involved a vertical, a deep and wide revetted open ditch with a landing about a foot higher than the take-off and a second vertical. The whole effort required a continuity of impulsion. The Orchard Rails was a large and solid obstacle with both a significant drop on the landing side and a choice of routes, with the shorter one involving an element more than 4' high. The In Flight, an optically hypnotic structure, was conceived as a variation on the traditional "Di-

amonds," but without a comparable degree of balance and proportion.

Fence 24A, B and C—the now-famous Ledyard Coffin, in the course since 1973—has always been a test of controlled boldness because: (1) the horse can't see the ditch in the middle until he is one stride in front of the first element; (2) he has to adjust his stride going down the slope, before jumping the ditch; and (3) he has to keep up his momentum, to continue up the slope and over the third element. Even though this fence causes fewer second refusals and eliminations than it used to, this obstacle still takes its toll in penalties.

The Table (fence 25) featured a sloping front of solid planks (like a chicken coop), which lessened the vertical course but also had a small dip in the ground on the approach. This made it more difficult—and caused some horses that were caught a bit off guard to bank it.

The Zig-Zag (fence 26, oak logs criss-crossed over a fieldstone wall) was not intended to present any particular jumping test as such, but rather was placed to encourage the competitors to take the shortest route over the next obstacle and in so doing to execute the most spectacular of the several options available.

The Eyelash (fence 27A, B & C), interestingly enough, took longer to lay out than all of the other obstacles on the course put together. The reason for this was the enormous amount of readjustment of both panels and rails that I went through in order to

end up with three curved sections that not only presented a graceful line and offered jumpable distances between elements, but that also achieved a proper balance between the problems presented by the longer route through the three elements, and the considerable drop involved in jumping the obstacle over the V at the extreme left. Just before the competition, the TD decided that the V should be lowered. This turned out to be an unfortunate decision because the great majority of horses negotiated the obstacle at this option, and very few took it through the three eyelash elements, which measured some 130 feet in length and which had taken hours and hours and hours of time to construct out of hard-to-come-by cedar.

As the next to last obstacle (fence 28), I put in a Double Brush Fence over a Water-Filled Ditch. My inspiration for this design was a similar obstacle I remembered from Badminton. I built it right up to maximum dimensions and added a degree of difficulty by constructing the base of the brush about eight inches above the lip of the ditch. This gave it the appearance of being much fiercer than it was and of not having a true ground line.

The final jump (fence 29) was a colorful Produce Stand (or Harvest Fence), designed with the two-fold purpose of bringing the horses home safely over a medium effort, straightforward obstacle and recognizing the time of year and the bounty of the area in an appropriate and attractive way. It accomplished both purposes.

In retrospect, it's always inter-

17 Weldon's Wall
Height 3'8"
Spread at bottom 9'8"

21a,b,c Rails and Grave
21a: Height 3'10"   21c: Height 3'10"
21b: Spread 7'

18 Woodcutter's Lot (Log Pile)
Height 3'10"
Spread 5'

22 Orchard Rails
Height 3'11"
Spread 5'
Drop 6'1"

19 Woodcutter's Lot (Saw Table)
Height 3'10"
Spread 5'8"

23 In Flight
Height 3'11"
Spread 5'8"

20 Tidworth
Height 3'9"
Spread 5'11"

24a,b,c Coffin
24a: Height 3'7"   *24c: Height 3'11"*
24b: Height 2'
Spread 4'10"

27a,b,c Eyelash
27a: Height 3'6"   *27c: Height 3'8"*
Spread 4'11"   *Height at*
Drop 6'6"   *bounce 2'10"*
27b: Height 3'8"

25 Table
Height 3'10"
Spread at bottom 7'1"
Spread at top 5'11"

28 Double Brush Fence Over Ditch
Height 4'7"
Spread 5'11"

26 Zig Zag Over Stone Wall
Height 3'11"

29 Produce Stand (Harvest Fence)
Height 3'5"
Spread 4'8"

esting to consider what might have been done differently. I personally feel that the Technical Delegate made some last-minute alterations which, in view of the final results, were not necessary. Lowering the V end of the Eyelash (fence 27) made this option by far the easier of the two, and by doing so, saw far too few horses take the much longer route through the three curved elements. The TD also "de-oxerized" both the Pine Log Oxer (fence 8) and the Orchard Rails (fence 22) because he felt that there were too many oxers on the course, and he was fearful that the combination of heavy going (principally on Roads and Tracks) and too many big oxers would take its toll. In view of the high percentage of clear rounds, it would appear that these two oxers could have been left in. More extensive gravel-filled and reinforced areas should have been engineered both in front of and on the landing of the Open Water (fence 7) and the Double Brush Fence over a Ditch (fence 28) because the horses sank in deeper than was truly safe at both of these obstacles. The disappointing design, to my way of thinking, was the In Flight (fence 23). The concept was original, but the result was unimpressive— perhaps because it was of too light a construction?

In conclusion, I think it is interesting to observe that the Ledyard '77 course, was viewed by the competitors as a real monster prior to the competition. The truth of the matter is that it rode very well.

J. Michael Plumb, Rider

Stories had drifted back to me about the enormous size of the Ledyard course. Several of the advanced riders had gone up to Hamilton (Mass.) to have a look, and some of them said that they weren't sure if there was a horse in the country that could get around. When I arrived on Wednesday before the event, I was most anxious to have a quick look around and I came to the same conclusion. It was big all right; it was a "big time course," a real International caliber course, but well within the realm of possibility.

Only the first and second fences were gifts, then after that the course posed problems at almost every fence, and that's the way it should be at that level. It was a matter of having your horse under control at all times, and knowing what you were about.

On Course

At the first fence, The Beech Logs, Laurenson was a little slow picking up speed, but he saw his fence, eyeballed it and went right on and attacked it. I like that.

We headed up the hill with the announcer's stand on our right, and then moved on down to a narrow place through the trees. I wondered if he was going to cheat me this time and put in a short one and pop the Stone Cradle. He did not; he jumped it really big. I had quite a good feeling inside of me. Just ahead, in a matter of yards, was the Ech-

elon Rails. This fence creates a strange optical illusion—if you approach it head on, it looks like a dozen or more posts sticking up in the air all by themselves. So we come in at a bit of an angle from the left, which makes it much more jumpable.

Now we have to head down through a wide grass alley way between the trees. The ditch and wall with the slanty rails is off the straight line, over to the right. This is a good wide fence that takes a bold galloping horse to see the problem and be drawn to it. Laurenson hasn't always been this way. But he clocks right on down to it bearing right. I let him pick his own pace, which is in excess of 570 mpm, so we are not losing any time.

Moving on down the hill, I can see the Birch Rails and Irish Bank through the trees. When walking the course, I was a bit concerned about this combination. Once up on the bank, a horse could get too greedy to get to the next fence. The birch fences on both sides are set at an angle so there is some maneuvering to do on the top. You have to jump up on the left of the bank, go to the right on the top, slide down the bank, jump over the ditch and then over the final birch rails. I ask Laurenson to show jump the first rails. He is very clever about the whole combination. He really is a very clever fellow.

We are out in the open again and heading on to the Open Ditch. It doesn't look very big on the approach, but at take-off it is another story. When walking the course, there was some talk about jumping into the water, but I didn't want any part of that. I think Laurenson has decided there are some ferocious tigers in the water just waiting to reach up and grab him if he doesn't jump good and clear. He makes a tremendous jump.

Now we head on up a hill, just below Mrs. Frederick Ayer's house on the way to the Pine Log fence. This was originally an oxer, but the far rail was removed just before the event. The footing looks a bit slick, but holds up really well. Actually the footing has been extremely good, considering the amount of rain we have had. (Later I learned that Tad Coffin had fallen off here when Bally Cor twisted badly, but Tad was clever enough to hang on until he was clear of the penalty zone.)

Galloping along, we pass above the Swimming Pool, cross the main avenue of the Ayer estate and arrive in another field where dwells the Creation on the Hill. Well named! Basically, it is two triangles. This jump gave more people more food for thought and more conversation than just about any other jump on the course, with the possible exception of the Eyelash. There are two obvious ways to do this obstacle. Jump through the triangle on the left side, and then over the left corner of the other triangle, or do the reverse on the right. The latter way appealed to my eye. Laurenson has jumped quite a number of corners since I always aim for them. If you don't make it a point to do so, then the tendency is to avoid corners completely, and you lose

a lot of time that way. Laurenson sees the line I pick for him and gets down to business.

It's not long before we are faced with the next obstacle down the same hill. When walking the course I was rather concerned with this fence, as it is big and you need a horse that's really trucking and jumping boldly. Laurenson eyes the Elephant Trap, comes right on down to it and—*wow!* It's a big, big fence.

We cross an avenue and are coming into another field. The Hobo's Hideaway is one of those jump-into-space fences; you touch down, then gallop down a bank, and cross a road. Laurenson comes in on a good long stride, sees the problem, sets over the top and drops down just like a bomb and moves right on down the hill and across the road. Very handy, just like a cat on a monorail.

We start on a long gallop up a big hill to the Golfer's Bench combination of two fences. The horse must jump the right-hand side and then do a U-turn back over it. Well, right now Laurenson really feels great—ready and strong, and I am only half way around the course. We jump over fine and have to make a real sharp turn so we don't go out of the penalty zone. That's the trick here. I'm making a bit of a mess of it, but he gets me out of trouble. We broke our momentum on the turn and it is hard to get going again.

That effort took a bit out of him, so I let him take a few deep breaths going back down the hill we just came up. The Bullfinch comes into view and he seems to

be back in business again. He feels as if he is jumping right over the top of the bushes—not taking any chances.

Laurenson is galloping on in a strong, very workmanlike manner, but as we cross the road, he begins to feel a little heavy on the front end. I decide to set him back a couple of times, particularly to alert him to the job ahead at the Swimming Pool. He is bold about water, but he has a hair-raising way of handling it. Just what I expected happens— I see the distance, go for it, and he lands in the water—plop, on all four feet! I almost come off, but we come out easily, thank goodness!

We continue on across another field and out onto the main part of the course. Weldon's Wall just ahead has me concerned because this is the type of fence (with water in front of an obstacle) where Laurenson has had trouble before. As we approach it, I see a long distance and go for it. He doesn't let me down! I really feel better now. My other horse, Better and Better, did not have a good fence here.

There is a long gallop to our next fence, rather our next two fences, since I plan to ride the Log Table and the Saw Table as a combination. It's rather like a pen jump. I let Laurenson move along now so as to make the time down the back track. He feels fine. We take the logs way over to the right, in order to have room for a sharp left-angled turn. We turn in the air over the fence, take three strides and are out over the right side of the Saw Table. He wasn't very sure of his exit and didn't exactly get drawn to it, but it was a safe maneuver. At least he seems to know what he is doing.

He's galloping on very strongly now and there is another long stretch ahead before the Tidworth. Our time is good. I think we have averaged 570 mpm. I can't help but think things are looking pretty good. But you never know what lies in store. We are coming out of the woods now. The take-off on the right side of the Tidworth is pretty dug up. The left side is lower but has more of a drop into a soft field on the landing side. We jump on the left and head on over to the right where there is a little road and firm footing.

Laurenson motors on into the next field where we have to swing wide up a hill to the Rails and Grave. It's an uphill effort starting with a vertical. Some riders jumped in from the side and went down into the ditch, but I understand that two riders who did this had stops, when the horses looked down into the ditch before dropping in. Laurenson is going well; I keep my leg on him and he just explodes right through the whole combination.

Now we continue up another hill in the direction of the International Barn. This hill is quite steep. Next we turn to the Orchard Rails. Laurenson still feels good and has a lot of gas left. I had planned to take the left side—it has less of a turn, but somehow I chickened out on that decision. If I got hung up there, everyone would say, what a jerk! So we make the wider

turn, and take the middle. The far rail was removed before the event started, but it's still a good, big fence.

We head on down the hill we had just come up. I let him roll on with his big, galloping stride. To the left around a corner is the In Flight fence. It's not big, but it has had me concerned from the beginning. It's not like any of the other fences; it looks as if it's maybe a hair on the flimsy side. A horse could hang a leg here. Mary Anne Tauskey had a fall here when Marcus Aurelius twisted really badly. This is a small fence that commands respect. I take hold of Laurenson a little and ask him to jump where I want him to. It works fine.

We're not too far from home now—six more fences to go. It's a pretty good gallop on up to the Coffin. Laurenson had a fall at a coffin-type fence at Blue Ridge, so I have a feeling there are some people who will be watching to see what he is going to do. Since everything has gone well up to this point, I feel that the Coffin isn't going to be a problem. I hope I'm right. He's over the first upright, takes a bit of a look at the ditch, and just keeps going —never a foot in the wrong place.

It's a good thing the galloping lanes are marked, for there are a lot of people on all sides of us as we head up to the Table. This fence is big: a 7 ft. 1 in. spread at the bottom, and 5'11" at the top, and a bit of a dip in the ground on the approach. Some horses were banking it. Laurenson is really in gear and makes a big leap. We land and turn to the right.

I can already see the Eyelash; it's just a matter of yards away. This obstacle provoked a lot of concern on the course walk. Beth Perkins and Hot Shot Shawn jumped it as a triple in and out, but this takes time. Another rider came down through the first chute from the top and jumped B and C as an in and out. The fastest and most dramatic way is over the end—the oxer— that has a 6'6" drop. My plan is the latter route, so we just keep on coming and from a long stride are over it, and are shooting down the big drop and on down the steep hill.

Now we really are on our way home. Laurenson has quite a bit left as we gallop on over the uneven ground toward the Double Brush over the Ditch. Two English riders fell here—Chris Collins and Fiona Moore. It is a very big, wide fence near the end of the course, when the horses are tired. The ground is quite soft and wet because the rain has collected here on the lowlands. Laurenson seems to know he is nearing home and the faster he gets on with it, the faster he will be back with his buddies. He makes a big leap over it.

We're heading up the last hill. He seems to be lengthening his stride toward the last fence, the Produce Stand, which is full of every sort of ripe fruits and vegetables imaginable. We're over it! And speeding toward home. I can really feel the excitement and elation, from that final burst of speed and the power that is pounding beneath me, and from knowing we have been successful.

World Championship Course, Lexington, Ky., September 1978

Roger Haller

Roger Haller, Designer

Course design has evolved over the past twenty years through the great surge of interest in the sport of eventing. The riders at the higher levels are more sophisticated than ever, and the course designers have to bear in mind that technical problems must be such that they pose questions for the horse and rider but within the limits of safety.

Questions of distances should be introduced at the Preliminary and Intermediate levels, so the horses will learn to shorten and lengthen into fences. Preliminary and Intermediate courses should also include questions of turning and pose problems of control. The horses must go forward in balance, with suppleness, and be bold.

The Advanced course puts all the components of cross-country riding together. The fences at this level can demand that the horses demonstrate long and short striding, balance, and turning skills, but a single obstacle can also combine all three requirements. The designer can present questions of boldness and control in repeated situations.

In 1976, when I was appointed course designer for the World Championships the first thing I wanted to fix in my mind was the difference between a course for a CCI, (Concours Complet International) and a CCIO, (Concours Complet International Officiel). I wanted to study the recent history of the development of the sport and see if my own ideas had been used by other designers, and if so, to study what they had done. I studied all the courses that had been used for CCIO's all the way back to the Berlin Olympic Games in 1936.

The first fact that struck me was that before the Rome Olympics in 1960 the sport was quite different. The fences were perhaps larger and more demanding physically, but the technical aspect of the courses was much more straightforward; the courses required tremendous stamina, but less sophistication. Rome changed the sport.

In my evaluation, I focused primarily on the courses at Rome in 1960, Tokyo in 1964, Mexico in 1968, Punchestown in 1970, Munich in 1972 and Burghley in 1974.

I made up a set of statistics concerning the types of fences, the distances of the courses, and the number of fences and combinations, and I studied the evolution of various types of obstacles, such as banks, ditches, and L's. I did all this homework to get the feeling of what other designers had done before.

The trend of the international courses, at Munich and Burghley, seemed to be to stress the technical aspects (distance and turning problems) and the sheer physical task (heights and spreads) had been de-emphasized. Only one course—Luhmuhlen—had caused problems to horses. Fifty to sixty percent of the field jumped clear, but the horses that could not make the big fences were injured.

A strong field of entries for the World Championship was expected, although the sheer cost of transporting horses to the United States was expected to limit the numbers somewhat. I knew that we could expect teams from some of the South American countries and that they might be less experienced than the European teams. I expected the entry to be more sophisticated overall than the field of competitors at the Montreal Olympics in 1976 but less experienced than the field that competed at the previous World Championships at Burghley in 1974. In a World Championship all countries have the right to start six riders, as opposed to four in Olympic competition.

Each Championship course is different. It is built on different terrain, the climate is different, and it also reflects changing trends in course design that seem to move in cycles. I wanted to create a course that would test the riders without building mountains. My goal was to build the harder parts of the course with more rider problems than horse problems. As it turned out the maximum size fences all were jumped clean, because they were single fences and any of the horses competing should be able to jump a big fence. I wanted to create a course that the riders should have been able to get around, if they rode intelligently. You expect a World Championship horse to have scope.

The site

As soon as the Championships had been assigned to the Kentucky Horse Park in Lexington, my first job was to inspect the actual grounds. While the Park lent itself ideally to hosting a CCIO, I found that the terrain did not include a great number of natural features. The terrain varies so much at Ledyard that it is easy to come up with new designs, but on the other hand Ledyard is in a more built-up area, so it does not have as much open land available. The size (acreage) of the Horse Park in Lexington was good for a CCIO.

My plan was to design a course that would be indigenous to America. It would of necessity be a parklike course with the flat-ter terrain. The footing appeared to be consistently beautiful.

I walked, and walked and walked over the land. I had a lot of ideas, some of which I eventually used, some of which I threw out. The whole track of my original course was completely altered after a year of study.

In 1976 a Preliminary course was set up at Lexington for a two-day event, partly to get a feel for the way a competition would go there, and partly to begin to train the thousands of volunteers who would be needed to run a World Championship competition. The course had great wide galloping lanes and I originally took the track of the course over the road behind the steeplechase course and into the neighboring farm. After the Preliminary event in 1976, we had a call from the owner of that farm, who told us that we could not cross the road, so we had to relocate the track of the course.

By 1976 however, I had enough ideas for fences and we were able to change the track around and run the course in the opposite direction.

In my mind, I divided the course into three major sections with a focal point in each one— the Bank at Old Fort Lexington, the Water complex, and the Serpent.

The idea for Old Fort Lexington came about as I tried to create a different type of bank jump. The history of pioneer Daniel Boone and Kentucky's early settlement inspired me to build an old frontier fort. The cabins were a natural addition. The idea of the bank came from the banks built at Rome in 1960 where there was a bounce bank, a much more sophisticated bank jump than anyone had seen before. The middle cabin of the first element was in reality a bank jump.

The water complex was probably the first one that included a Normandy Bank into water. The idea came about after a great deal of study of other water fences.

As for the Serpent, when I walked down to the crooked stream that ran through the park, I realized that I could design a lot of things around this natural feature.

The other combination that I spent some time on was the Dog Kennels. I had in mind a combination that would set up problems of distances, of shortening the horse's strides. Actually, I wanted to put the two triangles that I eventually put at Ledyard in 1977, The Creation on the Hill, in here, and the Kennels at Ledyard. But at Ledyard there was no convenient place for the Kennels. There were no other buildings on the hillside and no real reason for Kennels at that point. In the Horse Park, however, there were other buildings nearby, which made it a more logical place to build kennels.

The course

Fences 1 through 9 constituted an introduction to the course. The first fence was a standard sloping fence to get the horses galloping on the course.

The second fence was a solid oxer to make the horses sharp. It was built as a square obstacle so that the rider had to push on at it, and the horse had to start jumping well quickly. The horse had to pay attention and realize that it was no longer on the steeplechase.

Of all the obstacles on the course, the Park Pavilion, fences 3 and 4, turned out to be the ones I would like to have changed. The site was there and the Park officials liked the fence very much, but on hindsight I think I would have lowered this fence, or made them go into the pavilion and just jump out. It did fit into the park well, but it was perhaps too drastic a vertical problem to pose just at this point; had it been lower, I do not think we would have had the two falls there.

After I had sent in the plan of the course for approval by the FEI, I got a telegram in late May from the President of the Ground Jury saying that I had too many fences. I would have preferred to eliminate this fence, but instead we took out an upright gate that I had placed after Old Fort Lexington in the middle of that long gallop to the ditch and brush, and another fence between the Road Crossing and the Sinkhole. I wanted to remove the birch rails after the Head of the Lake, but the park people had already cut all the lumber and wanted the fence there because it fit so well into the hillside.

Fence 5 was the Diamonds, a different type of spread fence and one that the less sophisticated riders probably had not seen before.

At the Jenny Lane Crossing riders were faced with their first big decision—should they take a straight bold line across the two banks, or should they make a looping turn? They had to have their plan of attack in mind as they approached. Strangely enough, one rider started to go for the bold line and changed his mind in mid-course and pulled his horse around sharply to make the loop. I do not think changing your mind in the middle of a combination is a good idea. He was lucky and got through.

Fences 8 and 9—the Sinkhole combination—came at the end of the first section of the course. The fence offered three routes, one on the right (for a bold horse), where the rider had to be careful not to let the horse drift out; one through the middle, which resembled a coffin and required precise riding; and the third on the left, where the rider jumped in, fiddled around the tree, went along the ditch and found a way out. The American riders did not like this fence at all, but the English and the Germans, who have more experience in jumping coffins, were not as worried. There was an escape route if you got into trouble.

When Wolfgang Feld, the Technical Delegate, inspected the course the previous October he remarked that all the horses should be able to get this far in the course, but that this was the end of the fun, and the riders would have to start doing everything correctly from here on.

The middle part of the course, from fence 10 down to the Serpent, contained the real test for the competitors. After making them think about the Sinkhole, I gave them a breather in the form of a big (maximum dimension) Giant's Table—a fence out by itself in the middle of a galloping stretch. It was a big fence but nothing critical, and as it was it caused no problem at all.

The Kennels (fence 11A, B, and C) was the first real test of control and boldness. It was the easiest of the four major fences, and asked some fairly sophisticated questions. The rider could choose to take a double bounce slightly downhill, meaning that the horse had to be sharp and quick off the ground, or there was a diagonal line through the combination, which entailed jumping the kennel in the middle. If the flags had been set up a little differently I think we would have seen more riders attempt the second route, but the red flag was almost on the corner, which made the obstacle more difficult.

1 Logs & Shrubs
Height 3'11"
Spread 5'11"

2 Water Trough
Height 3'9"
Spread 5'7"

6,7 Jenny Lane Crossing
Height 3'9"
Spread 4'11"

3,4 Park Pavilion
Height 3'11"

8,9 Sinkhole
Height 3'7"—3'11"

5 Diamonds
Heights 3'9"—4'9"

10 Giant's Table
Height 3'11"
Spread 6'7"

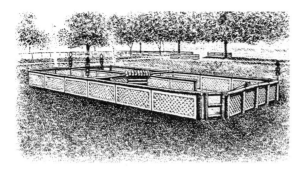

11a,b,c Kennels
Height each element 3'9"
Height kennel 4'3"

14a,b,c,d Old Fort Lexington (Bank)
Height bank 3'7"
Height stockade 2'
Distance between b&c 10'

12 Stack of Logs
Height 3'3"
Spread at top 6'7"
Spread at bottom 9'10"

15 Old Fort Lexington (Farmyard)
Height 3'11"
Spread 5'11"

13 Old Fort Lexington (Cabins and Shed)
Height 3'9"—4'3"
Spread 5'11"—7'10"

16 Ditch & Brush
Height brush 3'11"—4'7"
Spread left option 8'8"

I still think that the two triangles would have been a better problem to put here.

Fence 12 was a simple stack of logs, another maximum fence but it gave them a breather before the next real problem.

Now came the first really big complex, Old Fort Lexington, (fences 13, 14, and 15—all related), and the way you jumped the first element dictated how you would have to attack the main bank in the middle. I was trying to create a new kind of bank and I believe that I did just that. The main portion (the fort) had to be attacked, and the rider had to come as close to the ditch at the base of the bank as possible, to be able to jump high up onto the bank and to continue up over the fence on the top. When this combination was first built, the top fence was straight across, but when Kevin Freeman and Michael Page, who were the American advisers, accompanied Wolfgang Feld on his course inspection, we all looked at the fence and felt that something was wrong. We discussed it and decided that if we left the top stockade perfectly straight, the horse would take a full stride on top and there was a danger that an overly bold horse might launch itself into space on the far side and jump off without touching the bank on the way down.

We went back to study the fence several times and decided to set a section (the first part) of the rails back from the top to create a 10-foot bounce, which appeared to be a good solution. The construction crew got up on the bank and dug up the fence and

changed it in two hours flat. I think this made the fence much safer. I really did not want any horse leaping off the top and landing in a heap.

Fence 15, I must admit, did not turn out quite the way it should have, but we just ran out of logs. The corner on the right hand side should have offered a real jumping option with a rolled top; as it was, it turned out to be a non-jumping option. I did not want the riders to come down after the big effort at the bank and let the horses get disorganized; I wanted them to stay in balance during the recovery strides and I wanted to make the riders keep their wits about them.

As I mentioned earlier I had wanted to give them an upright gate during the next galloping stretch but that had to be one of the fences we eliminated. I wanted to give the riders a chance to relax before they had to cross the road and come to the Ditch and Brush. Originally I wanted to put the Footbridge here, but it did not work out because of the shape of the existing ditch. I did give the riders the option of taking the fence on the right hand side, or going down into the water and trotting over the brush if the horse seemed tired. After the championships, Joe Saito (the Japanese rider) thanked me for the options. He told me, "Without the options, I would never have gotten even as far as The Serpent."

The Head of the Lake complex was the most difficult fence for the horses. The riders had to choose whether to bounce the Normandy Bank into the lake, or to try to make the horses put in a

short stride. If they chose to ride for the bounce they had to go for it and suffer the consequences. The bank was faced with a steep turf slope rather than revetted with timbers so that the horse could see there was a chance to land on the slope and get in a stride to the bottom of the rails into the water. A Normandy Bank has to be attacked, so this fence was asking for boldness, but attacking it asked for speed into water, which is always a tricky problem due to the drag of the water. Speed into water invariably causes some falls, and this fence had four. Some of the riders did not find the right answer to the question.

Fences 18 and 19 led out of the water and the faults here were caused by lack of organization on the way out of the water. Tad Coffin on Bally Cor had some bad luck and broke some tack.

Fence 20, the Birch Rails, was the other fence I would have liked to take out. It was a lot to ask after the effort through the water.

I had to take the riders back over the stream at some point and the Footbridge seemed to be the answer. Perhaps it could have been easier but it did not cause much trouble. I gave them a chance to get their feet wet—it was fairly easy to trot through the water. I did not want to build a big fence at this point; I would rather they had a stop than a fall.

I needed to have a maximum oxer somewhere on the course and included it in the next fence, the Parallel Rails. The rider had a choice of taking a maximum spread or going around to take either of two smaller ones. The rider at this point should have been thinking about how the horse was jumping and how quick a response it was giving. As it was, most of the horses took the shortest way and there were absolutely no faults at this fence.

Then came the Serpent, fences 23–25, the key obstacle on the entire course. It was the first fence of its kind, a totally different fence, and it was the last of my three big focal points. I built zigzag rails over an existing zigzag ditch. The stream banks were of limestone so we had to dynamite the post holes and fill them with concrete to hold the uprights. That bothered me because it changed the structure of the footing. This fence was two-thirds of the way around the course. The whole course led up to this question, or series of questions. Included in the Serpent were questions of turning, balance, control, and of course, boldness. Besides presenting a summary of the technical questions all at once, this complex tested the rider's knowledge of the horse. If the horse was tired and losing his ability to respond quickly, there was a slower route through. It was an eye-opening experience to watch this fence being ridden. When we first looked at the fence Wolfgang Feld and I asked each other "How many horses do you think will go for the righthand side of the Vs and go for the faster route?" I guessed that 3 or 4 riders would try it, Wolfgang thought that even fewer would. As it was, many of the riders took the basic route and many came to grief. At this point the rider

might have assumed that the horse's engine was overheated and should have been able to slow down to cool off. The horse had to make a big jump over the first ditch and rail, come down and jump up over the second ditch and rail, and then jump into the water over the final rails. A horse that made any mistake at all did not have time to recover between elements. Riders do not always remember that horses change during the course of a round, and this competition was run under severely demanding conditions because of the heat and humidity.

Once through the Serpent, I had to get them back over the same ditch and the Open Water seemed to be the least offensive way through. The two horses that fell here probably did so because their riders were so relieved at getting through the Serpent safely that they just relaxed their attention.

The final portion of the course after the Serpent was designed as a recovery period.

The Rails and Drop at Fence 27 had me really worried. I was afraid that a tired horse would hook a leg and fall here. I did not like the ground formation but it was the only place I could take them back into the next field. In spite of my concern no horse had any faults.

I put the Sorghum Mill in the next flat stretch because I needed a relatively easy fence, but I wanted to design something native to the area that might give the riders pause and make them ride and think. It had to be show jumped.

For a final combination I

built the Maze around existing trees. When the course was still planned to run in the opposite direction, Old Fort Lexington would have been sited in the midst of these trees. I did not want them barreling into a big fence at this point. I considered this to be the recovery part of the course and I wanted them to ride without making mistakes, particularly if the horses were getting tired. The problem at the Maze was one of direction—if the rider was not correctly lined up the horse had ample opportunity to run out.

Fence 32, Hobo's Hideaway, was essentially a triple bar and covered up the drop in the ground, and the final Bank of Flowers was a fence that had to be respected. The last six efforts were designed with a tired horse in mind because I did not want any of them to fall down.

Looking back at the statistics I would probably say that perhaps some of the warm-up section of the course was too hard; the middle section was appropriate for a CCIO; and the final portion worked as I had hoped, it contained the right mixture of questions.

The crucial fences brought about mixed results: The bank (Old Fort Lexington) was new and an original and it jumped easier than most of the riders had expected; the water (the Head of the Lake Complex) was also a new concept and seemed appropriate for a CCIO. The Serpent caused a great many more falls than I would have liked; if I had to do it over, I would perhaps

17a,b Head of the Lake (Normandy Bank)
a: Spread 4'11"
b: Height 2'8"
  Drop into water 5'11"

21 Footbridge
Height 3'7"—3'11"

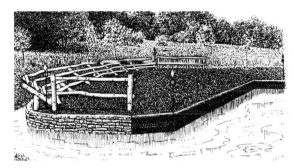

18,19 Head of the Lake (Bank & Rails)
18: height 3'3"
19: height 3'9"

22 Parallel Rails
Height 3'11"
Spread 5'3"—6'7"

20 Head of the Lake (Birch Rails)
Height 3'11"

23,24,25 The Serpent
24,25: height 3'9"
23: height 3'11"
23: spread 5'11"

26 Open Water
Spread 13′1″

29,30,31 Locust Maze
Height of brush 3′11″

27 Rails & Drop
Height 3′7″—3′11″
Drop 5′11″ (maximum)

32 Hobo's Hideaway
Height 3′9″
Spread 5′7″

28 Sorghum Mill
Height 3′7″—4′3″

33 Bank of Flowers
Height 3′9″
Spread 6′7″

move the third element, (I think the footing gave way in places), but I would not change very much. The heat and humidity had a great effect on the results and I wish the championships could have been run under better conditions, but I think that the course had meaning—those who rode without thinking found themselves caught out.

Ralph Hill, Rider

I was mentally prepared for a pretty rough course, because I had been told that the World Championships were usually more difficult than the Olympics. Tad Coffin had said that it was going to be "the course of the century." When we first walked it as a group, I thought, "Boy! These guys down here aren't kidding!" It was beautifully built and designed, but it was awesome, and it was imposing but not full of traps where horses get hurt—just *big.*

Mike Plumb felt it was a "horse and rider course" in that it was a thinking course for the rider as well as being a challenge to the horse. Walking it, the fences that struck us as the biggest problems were, first #8 and 9, The Sink Hole. There didn't seem to be any nice way through it. I was quite concerned about #11, The Dog Kennels. The most reasonable option here consisted of a 13'–13½' bounce going down hill. It was hard to imagine fitting a 17-hand horse into those short distances, particularly after coming off the Giant's Table oxer just before it where the horse

would have to reach out. #14, Old Fort Lexington was really imposing. I couldn't help but think, WOW, if my horse doesn't trust me and hesitates he'll never get his hind end up there—and that could be curtains. The water also gave me some pause. It was almost too much of a good thing—and an awfully big effort for a horse. The first part was quite enough without the second part.

The first time we walked the course our eyes were really big. After that it seemed within the realm of possibility, but we were still pretty staggered, particularly after we realized that there were actually eight combinations in total. This was asking an awful lot of our horses. The real "cruncher" were fences 23–25, the Serpent. This came two fences after the water and was a huge effort for a horse this late in the course, particularly after the energy expended in getting through the water combination.

All the riders had the same reaction—that the course "never let up." Tad declared that it was "Bromont times four."

Jack Le Goff gave some of the riders specific instructions on how to ride particular fences— what lines to take, and where exactly to jump an obstacle. Every night I'd write all this down and study it. He didn't give me too much advice because he said I knew my horse better than he did.

After walking the course three times, we were all worried about whether our horses were fit enough. This is one area where a rider never feels totally confident. Even though you've done

your homework, you can never be sure. The steeplechase was long and the ground undulating, and the cross-country was a maximum effort all the way. It was easy to have your doubts. Dad, who had walked the course with us and who knows Sarge as well as I do, felt the horse could handle it. This was reassuring.

On Course

Sarge seems to want to "get on with it" as we walk around outside the Starting Box. As the starter says "10 seconds," we enter the box. Now, the last part of the countdown. Sarge knows what that means. His head comes up, he's prancing in place, trying to root the reins out of my hands. This is all a good sign. My watch is set back to zero. I punch it and we're off! We're on course! What I want to do is get Sarge into his natural stride, listen to the "engine" and if all is going well, move on some and gamble a bit. I'd better concentrate on the first fence just ahead. Galloping along we head toward the right and then slightly back to the left to get a good approach to the Logs and Shrubs, which is maximum height. It rides well.

We head on alongside the steeplechase course. Now, Sarge is getting in gear as we gallop on over the deep velvety turf that's about as nice a footing as you'd find anywhere. We have to jump in and out of the Pavilion. I opt to handle it from the left to right, which means going around a tree on the left. I soon notice that our approach to this fence is a bit "deficient"—a bit slower than I wanted. Sarge is backing off a little more than I expected. We're in a tight spot! The only thing to do is sit quiet and get strong with the leg. This is my mistake. Sarge is going to have to pull more than 50% this time. We hit the fence, but he stays on his feet. He takes three strides and then we're out and on our way.

We have quite a long stretch over undulating ground until we get to the Diamonds, which is an airy looking fence that doesn't appeal to me very much. I'm still mad at myself for the mistake I just made. My plan is to jump the second panel from the white flag. Jack had said that if you do this be sure not to lose your right rein because if the horse jumped to the left he could land into the post. I'm going to be more aggressive this time. I see a nice spot and we're over it in good shape.

Now we have a short gallop to the Jenny Lane Crossing. This is basically a Road Crossing except the "out" part is not in line with the "in"—it is juxtapositioned to the left. My plan is to jump fence 6 on the left and 7 on the right and ride both at an angle. But the trick here is to let the horse know that there is no "open door" to the left down the lane. As we head for our approach, Sarge's ears are up. He's going forward nicely and jumps the first bank tidily. I take hold of my right rein and keep my left leg firmly on him on landing. We ride forward at an angle to the second bank. We're over and he lands galloping; this really

pleases me, because I know now that he's really in gear and that hopefully my mistake for the day is behind me. I tried to be careful not to mess with him at the combination as I will surely have to at the next two fences 8 and 9, another combination.

At this point we are still skirting the steeplechase course. We have quite a long gallop on our way to the Sinkhole, which is just about as appealing to me as its name. None of the ways through this are satisfactory. Someone said there is the crazy way, the bull way, and the chicken way—not a very good choice! I'm thinking that it was recommended we ride through the long way. But I feel there is a better way for Sarge. We jump in on the left and go down into the ditch. I have to pull on his teeth and make a sharp turn to the right and canter on the left lead along the length of the ditch, then take a left turn. Now we head toward the "out" part (fence 8), jump that, and we are on our way. I'm surprised—it really rode quite fast.

It's nice and flat on ahead. Now I'm thinking about getting Sarge back into a good rhythm as I want him to know that all that twisting and turning was just an illusion. This is not stadium jumping, but a big forward cross-country course. We can see the Giant's Table and as we come closer I remember that it's 3'11" high and 6'7" wide. He's never banked (jumped on and off) a wooden fence so I hope he won't now. He pricks his ears, and I see a nice spot. Sarge takes

off and lands right in stride—a really nice fence. The crowds cheer, which is encouraging.

We continue on up a slope, then head slightly downhill. I don't like what lies ahead too much. This is the Kennels—a maze of lattice work that's a real optical illusion. This combination is a real test of the horse. You have a short double bounce downhill that comes right after a big spread, the Giant's Table. After he has just jumped big and bold, I've got to cram my big guy into that little space. What runs through my mind is the fact that Sarge jumps slightly to the right. This should give us a bit more distance between fences. Three strides out I start to get him back, his hindquarters come underneath him, and he elevates in front. He's over the first part, over the second, now drifts to the right and out over the third element. He didn't even stub a toe. That mistake I made at the Pavilion sharpened him up, thank goodness. What a relief!

As we gallop on, I start to think about Fort Lexington, just two fences away. First we cross a road covered with tanbark, then jump the stack of logs, a big galloping fence. The last bounce backed Sarge off a bit because he had to really listen to me. Now I want him to come forward again, to get more aggressive. I'd say we are motoring along at about 570 mpm on our approach. I don't check him in front of this fence. I keep a good leg on him, his ears go up, and we're over. He has jumped it really well. I feel like I've got a lot of horse under me.

Sarge is galloping so lean and

long and he's being so cool about everything that it almost worries me. I wish he'd give me some definite sort of sign of how tired he is. There was quite a bit of controversy about the little cabins at Fort Lexington—jumping the middle one might encourage a horse to bank it. Sarge would jump the whole thing instead of doing that. Jack (Le Goff) thought the trajectory over the little log cabin on the right would be smaller and would require less of an effort. We head into this jump quite aggressively because I don't want my horse strung out on landing with the big Fort ahead. We're up and over and we have a nice straight line to the Fort.

We had been told to attack our fences, yet not to ride too hard at them, or the horse might get suspicious and have his confidence shaken. It is a fine line sort of thing. So many thoughts flash through my mind as that enormous Fort looms up. We are approaching the lip in front of it at about 500 mpm. There is no point in feeling nervous now—this is a do-or-die situation. Sarge is still cool as a cucumber—no chipping in, no pulling, no backing off. I wish I could yell Geronimo! He makes a powerful leap and we land further up the bank than I'd anticipated. Jack has said when you feel that front end come up, get on up and out of the bounce, and then right down the far side. What a good feeling to have a horse that is so honest and straightforward about it all.

I'd better get my act together; the next fence—the Farmyard—

is an easy place to get a run-out after the excitement of the Fort. I did remember to look up for this fence as we came off the bank of the Fort. We head into the left side and Sarge pricks his ears, then jumps nicely out over a trough at the end of it. At this point the crowds are cheering and going wild, which makes me feel good.

There is a long gallop ahead. Jack had told us that this would be a good place to let the horses have a breather, and to have a look at the watch. I'm glad he told us this because I'd have been tempted to press on here otherwise. We had picked our half-way point at the PortaJohns just ahead. My watch now reads 7 minutes. My time should be 6 minutes and 45 seconds at this point, so I am making pretty good time—and still have a lot of horse left. I take a deep breath. It's a darn good thing we are both fit; this course never lets up. The Ditch and Brush is right beside one of the main driveways of the park. It has a big water ditch in front of it and the brush itself is 4'11" high at the point where I plan to jump it. We are moving on down the hill at over 570 mpm. I can see a spot. As Sarge leaves the ground I touch him with my whip. I quickly apologize to him for this; it is really for my benefit. He really reaches out over the brush and ditch, but he's a bit cross with me for going to the stick.

I give him a pat as I do from time to time, which he likes. His ears come back, then forward, so I know he's listening. The crowds ahead look like an amphitheatre of people at the Lake.

This is an impressive combination! I think the thing to do is ride it like a Normandy bank and as if the ditch isn't there. We are coming at it at about 550 mpm. I take hold of his head at the pine trees, close my legs, he comes back a bit and up. We're over the ditch, into the bank, he nips over the top and shoots off into the water. Slightly more to the right than I anticipated, I'm in the "conservative" seat. We jog in the water now, slightly to the left, to get a straight line to the next section of the Lake.

Although the water is only 12"–14" deep, it is very tiring and we've been a long way, so I let him jog right up to the next bank (fence 19). Sarge feels powerful jumping up. The bank is 30 feet long before we come to the rails over the water and off the bank. He lands pretty heavily with a lot of concussion. There's a long hill ahead and I worry about that taking a lot out of him.

We were told not to press on up the hill but to let the horses take three or four strides to get their breath, get their minds organized again, and then pick them back up. We are heading toward the 4th panel from the left again. I put Sarge together with my legs and seat now as he is a bit strung out. We're over and he makes a real nice jump.

I let him get back into his stride again. We cross the road, go down a slope and head past the campgrounds on our left. The water has taken something out of him, but not as much as I expected. We gallop on and then

I test my horse's "motor." I keep wondering when the bottom might drop out of him! The only sign of any fatigue I've had is that he lands a bit heavier on the drops. When I discussed this fence with Tad (Coffin) he said to watch out for it, because I wanted to run right on down to it. He said I could stand my horse on his head if I wasn't careful. I slide the bit back and forth in Sarge's mouth and keep a good leg on him. His ears go back and he's mad because I'm messing with him, as though I'm questioning his ability. We jump on the right; he lands, and sort of skims over the water.

Next there's a long gallop up a pretty good incline. This is the last fence before the Serpent! These Parallel Rails offer several options. The fast way on the left is bigger, and the long way around (which Jack advised several of the individuals to take) is easier. I feel that I still have a lot of horse left, so I opt for the middle part; it's wide all right, but the back rail is visible. He's jumping it real nice. I feel a hind leg rub, but that's not bad. Now we're on our way down the long gallop to the Serpent!

These zigzag fences are the ones where you have to meet the fence "on the money" and be really sharp. The first part is the most imposing because it is big and airy, with a ditch underneath. I felt on this combination that if Sarge understood the first part, he'd be O.K. on the other two. The idea was to get this big guy over the first one, and take the shortest route between the other fences (the Gambler's

Way). I didn't want to break his rhythm by doing a lot of turning and twisting; just to keep the fences coming at him. He feels good enough to handle it this way. I set him back to 550 or 520 mpm, close the leg, and lengthen his frame toward the panel I've picked. I can feel him drift to the right on fence 23, and I use this to my advantage. He gives me a good fence.

We turn in the air, and as we land, I can see the next panel I want to jump. I keep him a little excited and keep riding at it. Bruce (Davidson) said that you have to go into this fence with a lot of impulsion and come out with what you have. Sarge's ears are flicking back and forth—he's still sharp. He lands into the bank, over fence 24. I expect him to peck but surprisingly, he doesn't.

After he takes one stride I head straight toward the second panel to the right of the white flag on fence 25. There are only about four or five strides to the last part of the Serpent. Bruce had said that this fence was a real knee-hanger. He suggested riding at the point of the V, so that the horses would get their knees up, then they would drift to the right. What a fence! It's so quiet that I can hear my heart beating. I close the leg and take a hold of Sarge's head. I can feel him raise up in front. I let him drift to the right, he rubs the fence a little with a hind leg, lands in the water, takes a stride, and is back on land again. The crowd is going bananas. I hadn't had any word except from Bruce about the way the course rode for him, so I didn't know about any of the

disasters other horses and riders had here.

Amazingly, I still have some horse left. He still feels good but it now takes me four or five strides to get him back in rhythm. It's a short gallop to the Open Water. Le Goff felt here that it would take less out of a horse if he jumped out and over it, rather than down into it. I leave it up to Sarge, but just let him know something is coming up, because it's hard to see the water. He thrusts off and lands heavily on the far side on the lip of the ditch, but I close the leg and we're off right away. He feels fine.

Now there's a long gallop in a hay field towards the Rails and Drop. I keep thinking, I've still quite a lot of horse left, but this can't be—another drop! We're still galloping and I hate to think of jarring him again on the landing of this drop; it doesn't seem fair. Jack says to keep a hold of the horse's head here and not to mess around with the "crest release" because he knows I show-jump a lot. You can't do that out here! We approach the fence coming off a turn, jump the middle of the rails, and I use the "conservative seat"—I lean back to help balance him. He lands quite heavily after the big drop but is away galloping.

We have another fence after a long gallop up a hill. We were told not to treat this fence lightly, because it is airy, it doesn't fit into this course, and a horse could easily have a fall here. You'd never live that down after going this far. So we cross a road that is covered with tanbark, and I take hold of Sarge's head, just enough to say, "Hey, there's a fence." He handles it well.

I'm already thinking of the Locust Maze ahead. I've come this far and I've still got some horse left, so I'm going to take the "Gambier's Route." Galloping on to the fence, I realize I've got to start to bring him back sooner, as he wants to hang on me a bit now. We head toward the little right-hand panel next to the red flag. I sit quietly, trying not to override. There is only 21 feet between that and the next brush fence. We're over both fences nicely. Now the trick is to grab the left rein and make that sharp turn. For a second I feel like I've lost my steering and we start to drift downhill! Now I've got him back, and he's making the turn toward the left part of the fence, and we're over it.

At this point we were told to "really start burning shells," so I close my legs. I can't believe it—he moves right out. We hit a good lick at about 570 mpm or better. I take back a little but not much, and his ears are a bit back on our approach because I'm hustling him, which he doesn't like much, but he gets over it fine. Reality hits me—we're almost there! This guy's really getting around! But there's still another fence left. We're really flying now, about 590–600 mpm.

We have a long gallop now to the last fence. There's no time to wave until you're over the last fence and through the finish flags. This is the only "gift" fence on the course, but is it really a gift with a tired horse? I take hold of him four strides out, see my distance, and he stands back to take off. We're through the finish flags! We keep on galloping and I pull up gradually as we gallop on up to the scales, 75 yards away. Sometimes if you pull up at the finish, that's it with a tired horse. You can't get him to the scales. I request permission to dismount, then throw my crop away. This is no time to make stupid mistakes. I pull off the tack. Sarge looks fine; winded, yes, but O.K.

We stay in the vet box for about 20 minutes until the vet says we can go. My groom, Susie Buchanan, leads Sarge back to the stables. Apparently when he passes fence 16, the Ditch and Brush, Sarge starts dancing around with excitement. He pulls Susie back to the barn.

This has been really exciting —to know that I had a horse in top condition to do what he did without hurting him. I'm really happy that he's ended his first big competition with a good feeling. He's given better than his 100% out there. He's quite a horse!

About the USCTA

Eileen Thomas
Executive Director, USCTA

Eileen Thomas (Photo by Warren Patriquin)

Eileen Thomas is no stranger to the international eventing world. She served as secretary to the British Pony Club and the British Combined Training Group for many years. Eileen has been the chief scorer at many leading international three-day events, including the 1971 European Championships at Burghley, England; the Badminton and Burghley Horse Trials in England, from 1968–1974; and both the 1974 World

Championships at Burghley and the 1978 World Championships in Lexington, Ky.

Eileen became Executive Secretary of the USCTA in 1974, and was named Executive Director in 1981. She has been instrumental in the growth of the USCTA, and her vast knowledge of all phases of eventing has made her a key figure in the sport's development in this country. No detail is too small to escape Eileen's sharp eye, and her efficient scoring system has been adopted throughout the U.S.

Eileen serves the eventing world with a cheerful smile and a cool efficiency. She is the lady with the answers to all of the questions.

The United States Combined Training Association, Inc. (USCTA) was formed in 1959 in order to fill a need—a need that had become increasingly more apparent since the United States Cavalry had been disbanded in 1948. Until that time, the U.S. Army had been responsible for training equestrian teams for international competition and, although the United States Equestrian Team (USET) was then created to continue the task of finding and training the international "stars," it became obvious that a much broader-based operation was required.

Horse Trials, the schooling and preparation grounds for future Three-Day Event horses and riders, were needed to be organized on a national basis, with definite standards and specifications. A grading system was also needed to ensure that horses progressed at an unhurried pace through the different levels of competition, in keeping with a systematic training program. Educational material, in the form of films and literature, was needed to promote the sport and to assist officials and competitors.

The USCTA rose to the challenge and its membership has grown from a mere handful of supporters and competitions in the early years, to nearly 6,000 members and 200 Events in

1981. By working closely with the American Horse Shows Association (AHSA), rules have been formulated and the list of officials, licensed by the AHSA, has continued to grow.

For organizational purposes, the country is divided into Areas, each Area being presided over by an Area Chairman. In almost every case, Area Championships are held at various levels and high score awards are also presented at the end of each year. In addition, high score awards on a national basis are offered by both the AHSA and the USCTA. There are also several Championship trophies that are offered on a national basis, such as the USCTA's Preliminary Horse Trial Championship, the AHSA's Young Riders and Intermediate Championship trophies, and two major trophies at the Advanced level that are presented by the USET.

The USCTA maintains a comprehensive film library, with subjects ranging from the education of jump judges to the full coverage of an Olympic Three-Day Event. It is also building up a library of printed material, containing educational publications for course builders, organizers, officials, veterinarians and competitors One of the USCTA's major contributions over the past few years has been the organization of numerous educational seminars and clinics throughout the country. Panelists and instructors for these clinics have been drawn from a nucleus of knowledgeable and experienced Combined Training riders and officials and many of the international 'stars' have donated their services to this educational program. Attendance fees have been kept to a minimum and an enormous number of people have been able to benefit from the expertise that has been made available to them through the auspices of the USCTA.

Membership of the USCTA is mandatory if you wish to compete in a USCTA competition at the Training level or above. There are three different membership categories—Life Membership, involving one initial fee; Full Membership, requiring an annual subscription; and

Family Membership, available where there is more than one person in a family wishing to join. Although membership is compulsory for active competitors, it does, however, bring with it a number of distinct advantages. As a Full, Life or Family Member, you will automatically receive a membership card and number. As a Full or Life Member, you will also receive a copy of the current Rule Book and both the Spring and Summer/Fall editions of the Horse Trials Omnibus Schedule. This Schedule, which is published twice a year, contains the prize lists of nearly every Registered event throughout the country. Where a prize list is not included, you are supplied with the name, address and telephone number of the Secretary so that, in every case, you are able to obtain full details of every registered competition. Also published in the Omnibus Schedule are all the dressage tests in current use at Horse Trials, plus the names and addresses of Area Chairmen, information on the grading system and on other local combined training associations, as well as detailed instructions on entering competitions and a supply of entry and stabling forms.

The USCTA also produces its very own glossy magazine, the *USCTA News*, which is automatically sent to all Full and Life Members. This is published every other month and contains informative articles, official news from the USCTA office, dates and results of events, and coverage of major competitions both at home and abroad. The magazine is illustrated throughout with numerous photographs.

As the sport of Combined Training grows in popularity and the demand for more and more quality competitions continues in all Areas, so, also, does the USCTA continue with its own efforts to sustain this growth through its membership, its educational clinics and publications, and its support of event organizers throughout the country.

Index